Best of the Best from the

SOUTHWEST

Cookbook

Selected Recipes from the
Favorite Cookbooks of
TEXAS, NEW MEXICO, and ARIZONA

KEITH ODOM

Located entirely in northern Arizona, Grand Canyon National Park encompasses 277 miles of the Colorado River and adjacent uplands. A World Heritage Site, the canyon is visited by over five million people each year.

Best of the Best from the

SOUTHWEST

Cookbook

Selected Recipes from the
Favorite Cookbooks of
TEXAS, NEW MEXICO, and ARIZONA

EDITED BY

Gwen McKee

AND

Barbara Moseley

QUAIL RIDGE PRESS
Preserving America's Food Heritage

Library of Congress Cataloging-in-Publication Data
Best of the best from the Southwest cookbook : selected recipes from the
favorite cookbooks of Texas, New Mexico, and Arizona / edited By Gwen
Mckee And Barbara Moseley. -- 1st ed.
    p. cm.
    Includes bibliographical references and index.
    ISBN-13: 978-1-934193-47-1
    ISBN-10: 1-934193-47-X
1. Cookery, American--Southwestern style. 2. Cookery--Texas.
3. Cookery--New Mexico. 4. Cookery--Arizona. I. McKee, Gwen.
II. Moseley, Barbara.
    TX715.2.S69B475 2010
    641.5979--dc22   2010000502

Book design by Cyndi Clark
Cover photo by Greg Campbell • Illustrations by Tupper England
Printed in South Korea by Tara TPS

ISBN-13: 978-1-934193-47-1 ISBN-10: 1-934193-47-X
First printing, June 2010

On the cover: Green Enchiladas with Spicy Sauce, page 134

QUAIL RIDGE PRESS
P. O. Box 123 • Brandon, MS 39043
info@quailridge.com• www.quailridge.com

CONTENTS

KEITH ODOM

At the base of sheer red cliffs in the canyon walls of Canyon de Chelly National Monument lies White House Ruins, Arizona, a cliff dwelling built by Native Americans between 350 and 1300 A.D.

Quest for the Best
Regional Cooking

In the Southwest, we tasted freshly made tortillas being turned by experienced hands in the street markets, as well as being massly turned out at a "tortilla factory" inside a Lubbock supermarket. These were warm and light and so fresh, well, it was ambitious to think we could duplicate that taste . . . but easy to understand why so many recipes using tortillas are so prevalent in this part of the country.

The peppery salsas are such a perfect accompaniment to southwestern cooking. "Green or red?" you may be asked, and each is so authentically delicious. The spicy chilis and stews and beautifully seasoned dishes with spicy sounding names like tacos, fajitas, enchiladas, empanadas, quesadillas . . . are so much a part of the whole landscape of the Southwest. When you are there, you can smell these pungent aromas wherever you go, and it all adds to a totally delicious flavor experience.

Traveling to every state in the United States in search of the best cookbooks and recipes took Barbara and me the better part of 25 years. What started in our home state of Mississippi with one cookbook, grew to include our neighboring states, then as each one neared completion, we reached out farther and farther away from home to explore the cuisines of states far and wide. The experience has been one that has enabled us to bring home each new state's recipes to become ours forever.

But nothing seems so special and dear as when you share it with others who you know will enjoy it as much as you do. Our BEST OF THE BEST STATE COOKBOOKS are chosen favorite recipes that we are proud to have brought from each state home to you, wherever you are. I wish we could introduce you to the many people we have met in every state who were proud of their cooking heritage and eager to show us just how good their recipes were . . . and are! Sometimes it was

a particular local ingredient, or the way they kneaded the dough, or browned the flour, or marinated the meat, or maybe a secret method they used to make something particularly unique to their way of cooking. It has truly been a delicious experience!

We loved the liveliness . . . the colors . . . the landscape . . . the whole atmosphere of the Southwest—we loved it all! We have been blessed to have traveled all over the incredibly beautiful states of Texas, New Mexico, and Arizona. It was so interesting and so much fun that we have included herein lots more than just recipes, but also some of our photos and interesting tidbits about places that we found unique and fascinating.

Put a little spice in your life and on your plate . . . come on in to the tantalizing tastes of the American Southwest.

Gwen McKee

Gwen McKee and Barbara Moseley, editors of
BEST OF THE BEST STATE COOKBOOK SERIES

BEVERAGES and APPETIZERS

The East Texas Oil Museum in Kilgore College is a tribute to the independent oil producers and wildcatters who discovered oil in the early 1930s. The resulting "Oil Boom" permanently transformed the economy of Texas, bringing industry and wealth to the state. Texas is the nation's leading producer of oil and natural gas.

Almond Tea Punch

1 cup sugar
½ cup lemon juice
2 tablespoons almond extract
1 tablespoon vanilla extract
1 cup very strong tea

1 quart water
1 quart ginger ale
Mint sprigs
Lemon

Mix sugar, lemon juice, almond and vanilla extracts, and tea together. Then add water and ginger ale. Serve over lots of crushed ice. Garnish with mint sprigs and lemon.

The Second Typically Texas Cookbook (Texas II)

Mint Tea

4 tea bags
8–10 sprigs mint
1 quart boiling water
⅔ cup lemon juice

⅓ cup orange juice
1¼ cups sugar
3 cups hot water

Put tea bags, mint, and boiling water in a covered container. Let set for 15 minutes. Mix all other ingredients in another container. Mix all together; serve over ice. Yields ½ gallon.

Scrumptious (Texas)

Lake Austin Iced Tea

2 (6-ounce) cans frozen
  lemonade concentrate,
  undiluted
1 (6-ounce) can frozen orange
  juice concentrate, undiluted

1 cup sugar, or to taste
6 cups water
2 cups strong-brewed tea
1½ cups bourbon

Combine all ingredients in 1-gallon container. Blend well. Serve in tall glasses over crushed ice. Makes approximately 13 cups.

Per 1-cup serving; Cal 193; Prot .391g; Carb 32.9g; Fat .1g; Chol 0mg; Sod 6.24mg.

Changing Thymes (Texas II)

Texas Sunrise

4 cups cran-raspberry juice
2 cups pineapple juice
2 cups orange juice

2 cups club soda
1 lime
1 cup whole strawberries

Combine cran-raspberry, pineapple, and orange juices in punch bowl or large pitcher. Add club soda. Cut lime into thin round slices, discarding ends. Float some or all of slices in punch. Stir in strawberries. Add ice, if desired, and serve. Makes approximately 10 cups.

Per ½-cup serving: Cal 62; Prot .361g; Carb 15.5g; Fat .1g; Chol 0mg; Sod 6.58mg.

Changing Thymes (Texas II)

Tequila Slush

1 (6-ounce) can frozen lime juice
2 (6-ounce) cans frozen limeade
1 (6-ounce) can orange juice
6 (6-ounce) cans water

1 quart bottle Wink or similar
  drink
⅓–½ bottle tequila

Mix ingredients and freeze. Remove from freezer 30 minutes before serving and stir until slushy with a spoon. Can be refrozen and kept indefinitely.

La Piñata (Texas)

Strawberry Margarita Slush

1½ cups frozen sliced
  strawberries with sugar, thawed
¼ cup tequila
¼ cup triple sec
¾ cup sweet and sour bar mix

1½ cups frozen limeade
  concentrate
1 cup water
2–3 tablespoons simple syrup
  (optional, to taste)

Mix all ingredients together and place in plastic container to freeze overnight (or at least 8 hours). Remove from freezer and buzz briefly in a blender or set out a few minutes to thaw slightly before serving. Makes 5 cups.

Gourmet Gringo (Arizona)

Perfect Margaritas

Be prepared! These high-octane margaritas just might sweep some of your guests off their feet. They are wonderfully flavored and potent. For the very best margaritas, always squeeze fresh limes (preferably the juicy, thin-skinned, yellowish Mexican variety, which have the traditional pungent flavor.) Whenever I am near the Mexican border or in the Caribbean, I lay aside quantities of the freshly squeezed juice of these limes in half-pint freezer containers or jars and bring them home solidly frozen. In a pinch the dark green, thicker-skinned Persian limes will work, too. Be sure to keep the juice frozen until you use it. Always buy at least 80-proof tequila, made from the blue agave plant.

8 fresh limes, preferably Mexican variety
Coarse salt
½ cup triple sec, or to taste
1½ cups 80- to 92-proof pure agave tequila (white preferred)
⅓ of a fresh egg white, beaten with a fork
Crushed ice

Squeeze the limes, being certain to get all the flesh plus the juice. Measure and use only ½ cup juice. Reserve the rest. Prepare the glasses. If salt is desired, rub one of the lime rinds around the top rim of each glass. Crunch the glasses into the salt and place in the freezer, allowing at least 30 minutes to frost.

Meanwhile, prepare the margaritas by placing the lime juice, triple sec, tequila, and egg white in the blender. Add enough ice to fill the blender about halfway.

Process. If the texture is not slushy enough, add ice to get the desired texture. Taste and add more triple sec if not sweet enough. Serve in the frosted glasses, either straight up or over ice. Yields 4 large margaritas.

Note: You can freeze leftover margaritas for at least a month.

Fiestas for Four Seasons (New Mexico)

Libba's Bloody Marys

1 (46-ounce) can tomato juice
1 can beef consommé or beef
    bouillon soup, undiluted
1 cup lemon juice
2 tablespoons Worcestershire
½ teaspoon sugar, if desired

2 teaspoons celery salt
½ teaspoon pepper
1 teaspoon salt
1 teaspoon Tabasco
1½ soup cans vodka

Mix all together and serve over ice with fresh lime wedge and celery sticks. Also can add 1 slice cucumber to glass for an extra flavor! Serves 8.

Spindletop International Cooks (Texas)

My Kinda Cocoa

This is strictly an adult drink for those cold winter nights when coffee won't do—and chocolate will.

1 tablespoon cocoa
3 teaspoons sugar
1 ounce tequila

1 ounce Kahlúa
1 cup hot milk
Whipped cream

Spoon the cocoa and sugar into the bottom of a large mug or heavy glass. Stir in tequila and Kahlúa, pour in the hot milk, and stir well. Top with a dollop of whipped cream and serve. Serves 1.

The Tequila Cook Book (New Mexico)

Champurado

(Original Mexican Cocoa)

2 quarts milk
3 (2-inch) cinnamon sticks
½ cup cocoa
1 cup sugar

1 teaspoon vanilla
¼ cup cornmeal
½ cup milk

In saucepan, combine milk and cinnamon sticks. Heat until almost boiling. Combine cocoa, sugar, vanilla, cornmeal, and ½ cup milk. Stir to make a thick sauce. Pour cocoa sauce into heated milk, stirring constantly with a wire whip or a rotary beater (5 minutes). Serve at once. Very delicious served with sopapillas or bunuelos. Serves 8–10.

South Texas Mexican Cook Book (Texas II)

Black-Eyed Pea Dip

2 cups cooked black-eyed peas
1 stick margarine, melted
1 jalapeño pepper
½ teaspoon juice of pepper
1 medium onion, chopped

1 clove garlic
4 ounces grated Cheddar cheese
¾–1 cup milk (if needed for
  consistency)

Mix in blender first 6 ingredients; then place in saucepan. Add cheese and milk as needed for consistency. Stir over heat until cheese melts. Serve hot or cold.

The Pride of Texas (Texas)

Texas Caviar

1 pound dry black-eyed peas
2 cups Italian salad dressing
2 cups diced green bell pepper
½ cup finely chopped green
  onion
½ cup chopped jalapeño
  peppers

1 (3-ounce) jar diced pimento,
  drained
1 tablespoon finely minced garlic
Salt to taste
Hot pepper sauce to taste

Soak black-eyed peas in enough water to cover for 6 hours or overnight. Drain well.

Transfer peas to saucepan; add enough water to cover. Bring to boil over high heat. Reduce heat; allow to boil until tender, about 45 minutes. Do not overcook. Drain well, then transfer to large bowl. Blend in Italian dressing, and let cool. Add remaining ingredients; mix well. Refrigerate. Serve with tortilla chips. Yields 7½ cups.

Note: This dish can also be served on a lettuce leaf as a salad. Serve with grilled chicken for a cool summer meal.

Coastal Cuisine (Texas II)

Guacamole de Suzanne
(Avocado Sauce)

3 large avocados, chopped	2 small chiles, chopped
1 medium-size onion, peeled and chopped	1 tablespoon olive oil
	1 teaspoon wine vinegar or lemon juice
1 medium-size tomato, peeled and chopped	2 teaspoons salt

Mix all ingredients (except ½ avocado) until creamy then chop the remaining half avocado in cubes and add. Taste for seasoning. Chill. If made in advance, be sure to store in refrigerator with the avocado seeds placed in the sauce and sprinkle with lemon juice to prevent its darkening. Serve as a dip with toasted tortillas, or for a salad in lettuce cups. Serves 8.

Variation: If chiles are not available, use canned Mexican hot sauce to taste.

From My Apron Pocket (Texas)

Chunky Guacamole

1 large ripe avocado	3 long green chiles
1 medium tomato	Juice of ½ lemon
1 small onion	Salt to taste
1 small bell pepper	

Chop all the ingredients fine. Do not mash. Use fresh roasted and peeled chiles, but, if they are not available, use canned or frozen. Mix together with the lemon juice and add salt to taste. Serve as a dip or as a salad with lettuce and corn chips.

The Best from New Mexico Kitchens (New Mexico)

Cloudcroft is a small village in Otero County, New Mexico, within the Lincoln National Forest whose population is only 750–800. At 8,600 feet above sea level in an otherwise arid region, the mild summer makes it a popular tourist attraction in West Texas and New Mexico. It was named by Fodors in 2002 as the Number 3 "Most Overlooked and Underrated Destination Spot." Though two large ground terminals for the Tracking and Data Relay Satellite System are located near Cloudcroft, tourism remains the primary economic driver of the village.

Great Guacamole

Try it! You won't believe it!

1 (10-ounce) package frozen asparagus spears, cooked
¾ cup non-chunky picante sauce
½ cup diced fresh tomatoes
1 teaspoon oregano
1½ teaspoons cumin
2 tablespoons Healthy Choice Fat Free Cream Cheese
1¼ teaspoons cilantro
⅛ teaspoon garlic powder
Dash of garlic salt and chili powder, or to taste
1 package dry Butter Buds

Blend all ingredients in blender or food processor until smooth. Chill and serve. Serves 8.

Per Serving: Cal 54; Fat 0; % Fat 0; Prot 5.1g; Carb 8.1g; Sod 469mg; Chol 0.

The Lite Switch (Texas II)

Avocado Logs

1 cup mashed avocado
1½ cups dry roasted cashew nuts, chopped
8 ounces cream cheese, softened
½ cup grated sharp Cheddar cheese
2 teaspoons lime juice
1 garlic clove, crushed and minced
½ teaspoon Worcestershire
½ teaspoon salt
Dash of Tabasco
Paprika

Combine all ingredients except paprika, and mix well. Cover mixture and refrigerate 30 minutes. Divide mixture in half and shape each into roll. Sprinkle wax paper with paprika, turning roll to cover with paprika. Wrap each roll in foil and refrigerate until ready to serve. Slice and serve with crackers. May be made up to 2 days ahead of serving. Yields 2 logs.

Of Magnolia and Mesquite (Texas)

Pico de Gallo

1 bundle green onions and stalks,
  chopped
1 medium tomato, diced
1 large Anaheim pepper, finely
  chopped

1 teaspoon salt
2 teaspoons fresh cilantro,
  chopped
1 can Ro-Tel tomatoes

Mix all ingredients and place in covered bowl in refrigerator for 5–6 hours. Serve on tacos or use as a dip.

"I'm Glad I Ate When I Did, 'Cause I'm Not Hungry Now" (Texas)

Fiesta Salsa

A mild salsa that can be used on tacos and enchiladas. Especially good heated and poured over thinly sliced strips of steak or roast beef. For spicier taste, use more green chiles.

4 fresh tomatoes, chopped
2 fresh green chiles, finely
  chopped, or 1 (4-ounce) can
  chopped green chiles
1 large Bermuda onion, chopped
1 green bell pepper, chopped
1 tablespoon sugar

1 tablespoon red wine vinegar
1 teaspoon olive oil
Salt and pepper to taste
2 tablespoons chopped fresh
  cilantro
¼ teaspoon oregano

Mix all ingredients and refrigerate. Yields 2 cups.

Purple Sage and Other Pleasures (Arizona)

Though many people picture New Mexico as desert terrain, one-fourth of the state is actually filled with forests. In fact, New Mexico has seven National Forests including one of the nation's largest, the 3.3 million acre Gila National Forest and Wilderness. Terrain ranges from rugged mountains and deep canyons to semi-desert. Due to the extremely rugged terrain, the area is largely unspoiled. There are several hot springs in Gila National Forest, including Middle Fork Hot Springs, Jordan Hot Springs, and Turkey Creek Hot Springs. Gila contains more publicly owned land than any other national forest outside of Alaska.

Roasted Rainbow Salsa

3 large green chiles, such as
  Anaheims or poblanos
2 large firm tomatoes
1 yellow onion
1 red onion
1 head garlic
1 red bell pepper

1 yellow bell pepper
1 green bell pepper
½ cup chopped cilantro
Juice of ½ lemon
1 clove fresh garlic, minced
Salt and pepper to taste

Spray grill with cooking spray to prevent sticking and preheat to high.

Place whole vegetables directly on the grill and roast the chiles, tomatoes, onions, garlic, and peppers, turning frequently, until the skins are charred all over.

Remove the vegetables from the grill and place in a brown paper bag or a large bowl. Fold the bag over or cover the bowl and let sit at least 15 minutes, until vegetables are cool enough to handle. The charred skins should easily slip off the chiles, tomatoes, and peppers; use a paring knife to help remove the outer layers of the onions and garlic.

Cut vegetables into large chunks and place in a food processor or blender. Gently pulse to the desired consistency (do not overprocess). Place in a large bowl and add cilantro, lemon juice, fresh garlic, salt, and pepper. Chill at least 4 hours, preferably overnight. Makes about 4 cups.

Chips, Dips, & Salsas (Arizona)

When storing fresh chiles, wash and dry the chiles, wrap them in paper towels, and store in the crisper section of the refrigerator. Do not store in plastic bags as moisture will accumulate and hasten spoiling.

Salsa Picante

In 1992 the folks who keep track of such things officially declared picante sauce as the number one condiment in the United States, surpassing ketchup, mayonnaise, mustard, and the lot. The most amazing thing about this statistic, outside of the fact that it took 'em so long, is that most people have never even had the good stuff! Almost all commercially bottled hot sauces have to be cooked, for shelf-life reasons; and consequently they lack all the vitality, fresh taste, and crunch that a homemade salsa delivers. So make your own!

This recipe is at its very, very best the day it is made, but would keep in the refrigerator for about a week, if you let it, which you won't. Good fresh tomatoes, when you can get them, instead of the canned, make the very best of all salsas.

1 (14-ounce) can of tomatoes
with juice (or 4 fresh)
¼ onion, coarsely chopped
2 green onions, coarsely
chopped
1 large clove garlic, chopped
2 tablespoons tomato purée
(optional)

3 tablespoons fresh cilantro,
chopped
2 serrano peppers, chopped
Juice from ½ lime
Pinch of sugar
Pinch of salt

Pulse all ingredients in a food processor to the desired consistency. Yields approximately 3 cups.

Calories: 3; Fat per tablespoon: trace.

Lean Star Cuisine (Texas II)

Sombrero Spread

2 teaspoons salt
2 pounds ground beef
2 cups chopped onion
1 (14-ounce) bottle Heinz hot
ketchup
5 teaspoons chili powder

1 teaspoon comino seed
1 pound cooked pinto beans, or
1–2 cans
2 cups shredded American cheese
1 cup chopped stuffed olives
Corn chips or tostados

Spread salt in frying pan and heat. (Oil may be used, if preferred). Add beef, stirring with fork. When moist, add 1 cup onions. Continue stirring until beef and onions brown. Stir in ketchup, chili powder, and comino seed. Mash and add pinto beans. Heat until blended. May be refrigerated or frozen. More salt, Tabasco, Worcestershire, or sugar to taste may be added.

When ready to serve, heat and place in a large chafing dish. Pile olives in the center and surround with a large ring of onions and an outer ring of cheese. Olé—a sombrero! Serve with corn chips or tostados. Serves 40.

San Antonio Cookbook II (Texas)

Southwestern Corn Dip

2 (10-ounce) packages frozen
corn, cooked and drained
2 cups grated sharp Cheddar
cheese
1 (4-ounce) can diced
pimentos, drained
1½ tablespoons chopped
jalapeños

2 tablespoons chopped cilantro
1 cup sour cream
½ cup mayonnaise
¼ teaspoon Tabasco
Salt to taste
Tortilla chips for dipping

In large bowl, combine all ingredients; cover; refrigerate. Serve with chips. It's that simple! Yields approximately 7 sensational cups!

Great Flavors of Texas (Texas II)

Seven Layer Fiesta Dip

24 ounces refried beans
6 ripe avocados
2 tablespoons lemon juice
1 cup sour cream
4 tablespoons mayonnaise
1 package taco seasoning mix

1 bunch green onions
3 medium tomatoes
1 small can sliced black olives
1 (8-ounce) package shredded
 Cheddar cheese

In a large dish, spread beans. Layer mashed avocados over the beans and sprinkle with lemon juice. Mix sour cream, mayonnaise, and taco seasoning mix, then spread over avocados. Chop green onions and tomatoes for the fourth and fifth layers. Spread olives on top; sprinkle with Cheddar cheese. Chill. Serve with tortilla chips.

Red, White & Blue Favorites (Arizona)

Many Layered Nacho Dip

Watch it disappear!

1 (16-ounce) can refried beans
1 package taco seasoning mix
1 (8-ounce) carton sour cream
1 (6-ounce) carton frozen
 avocado dip, thawed
1 (4½-ounce) jar stuffed green
 olives, or black olives, chopped
 (save a few for garnish)

2 large tomatoes, diced
1 small onion or green onions,
 chopped
1 (4-ounce) can diced green chiles
 (or fresh)
1½ cups grated Monterey
 Jack or Cheddar cheese
Paprika

Combine beans and taco seasoning, stirring well. Spread in a greased 12x8x2-inch dish. Layer remaining ingredients as listed, ending with cheese. Sprinkle with paprika and place a few olives on top. Refrigerate until serving time. Good served with blue corn tortilla chips.

Saint Joseph's Really Grande Cookbook (New Mexico)

Chili Parlor Nachos

Eating these nachos—mounded high, mortared together with melted cheese, and napped with steaming chili con carne—is an exercise in manual dexterity and greed. Provide plenty of napkins. In Texas there are some pretty good brands of canned chili for sale, but in the rest of the country, you may prefer to use homemade.

8 ounces unspiced, lightly salted, commercially prepared tortilla chips, or homemade tostaditas*

2½ cups (about 10 ounces) grated medium-sharp Cheddar cheese

6 pickled jalapeño chiles, stemmed and minced

1½ cups chili with beans

1 medium onion, peeled and diced (about 1 cup)

4 ounces sour cream, whisked until smooth and shiny

Position a rack in the upper third of the oven and preheat the oven to 425°. Layer half of the tostaditas in a round 10-inch ovenproof serving dish (we use a white ceramic quiche dish). Scatter half the cheese and half the jalapeños over these tostaditas. Bake 10–12 minutes, or until the cheese is melted and the tostaditas are lightly browned.

Meanwhile, in a small saucepan over medium heat, bring the chili to a simmer, stirring occasionally. Pour the chili evenly over the hot nachos. Sprinkle the onions evenly over the chili, top the entire business with the sour cream, and serve immediately. Serves 4–6.

*Tostaditas are corn tortilla chips, but they are not Doritos and they are not Fritos. To make: Fry 6-inch yellow or blue corn tortillas cut into 6 wedges in deep hot corn oil till crisp; drain on absorbent paper and salt lightly.

Texas Border Cookbook (Texas II)

The "eat, drink, and be merry" city, Austin, Texas, hosts the most restaurants and bars per capita than any other city in America. It also hosts the popular live TV show, "Austin City Limits," and is designated "The Live Music Capital of the World."

⓵

Heavy-Duty Nacho Sauce

For nachos, you can always heat a jar of Cheez-Whiz in the microwave and pour it over corn chips. OR you could make this beer-cheese sauce. It is so good that you can dip tortilla chips or even steamed flour tortillas in it—and call it a meal.

1 cup chopped onion
2 medium-size cloves garlic, crushed
¼ cup olive oil
½ teaspoon ground cumin
½ teaspoon ground coriander
½ teaspoon mild red chili powder, or more to taste
1 teaspoon salt
¼ teaspoon freshly ground black pepper
1 bell pepper, chopped
2 tomatoes, chopped
¼ cup flour
1 (12-ounce) can beer, at room temperature
2 cups grated brick or Monterey Jack cheese

Sauté onion and garlic in olive oil with spices and salt. When onion is translucent, add peppers and tomatoes; sauté 10 minutes more. Stir in the flour and cook 5–10 minutes. Add the beer and cook over medium heat another 15 minutes, stirring often. Cover and heat very low and let simmer an hour or two, stirring every 15 minutes. Uncover, remove from heat, and let cool, about 45 minutes. To serve, reheat slowly, sprinkle in the cheese as it melts. Serve hot.

License to Cook New Mexico Style (New Mexico)

Jalapeño Pie

1 (11-ounce) can jalapeño peppers
2 cups grated Cheddar cheese
3 eggs, beaten
Salt and pepper to taste

Seed and chop peppers. Place peppers in greased 9-inch pie plate. Sprinkle cheese over peppers. Pour seasoned eggs over cheese. Bake 20 minutes at 400°. Cut into small slices and serve.

The Four Ingredient Cookbook (Texas II)

Chile Cheese Cubes

8 eggs
½ cup all-purpose flour
1 teaspoon baking powder
¾ teaspoon salt
1 (12-ounce) package grated
  Monterey Jack cheese

1½ cups small-curd cottage
  cheese
2 (4-ounce) cans mild green
  chiles, drained, seeded and
  chopped

In large mixing bowl, beat eggs until light (4–5 minutes). Stir together flour, baking powder, and salt. Add to eggs, and mix well. Fold in cheeses and chiles. Turn into greased 9x9x2-inch baking dish. Bake at 350° for 40 minutes. Remove from oven and let stand for 10 minutes. Cut into small squares, and serve hot. Yields 36–48 appetizers.

Tasteful Traditions (Texas)

Caliente Cheese Fritters

3 eggs, separated
2 cups corn, canned or fresh
½ teaspoon salt
¼ teaspoon black pepper
1 teaspoon baking powder
¾ cup all-purpose flour
1 cup finely shredded Cheddar
  cheese

½ cup canned green chiles,
  chopped
¼ cup chopped red bell pepper
¼ cup finely chopped onion
Oil for frying
Salsa and sour cream for garnish
  (optional)

Beat egg whites until almost stiff. Pour corn into a separate mixing bowl. Add to corn the beaten yolks, salt, pepper, baking powder, flour, cheese, chiles, red pepper, and onion. Mix well with a wooden spoon or spatula. Gently fold in beaten egg whites.

Heat about 1 inch of oil in skillet. When the oil gets hot, drop fritters by spoonfuls. Brown on both sides. Drain on paper towels. Serve with salsa and a dollop of sour cream on the side, if desired. Makes 8–10 appetizer servings.

Savory Southwest (Arizona)

Cream Cheese Puffs

4 ounces cream cheese, softened
¾ teaspoon grated onion
¼ cup homemade mayonnaise
1 tablespoon chopped chives

⅛ teaspoon cayenne
⅛ cup grated Parmesan cheese
½ small loaf white bread

In a small bowl combine first 6 ingredients and mix well. Cut bread into circles (1½ inches round) and spread each with cheese mixture. Bake in 350° oven for 15 minutes; longer for crisper puff. The bread may be cut and spread with cheese mixture and then frozen. Bake when ready to use. Yields 2 dozen puffs.

Amarillo Junior League Cookbook (Texas)

Green Chile Pinwheels

8 ounces sharp Cheddar
  cheese, grated
8 ounces extra sharp Cheddar
  cheese, grated
2 cups all-purpose flour

¼ pound butter, softened
3 tablespoons water
Chopped green chiles to taste
  (about 2 small cans)

Combine cheeses and flour, mixing thoroughly so cheese is coated with flour. Add butter and water and work mixture with hands until well blended. Divide cheese mixture into 4 parts and form each into a ball. Roll between 2 sheets of wax paper, like pie crust. Remove top sheet of wax paper and cover entire cheese surface with chiles. Lift edge and roll as you would a jellyroll. Twist ends of wax paper and refrigerate for at least 30 minutes before slicing. At this point they may be frozen for later baking, or stored in refrigerator for up to a week.

When ready to bake, preheat oven to 350°. Slice rolls about ¼ inch thick. Place on ungreased cookie sheets and bake 12–15 minutes or until golden. These freeze well.

Good Sam Celebrates 15 Years of Love (New Mexico)

Stuffed Jalapeño "Mice"

These darling appetizers look meek, but roar in your mouth. The cheese counteracts most of the heat, but there's still a nice bite to the finish.

½ cup crumbled feta cheese
1 tablespoon extra virgin
   olive oil
1 teaspoon finely chopped
   garlic
1 teaspoon coarsely chopped
   fresh oregano

¼ teaspoon freshly ground
   black pepper
7 kalamata olives, pitted and
   coarsely chopped
16 jalapeño chiles, roasted and
   peeled
Salt to taste

In a small bowl, with a fork mix together feta, olive oil, garlic, oregano, pepper, and 6 of the chopped olives until well blended. Cover and refrigerate while preparing the chiles.

With the tip of a small, sharp knife, slice each chile open lengthwise from the base of its stem to the tip, leaving the stem attached. Open it up flat and remove the seeds and ribs. Lightly salt the inside of each chile.

With a teaspoon, neatly mound the filling in the center of each chile, distributing it evenly. Close the sides of each chile around the filling.

Place the chiles, seam side down, on a small serving platter, all pointing in the same direction like scurrying mice. With the pieces of reserved chopped olive, give each mouse two little black eyes, pressing them gently into each chile near its narrow tip, opposite the stem (tail) end. Serve immediately.

Note: These can be stuffed a day ahead, covered, and refrigerated.

Recipe by Chef John Rivera Sedlar
Savor the Southwest (Arizona)

Armadillo Eggs

½ pound Monterey Jack
  cheese, grated
½ pound hot bulk Texas
  sausage
1½ cups buttermilk biscuit
  mix

15 medium jalapeño peppers,
  canned
½ pound Monterey Jack cheese,
  cubed (or with jalapeños)
1 box Shake 'n Bake for Pork
2 eggs, beaten

Mix cheese and sausage; add biscuit mix ½ cup at a time until thoroughly mixed. The mixture will become a very stiff dough and should be kneaded several minutes. Set aside. Slit and seed jalapeños. Stuff each pepper with a cube of cheese and pinch the pepper closed around the cheese. Pinch off a bit of the cheese-sausage mixture and pat into a flat pancake about ¼ inch thick. Place the cheese-stuffed pepper in the middle of the pancake and wrap pepper completely with dough, being sure that all edges and ends are sealed completely. Roll the dough-covered pepper back and forth in your hands to mold egg shape. Roll each "egg" in Shake 'n Bake until coated. Dip armadillo eggs in beaten eggs and Shake 'n Bake again. At this point, the armadillo eggs may be baked or frozen. To serve, bake in slow oven about 300° for 20–25 minutes. If the cheese begins to bubble out, remove from the oven. The "eggs" will seem soft to the touch, but upon cooling will crust nicely. Best served slightly warm. Yields 15 eggs.

Potluck on the Pedernales (Texas II)

TOM FRIEDEL

The armadillo has long been associated with Texas, having emigrated from South America. Once hunted for its meat, the armadillo is now more of a tourist attraction, and its "shell" (actually a super thick skin) is often fashioned into assorted baskets and gift items.

Stuffed Jalapeño Chile Peppers

If you can find the red-ripe jalapeño chiles, you are in for a treat. The mature pepper has a rich warm flavor. I fix these stuffed jewels as often as I can.

18 ripe red jalapeño chiles
1 (8-ounce) package cream
  cheese, softened
2 tablespoons lime juice
1 teaspoon ground cumin
1 teaspoon ground red New
  Mexico chile

Dash of fresh-ground black
  pepper
2 tablespoons vegetable oil
½ cup chopped pecans
½ small white onion, chopped
Cilantro, finely chopped

Cut jalapeños in half lengthwise. Remove seeds and devein. Set aside. In a medium bowl, combine all ingredients except pecans, onion, and cilantro. Beat with electric mixer until smooth. Stir in pecans and onion. Stuff jalapeños with cream cheese till slightly rounded. Cover and refrigerate at least 8 hours. Serve sprinkled with cilantro.

Sassy Southwest Cooking (New Mexico)

New Mexico Cherry Bombs

The word bomb is only a slight exaggeration. For a much milder version, use cherry peppers.

24 jalapeño chiles
8 ounces Monterey Jack or
  Cheddar cheese, sliced

Flour for dredging
2 eggs, beaten
Vegetable oil for deep-fat frying

Slit each pepper, remove the seeds with a small spoon or knife, and stuff the peppers with slices of cheese. If necessary, insert a tooth-pick to hold the peppers together. Dip each chile in the flour, then the egg, then the flour again. Fry in 350° oil until golden brown. Drain and serve. Yields 24. Heat scale 8.

Variations: Stuff the chiles with chorizo, or ground meat with cheese.

Fiery Appetizers (New Mexico)

Mushroom Croustades

**24 slices white bread, very thinly   Soft butter
sliced**

Cut 24 croustades, using a 3-inch cutter, fluted or plain. Coat each heavily with butter. Fit bread into tiny muffin tins. Bake in a 400° oven for 10 minutes. Do not overbrown.

FILLING: MUSHROOM DUXELLES

4 tablespoons butter
**3 tablespoons finely chopped
  green onions**
½ pound mushrooms, chopped
2 tablespoons flour
1 cup heavy cream
½ teaspoon salt

¼ teaspoon cayenne
**1 tablespoon finely chopped
  chives**
½ teaspoon lemon juice
**2 tablespoons grated Parmesan
  cheese**

Heat butter until foam subsides. Add onions and sauté for 4 minutes. Stir in mushrooms. Sauté until moisture evaporates. Remove from heat. Sprinkle in flour. Stir. Add cream. Bring to a boil and simmer 1 minute. Add salt, cayenne, chives, and lemon juice. Refrigerate. Spoon into croustades. Sprinkle with cheese and dot with butter. Bake in a 350° oven for 10 minutes. Freezes beautifully. Serves 8–12.

Amarillo Junior League Cookbook (Texas)

Deep-Fried Mushrooms

1 pound fresh mushrooms
2 eggs, slightly beaten

Flour
Bread crumbs

Wash and clean mushrooms. Cut large ones in half. Dip in flour, eggs and bread crumbs. Deep-fry in oil. Serve with mustard dip.

MUSTARD DIP FOR VEGETABLES AND FRIED MUSHROOMS:

1 cup sour cream
**1 cup Miracle Whip salad
  dressing**
3 tablespoons Dijon mustard
¼ cup chopped onion

1 clove garlic
Dash of salt
3 dashes Worcestershire
Paprika

Combine all ingredients. Sprinkle paprika on top. Serve with raw vegetables. Delicious with fried mushrooms.

Hullabaloo in the Kitchen (Texas)

Tangy Chicken Tidbits

For a terrific tangy variation, skewer these tidbits, alternating the chicken with cherry tomatoes, and baste with the cayenne sauce while grilling.

3 tablespoons butter
1 tablespoon sesame oil
1 teaspoon cayenne powder
½ cup Dijon-style mustard
⅓ cup cider vinegar
2 tablespoons brown sugar,
  firmly packed

3 tablespoons honey
1 tablespoon soy sauce
2 pounds boneless chicken
  breast, skinned and cut into
  1-inch cubes

Melt the butter and oil in a pan, add the remaining ingredients, except the chicken, and simmer for 5 minutes. Add the chicken and sauté until the chicken is browned on all sides, 10–15 minutes. Serve the chicken, along with the sauce, in a chafing dish with toothpicks. Garnish with parsley. Yields 50–60. Heat scale 4.

Fiery Appetizers (New Mexico)

Seafood Spread

1 (8-ounce) package cream
  cheese, softened
⅓ cup mayonnaise
⅓ cup sour cream
3 hard-boiled eggs, mashed
1 (8-ounce) can crabmeat,
  flaked

1 (8-ounce) can tiny shrimp,
  drained and chopped
¼ onion, very finely chopped
1 stalk celery, very finely
  chopped
1 teaspoon Creole seasoning
Several dashes Tabasco

Combine cream cheese, mayonnaise, sour cream, and boiled eggs in mixer bowl. Beat until fairly smooth. Add crabmeat, shrimp, onion, celery, Creole seasoning, and Tabasco; mix well. Serve with crackers; this can also be used as a dip or to make good sandwiches.

I Cook - You Clean (Texas II)

Spicy Hot Crab Dip

An elegant entrée when served over rice or in pastry shells.

1 (8-ounce) package cream
   cheese, softened
1 tablespoon milk
8 ounces fresh lump crabmeat
2 tablespoons sherry
1 teaspoon Worcestershire
½ teaspoon garlic powder

1 teaspoon Tabasco
Juice of ½ lemon
2 tablespoons grated onion
2 teaspoons prepared horseradish
¼ teaspoon salt
Dash of cayenne pepper

Preheat oven to 375°. Combine cream cheese and milk. Blend thoroughly. Add remaining ingredients. Blend well. Spread mixture in a baking dish. Bake 15–20 minutes. Serve with assorted crackers. Serves 12–15.

Necessities and Temptations (Texas II)

Shrimp-Crab Mousse

1 (10¾-ounce) can condensed
   cream of mushroom soup
1 (8-ounce) package cream
   cheese
1 envelope unflavored gelatin

1 cup finely chopped onion
1 cup finely chopped celery
1 cup real mayonnaise
1 (6-ounce) can lump crabmeat
1 cup cooked salad shrimp

In saucepan, heat soup, cream cheese, and gelatin until warm and blended. Working with ½ mixture at a time, add remaining ingredients; mix until smooth. Grease a favorite seafood mold very well; fill with mousse mixture. Chill overnight.

Unmold and garnish as desired. Serve with crackers or vegetable sticks. Serves 10–12.

Coastal Cuisine (Texas II)

Garlic Shrimp

Shrimp, cooked, peeled and
  deveined
8 cloves garlic
1 teaspoon thyme
1 teaspoon dry mustard

Juice of one dozen lemons
Dash of oregano
Dash of cayenne
Salt and pepper to taste

Pour sauce over shrimp and refrigerate 12–24 hours. Serve as hors d'oeuvres.

Trading Secrets (Texas)

Texas Shrimp Pâté

1 (10-ounce) can tomato soup,
  undiluted
1 package plain gelatin
3 tablespoons cold water
1 (8-ounce) package cream
  cheese, softened
¾ cup mayonnaise

1 small onion, grated
1 cup finely chopped celery
Dash of cayenne pepper
1 small can shrimp, drained and
  chopped, or 1 cup cooked
  shrimp
Parsley sprigs

Heat soup. Remove from heat. Dissolve gelatin in cold water. Add to soup. Stir well. Add all ingredients except parsley and mix well. Spoon into oiled 4-cup mold. I use a Texas-shaped cake pan. Chill. Unmold and garnish with parsley; serve with crackers.

Variations: You may substitute 1 can of mushroom soup for the tomato soup and 1 small can crabmeat, flaked, for the shrimp, and spoon into an oiled fish mold.

A Different Taste of Paris (Texas)

Shrimp Bubbles

1 (4½-ounce) can tiny
  shrimp, drained and flaked
¼ cup real mayonnaise
1 teaspoon instant onion

½ teaspoon Ac'cent
¼ teaspoon creamed
  horseradish
2 cans Pillsbury Crescent Rolls

Mix shrimp, mayonnaise, onion, Ac'cent, and horseradish well. Cut each triangle of rolls in half to make 32. Place a scant amount of shrimp mixture on each triangle. Roll up and pinch dough to seal. Bake at 375° until brown. This also makes a good spread for crackers.

Feast of Goodness (Texas II)

Mexican Party Mix

4 tablespoons margarine
2 teaspoons chili powder
¼ teaspoon garlic salt
¼ teaspoon onion salt

7 cups Kellogg's Crispix
2 cups Chili Cheese Fritos
¾ cup peanuts
¼ cup grated Parmesan cheese

Melt margarine in microwave or saucepan; add the spices. Toss cereal, Fritos, and peanuts in a 9x13-inch pan or roaster pan. Pour margarine mixture over and toss to coat thoroughly. Bake in preheated oven at 250° for 15 minutes. Remove from oven; toss with Parmesan cheese to coat and return to oven for 30 minutes longer. Stir after 15 minutes. Spread on paper towels to cool. Yields about 10 cups.

The Mexican Collection (Texas II)

Texas, Arizona, New Mexico, and California all border Mexico. Texas has the longest stretch of the international border between the United States and Mexico, while California has the shortest. It is the most frequently crossed international border in the world, with about 250 million people crossing every year.

Indienne Cashew Spread

½ cup chopped cashews
5 tablespoons Major Grey's
   Chutney, chopped
½ teaspoon lemon juice

1 (8-ounce) package cream
   cheese, softened
¼ teaspoon curry powder
Apple rings (or Triscuits)

Mix together the cashews, chutney, lemon juice, cream cheese, and curry powder. Spread on cool, unpeeled apple rings (or Triscuit crackers). Covers 15 apple rings.

Recipes from the Cotton Patch (New Mexico)

Barbecued Pecans

2 tablespoons margarine
¼ cup Worcestershire
1 tablespoon ketchup

2 dashes of hot sauce
4 cups pecan halves
Salt

Melt margarine in a large saucepan; add Worcestershire, ketchup and hot sauce. Stir in pecans. Spoon into glass baking dish and spread evenly. Toast at 400° about 20 minutes, stirring frequently. Turn out on absorbent towels and sprinkle with salt.

The Dallas Pecan Cookbook (Texas)

BREAD and BREAKFAST

GWEN McKEE

The architect of the Loretto chapel in Santa Fe, New Mexico, died suddenly during construction, with the structure lacking any type of stairway to the choir loft. Needing a way to get up to the choir loft, the nuns prayed for nine days. Then a stranger appeared and told the nuns he would build a staircase but that he needed total privacy and locked himself in the chapel for three months. The resulting spiral staircase ascends twenty feet, making two revolutions up to the choir loft without the use of nails or apparent center support, and is made entirely of non-native wood. The identity of the carpenter is not known, since he left before being paid. Many feel it was a miracle. In 1887—ten years after it was built—a railing was added and the outer spiral was fastened to an adjacent pillar.

Biscuits and Sausage Gravy

3 cups biscuit mix
¾ cup milk
½ pound pork sausage
½ stick margarine

⅓ cup flour
3½ cups milk
½ teaspoon salt
½ teaspoon pepper

Combine biscuit mix and milk; stir. Roll dough on floured wax paper to ¾-inch thickness; cut with biscuit cutter. Place on a greased baking sheet. Bake at 400° for 12–15 minutes or until golden.

For gravy, crumble and brown sausage in skillet. Drain, reserving 1 tablespoon drippings in skillet. Set sausage aside. Add margarine to drippings; melt margarine. Add flour and cook 1 minute, stirring constantly. Gradually add milk; cook over medium heat, stirring constantly until thickened. Stir in seasonings and sausage. Cook until heated, stirring constantly. Serve sausage gravy over cooked biscuits. Serves 6–8.

Great Tastes of Texas (Texas II)

Creole Cheese Sticks

2 tablespoons unsalted margarine
¾ cup water
1 packet Butter Buds
1 teaspoon Tony's Creole
　Seasoning (or ¼ teaspoon each:
　thyme, celery seed, marjoram,
　and white pepper, if Tony's not
　available)

1 loaf Pepperidge Farm wheat
　bread, sliced extra thin
1 small can Parmesan cheese

In boiler, melt margarine with water, Butter Buds, and seasoning. Keep warm 5 minutes before brushing each slice of bread, both sides, with mixture. Slice each slice into 3 fingers.

In a flat pan, put Parmesan cheese. Press to coat each bread finger on both sides. Bake in preheated 350° oven only until lightly brown and crunchy.

La Galerie Perroquet Food Fare (Texas)

Texas Beer Bread

3 cups self-rising flour
¼ cup sugar
1 can Lite beer

1 egg, beaten
1 tablespoon water
Melted butter

Mix flour and sugar in bowl. Add beer; watch it foam, and mix just until blended. Pour into buttered loaf pan, preferably glass. Combine egg with water and brush top of loaf. Let rise 10 minutes. Bake at 350° for 40–45 minutes. Brush top with butter while hot. Great for last minute.

Lone Star Legacy (Texas II)

Betty Ewing's Jalapeño Cornbread

1 cup cornmeal
1 tablespoon sugar
½ tablespoon baking powder
1 teaspoon salt
2 eggs, beaten
½ cup bacon drippings
1 (16-ounce) can cream-style corn

1 large onion, diced
½–¾ pound Cheddar cheese, grated
¼ cup diced jalapeño pepper, seeds removed
⅛ cup diced pimento
1 pod garlic, squeezed thru press
1 tablespoon Pace's Hot Sauce

Mix above ingredients in order of succession. Pour into well-greased casserole. Bake at 400° for 35 minutes.

March of Dimes Gourmet Gala Cookbook (Texas)

Cowboy Cornbread

½ cup vegetable shortening
2 cups self-rising yellow cornmeal mix
1 (8½-ounce) can cream-style corn
1 (8-ounce) carton sour cream

1 cup shredded sharp Cheddar cheese
2 eggs, beaten
1 (4-ounce) can chopped green chiles, undrained

Preheat oven to 400°. Melt shortening in a 9-inch square baking pan. Tilt pan to coat bottom evenly. Mix remaining ingredients. Add melted shortening. Mix until well blended. Pour into hot pan. Bake 30 minutes or until golden brown. Yields 9 servings.

Wild About Texas (Texas II)

Peanut-Carrot-Pineapple Holiday Bread

3 cups all-purpose flour, sifted
1 teaspoon baking soda
1 teaspoon salt
1 teaspoon cinnamon
3 eggs, beaten
3 cups sugar

1 cup cooking oil
2 cups finely grated carrots
1 (9-ounce) can crushed
  pineapple, drained
2 teaspoons vanilla
1 cup chopped peanuts

Sift flour, baking soda, salt, and cinnamon together. Place eggs and sugar in mixer bowl. Beat at medium speed until mixed. Beat in oil, a small amount at a time. Stir in flour mixture, carrots, pineapple, vanilla, and peanuts. Pour batter in 2 greased loaf pans. Makes 2 small loaves. Bake at 350° for 60 minutes.

Peanut Palate Pleasers from Portales (New Mexico)

Holiday Treasure Loaf

1 cup all-purpose flour, sifted
1 cup sugar
½ teaspoon salt
½ teaspoon baking powder
3 cups pitted dates, whole

1 (8-ounce) jar Maraschino
  cherries, whole
1 pound walnut meats, whole
4 eggs
1 teaspoon vanilla

Sift dry ingredients into a large bowl. Add dates, cherries, and nuts to flour and coat well. Beat eggs well and add vanilla and pour into first mixture. Mix thoroughly with hands.

Line greased pan (5½x9½x2¾-inch) with heavy brown paper and grease paper well. Bake at 325° for 1¾–2 hours, or until "pick" clean. Remove from pan and wrap in a brandy-moistened cloth, then foil. Let stand a day or two. Fruit juice may be used instead of brandy. Serves 10.

The Dog-Gone Delicious Cookbook (Arizona)

Mom's Apple Bread

3 eggs
1 cup oil
2 cups sugar
2 cups all-purpose flour
1 teaspoon vanilla

1 teaspoon cinnamon
1 teaspoon baking soda
Dash of salt
2 cups chopped apples
1 cup chopped nuts

Mix eggs, oil, and sugar in large bowl. Add flour, vanilla, cinnamon, baking soda, salt, apples, and nuts. Pour into greased loaf pans. Bake one hour at 350°. Makes 3 loaves.

What's Cookin' at Casa (New Mexico)

Easy Eggnog Bread

This bread is wonderful with Swiss, Cheddar, or brick cheeses and cold meats . . . especially for a quick supper during the Christmas season.

3 cups all-purpose flour
¾ cup sugar
1 tablespoon baking powder
1 teaspoon salt
½ teaspoon nutmeg
1 egg, beaten

¼ cup butter, melted
1½ cups eggnog
¾ cup chopped walnuts or
    pecans
¾ cup candied fruits

In large mixing bowl, sift together flour, sugar, baking powder, salt, and nutmeg. Combine egg, butter, and eggnog. Add to dry ingredients; stir until thoroughly mixed. Add nuts and fruits. Bake in greased loaf pan 60–70 minutes at 350°. Cool on wire rack. Yields 1 loaf.

Cook 'em Horns (Texas)

AZ NM The sun shines in southern Arizona 85% of the time, which is considerably more sunshine than Florida or Hawaii. Tucson enjoys more sunshine than any other city in the United States, about 350 days each year. Farmington, New Mexico, recorded 779 days of consecutive sunshine from December 16, 1961, to February 2, 1964.

Banana Oatmeal Muffins

1 cup all-purpose flour
½ cup sugar
2 teaspoons baking powder
½ teaspoon baking soda
½ teaspoon salt
⅔ cup old-fashioned oats

¼ cup finely chopped pecans
1 egg
½ cup milk
2 tablespoons oil
½ cup mashed bananas

Combine flour, sugar, baking powder, baking soda, and salt in a medium mixing bowl. Stir in oats and nuts. In a small bowl slightly beat egg; add milk and beat. Stir in oil and bananas. Add to dry ingredients. Fill greased muffin tins ⅔ full. Bake at 425° for about 15 minutes.

Not Just Bacon & Eggs (Texas II)

Mom's Streusel-Filled Coffee Cake

This recipe has been in my family for generations. I can't remember celebrating a holiday and not having "Mom's Coffee Cake" warm from the oven. My guests at the Inn love this recipe.

CAKE:
3½ cups all-purpose flour
1 tablespoon baking powder
1 teaspoon salt
1½ cups sugar

½ cup shortening
2 eggs
1 cup milk
1 tablespoon vanilla

STREUSEL:
1 cup brown sugar
2 tablespoons cinnamon
¼ cup flour

¼ cup melted butter
1 cup chopped nuts

Mix cake ingredients well and place half of the batter in the bottom of a greased springform pan. Mix the streusel ingredients together with a fork. Add half the streusel over cake batter, then add the rest of the batter and top with remaining streusel. Bake in a preheated oven at 350° for about 45 minutes.

Inn on the Rio's Favorite Recipes (New Mexico)

Rich Pineapple Coffee Cake

Your guests will want this moist, very rich coffee cake recipe!

1½ cups sugar
2 cups all-purpose flour
1 teaspoon baking soda
½ teaspoon salt
2 eggs, beaten

2 cups crushed pineapple,
 slightly drained
½ cup brown sugar
½ cup chopped pecans

TOPPING:

½ cup margarine
¾ cup sugar

1 cup evaporated milk
½ teaspoon vanilla

Preheat oven to 325°. In a large mixing bowl, combine sugar, flour, baking soda, salt, eggs, and pineapple. In a greased and floured 7x11-inch pan, pour mixture. In a separate bowl, mix brown sugar and pecans. Sprinkle over batter. Bake 30 minutes. Begin making Topping about 10 minutes before cake is done. In a saucepan, mix together margarine, sugar, and evaporated milk. Boil over medium-low heat for 2 minutes. Stir in vanilla. Spoon over hot cake. Yields 0 servings.

Variation: Use ½ Topping.

Celebrate San Antonio (Texas II)

Taos Pueblo is an ancient pueblo belonging to a Taos (Northern Tiwa) speaking Native American tribe of Pueblo people. About 130 people live in it full-time. A reservation of 95,000 acres is attached to the pueblo, and about 1,900 people live in this area. It was designated a National Historic Landmark on October 9, 1960, and in 1992 became a World Heritage Site. Approximately 1,000 years old, it lies about one mile north of the modern city of Taos, New Mexico.

GWEN McKEE

Quick Crescent Caramel Rolls

8 tablespoons margarine, divided
¾ cup firmly packed brown sugar
¼ cup water
½ cup chopped pecans (optional)

2 (8-ounce) cans refrigerated crescent dinner rolls
¼ cup sugar
2 teaspoons cinnamon

In ungreased 9x13-inch pan, melt 5 tablespoons margarine in oven. Stir in brown sugar, water, and pecans. Set aside. Separate each can of roll dough into 4 rectangles. Pinch perforations together to seal. Spread with 3 tablespoons softened margarine. Combine sugar and cinnamon; sprinkle over dough. Starting at shorter side, roll up each rectangle. Cut each roll into 4 slices, making 32 pieces. Place cut side down in prepared pan. Bake at 375° for 20–25 minutes until golden brown. Invert immediately to remove from pan. Serve warm. Yields 32 rolls.

Hint: To reheat, wrap in foil and warm at 350° for 10–15 minutes.

Homecoming (Texas II)

Empanadas de Fruta

1½ cups all-purpose flour
1 teaspoon baking powder
1 teaspoon salt

8 tablespoons shortening
4–6 tablespoons water
Butter or margarine (optional)

Sift flour, baking powder, and salt together. Cut in shortening and mix well. Add enough water to make dough easy to handle. Roll out dough to ⅛-inch thickness. Cut in rounds 3–4 inches in diameter. Fill each round with fruit. Press edges of dough together. Brush with butter and bake until brown.

FRUIT FILLING:
2 cups canned fruit, drained
1 cup sugar

1 teaspoon cinnamon
½ teaspoon cloves

Blend all thoroughly. Fill pastry rounds.

Recipes from Hatch (New Mexico)

Out of This World Pecan Waffles

2½ cups all-purpose flour
4 teaspoons baking powder
1½ tablespoons sugar
¾ teaspoon salt

¾ cup oil
2¼ cups milk
2 eggs, beaten
½ cup ground pecans

Measure and sift dry ingredients together. Mix oil with milk and eggs. Stir into dry ingredients. Mix until smooth. Add pecans and mix well. Bake immediately or let set in the refrigerator overnight. They will keep well covered for 2 weeks. Easy and good.

The Authorized Texas Ranger Cookbook (Texas II)

Bobbi's Apple Pancakes

"I use it for recruits," says Bobbi Olson, wife of Lute Olson, UA basketball coach. "They love it, and want their mothers to have the recipe."

CINNAMON SYRUP:

2 cups light corn syrup
4 cups sugar
1 cup water

1 tablespoon cinnamon
2 cups evaporated milk

Combine all ingredients except the milk and bring to a full boil in a medium size pot. Cook for 2 minutes, stirring constantly. Let cool a full 5 minutes. Add milk, and serve warm.

BATTER:

2 medium-size green apples,
    (Jonathan or Granny Smith),
    peeled, cored, and chopped
2 eggs
2 tablespoons sugar

2 tablespoons butter, softened
2 cups evaporated milk
2 cups Bisquick All-Purpose
    Baking Mix

While waiting for the syrup to cool, mix all the batter ingredients in a large bowl. Spoon onto a greased pancake grill or frying pan and cook over medium-high heat. Serves 4.

The Arizona Celebrity Cookbook (Arizona)

Apple Fritters

1 egg	½ teaspoon salt
⅓ cup milk	1½ cups grated fresh apple, or
1 cup all-purpose flour	1 can apple pie filling
1½ teaspoons baking powder	Powdered sugar

Beat egg well, then mix with milk. Blend flour, baking powder, and salt into egg mixture. Stir in apples. Drop by tablespoonsful into hot grease. Deep-fry at 350° until golden brown. Roll hot fritters in powdered sugar. If you like a sweeter fritter, add ¼ cup sugar and 1 teaspoon cinnamon to batter. Canned chunk pineapple can be used instead of apples.

    These are best hot, just out of the fryer, but are pretty good for a couple of hours if they last that long. Yields 3 dozen.

Scrumptious (Texas)

Pan Fried Apples, 1919

These make a great camp meal anywhere, even at the backyard barbecue.

3 or 4 large, tart apples, cored and sliced	⅓ cup wild honey or brown sugar
2 tablespoons bacon drippings or butter	Salt and cinnamon

Heat apple slices in hot bacon drippings in skillet until they soften, stirring to turn over. Add honey or brown sugar and a little salt and cinnamon, if available. If not, honey or sugar will glaze the slices if allowed to remain on the fire, covered, 5–10 minutes, depending on heat.

Arizona Highways Heritage Cookbook (Arizona)

Huevos Rancheros

Although usually associated with breakfast, Huevos Rancheros is a hearty regional favorite at any time of the day, almost always accompanied by "refried" beans.

**Oil, preferably corn or canola,
  to a depth of ½ inch**
6 (5-inch) corn tortillas
12 eggs

**2–3 cups green chile sauce,
  warmed**
**Shredded lettuce and chopped
  tomato, for garnish**

Arrange several layers of paper towels near the stove.

Heat the oil in a large skillet until it ripples. With tongs, dip a tortilla into the hot oil and cook it until it is softened and pliable, a matter of seconds. Remove the tortilla immediately and drain it on the paper towels. If you don't act quickly enough, the tortilla will become crisp. Repeat with the rest of the tortillas. Carefully pour out of the skillet all but enough oil to generously coat its surface. Reserve the extra oil.

Arrange each tortilla on a plate and set aside. Place the skillet back on the stove and heat the oil over low heat. Fry the eggs, 2–3 at a time, turning once after the whites have set and the yolk has thickened. (For health reasons, each should be fried until the yolk sets.) Top each tortilla with two eggs, arranged side by side. Continue until all the eggs are fried, adding a bit of the reserved oil when the skillet becomes dry. Pour ⅓–½ cup of green chile sauce over each serving. Garnish the plates with lettuce and tomato. Serve with scoops of "refried" beans and Spanish rice, if desired.

The Rancho de Chimayó Cookbook (New Mexico)

Huevos Rancheros
(Eggs Ranch Style)

4 slices bacon
1 medium onion, chopped
2 ribs celery, chopped
1 can Ro-Tel tomatoes and green
   chiles

1 (14½-ounce) can whole
   tomatoes
4 eggs
4 corn tortillas
Grated Cheddar cheese

Fry bacon crisp and put aside for later. Sauté onion and celery in 2 tablespoons bacon drippings. Add both cans of tomatoes to the sautéed mixture. Let simmer till liquid cooks down some. Make a little "well" in the mixture for each egg. (Depending on size of skillet—you may be able to cook only 3 eggs at a time). Place a whole egg in each "well"; cover and let simmer till desired doneness. Serve each egg on a warm tortilla and cover with tomato mixture. Sprinkle grated cheese and crumbled bacon on top of each serving.

A Taste of Victoria (Texas)

Southwest Breakfast Omelet

8 slices white bread, buttered
2 cups grated Cheddar or
   longhorn cheese (retain
   ¼ cup to sprinkle on top
   before baking)
1 onion, diced
1 pound mushrooms, sliced

1 (7-ounce) can chopped green
   chiles
4 eggs
1½ teaspoons salt
¼ teaspoon pepper
½ teaspoon table mustard
3 cups milk

Put 4 slices of bread in bottom of casserole dish. Sprinkle with half the cheese and half of onion, mushrooms, and chiles. Add another layer of bread and remainder of cheese, onion, mushrooms, and chiles. Beat eggs with seasonings, adding milk. Pour over bread and sprinkle additional cheese over top. Bake for 1 hour at 350°. Cover with foil for the first 40 minutes. Let stand about 10 minutes before serving. (Can be made the night before, covered with foil, and put in the refrigerator.) Serves 8.

Padre Kino's Favorite Meatloaf (Arizona)

Company Eggs and Cheese

14–15 slices white sandwich
bread
1 cup grated sharp Cheddar
cheese
1 cup grated Monterey Jack
cheese
1 (4-ounce) can chopped
green chiles

7 eggs
½ tablespoon dry mustard
1 teaspoon salt
3 cups milk
1 cup crushed cornflakes, or
enough to cover
¼ cup melted butter

Preheat oven to 350°. Remove crusts from bread and cut slices in half. Place half the bread in a buttered 9x13-inch pan. Layer with Cheddar cheese, Monterey Jack cheese, and green chiles. Cover with remaining bread. Beat eggs with dry mustard, salt, and milk. Pour over casserole and let stand in refrigerator 12 hours or overnight. Before baking, cover with cornflakes and drizzle with butter. Bake for 30–40 minutes at 350°. Makes 8–12 servings.

Cooking with Kiwanis (New Mexico)

Saucy Eggs Mornay

6 thin slices ham
Butter or margarine
3 English muffins, split, buttered
and toasted

6 eggs, poached
1 tablespoon chopped chives

Lightly brown ham in small amount of butter. Place ham slice on each muffin half and top with poached egg. Keep warm while preparing Mornay Sauce. Pour Mornay Sauce over eggs and sprinkle with chives. Serve immediately. Serves 3–6.

MORNAY SAUCE:

3 tablespoons butter or margarine
3 tablespoons flour
¾ teaspoon salt
¼ teaspoon nutmeg

Dash of pepper
1 cup light cream
¼ cup dry white wine
⅓ cup shredded Swiss cheese

Melt butter in saucepan. Blend in flour, salt, nutmeg, and pepper. Stir until smooth and bubbly. Add cream all at once and cook quickly, stirring constantly until mixture thickens and bubbles. Stir in wine. Add cheese and stir until melted. Use at once.

Becky's Brunch & Breakfast Book (Texas)

Green Chilaquiles Omelet

These beauties can be made in relays and kept warm in the oven, or you can make a double recipe in an 8-inch omelet pan and cut the omelet in quarters to serve. They look very pretty garnished with tomato quarters and a sprig of fresh coriander.

1 corn tortilla	½ cup green chile sauce, heated
Oil for frying	½ cup grated Monterey Jack
Salt	cheese (or Cheddar)
Ground cumin	1 tablespoon butter
2 eggs	

Cut the tortilla's round edges off so you have a square. Cut the square in half, stack the halves, and cut into matchstick strips. Fry in hot oil until crisp, drain on paper towels, and sprinkle with salt and a little cumin immediately. Beat eggs in a bowl with a little salt, and have sauce and cheese ready.

Melt butter in a 6-inch omelet pan over medium heat. When it sizzles, pour the eggs in. When they start to set, lift the edges with a fork to let unset egg run under, then spread with sauce. Keep lifting the edges to let any runny egg under, but don't let the omelet over-cook—the edges should be set, but the top should still be a little undercooked. Remove from the heat; sprinkle with tortilla strips, and then cheese. Run under a broiler for a minute or so to melt the cheese, then slip face up onto a plate. Serves 1.

The Aficionado's Southwestern Cooking (New Mexico)

Early Morning Casserole

1 pound sausage	1 can mushroom soup
4 tablespoons margarine	1 can chopped green chiles
12 eggs	Grated cheese

Scramble and cook sausage until brown. Drain on paper towels and put in ovenproof pan. Melt butter in skillet; scramble eggs until soft. Pour over sausage and add mushroom soup (undiluted). Add chopped chiles and cover with grated cheese. Bake at 350° for 10 minutes or until heated through.

Amistad Community Recipes (New Mexico)

Oak Creek Eggs

Vegetable oil
2 (6-inch) flour tortillas
2 ounces chorizo
2 eggs

2 black olives
2 ounces (¼ cup) Cilantro
  Hollandaise

Heat oil in deep heavy pot to 350°. Drop in flour tortilla and push down with a 2-ounce ladle and cook until golden brown and holds the shape of a cup. Repeat with second tortilla. Cook chorizo and poach the eggs. Spoon half of the chorizo in each tortilla cup and place egg over chorizo. Ladle 1 ounce of Cilantro Hollandaise over each egg. Garnish each with a black olive and serve with home fries or hash browns.

CILANTRO HOLLANDAISE:

2 egg yolks
1 teaspoon water
4 ounces (½ cup) clarified
  butter
¼ cup lemon juice

Dash of Tabasco
Dash of Worcestershire
¼ bunch cilantro, chopped
1 teaspoon white wine
Pinch of garlic

Beat egg yolks with water in a double boiler over low heat until eggs become fluffy (do not let eggs stick to the bowl). Slowly drizzle in the butter while beating rapidly. Stir in lemon, Tabasco, Worcestershire, cilantro, wine, and garlic. Serves 2.

Sedona Cook Book (Arizona)

Tex-Mex Brunch or Supper

12 eggs, beaten
2 cups cream-style corn
1 tablespoon Worcestershire
4 cups (1 pound) sharp
  Cheddar cheese

2 (4-ounce) cans green
  chiles, drained and chopped
1 tablespoon salt
½ teaspoon red pepper

Preheat oven to 325°. In large bowl, combine all ingredients; beat until well mixed. Pour into greased or Pam-sprayed 9x13-inch baking dish. May prepare ahead of use up to this point; cover and refrigerate up to 24 hours in advance. Bake 1 hour 15 minutes, or until firm to touch, at 325°. Serves 10–12.

Note: Good served with fresh fruit and buttered bread sticks.

Collectibles III (Texas II)

Brunch Eggs

CHEESE SAUCE:

2 tablespoons butter
2 tablespoons all-purpose flour
½ teaspoon salt
⅛ teaspoon pepper

2 cups milk
1 cup (4-ounces) processed
   American cheese, shredded

Melt butter and blend in flour, salt and pepper. Slowly pour in milk, cooking and stirring constantly until thickened and smooth. Stir in cheese and stir until melted.

EGGS:

1 cup (4-ounces) diced
   Canadian bacon
¼ cup chopped green onions
3 tablespoons butter or margarine
12 eggs, beaten
1 (3-ounce) can mushroom
   pieces, drained

4 teaspoons butter or margarine,
   melted
2¼ cups soft bread crumbs
   (3 slices)
⅛ teaspoon paprika

In a large skillet, cook Canadian bacon and onion in the 3 table-spoons of butter until onion is tender but not brown. Add eggs and scramble just until set. Fold mushrooms and cooked eggs into Cheese Sauce. Turn into a 12x7x2-inch baking dish. Combine remaining melted butter, crumbs, and paprika, and sprinkle on top of eggs. Cover and chill until 30 minutes before serving. Bake, uncovered, in 350° oven for 30 minutes. Serves 10.

Cookin' Wise (Texas)

Six Shooter Casserole

1 (2-pound) package thawed hash brown potatoes
1 pound chopped ham, sausage, or bacon, cooked and crumbled
1 (8-ounce) can chopped green chiles
12–14 eggs
1 teaspoon salt
½ teaspoon pepper
⅓ teaspoon dry mustard
½ cup milk
1 cup grated Cheddar cheese

Layer potatoes, meat, and chiles in greased 9x13-inch baking dish or evenly into individual ramekins. Beat together eggs, salt, pepper, dry mustard, and milk. Pour over top of casserole. Sprinkle with grated cheese. Bake at 350° for 1 hour. Can be prepared and refrigerated overnight. Garnish with salsa. Makes 12 servings.

What's Cooking Inn Arizona (Arizona)

Farmer's Breakfast

Great for a change

6 slices bacon, cut into 3-inch pieces
3 medium-size potatoes, cooked, peeled, and cubed
¼ cup chopped green bell pepper
¼ cup chopped onion
1 cup grated Cheddar cheese
6 raw eggs
1 teaspoon Knorr Swiss Aromat Seasoning for Meat
½ teaspoon salt
¼ teaspoon black pepper

1. In a large skillet using low heat, fry bacon until crisp; remove and drain bacon. Leave 3 tablespoons of bacon drippings in the skillet.
2. Add potatoes, peppers, and onions to the skillet and cook about 5 minutes or until potatoes are browned.
3. Sprinkle cheese over potatoes and stir until cheese melts.
4. Break eggs into skillet, add the seasonings, and stirring gently, cook mixture until eggs are done.
5. Sprinkle top with bacon pieces and serve. Serves 6.

Leaving Home (Texas)

Spicy Southwest Bake

As a busy innkeeper, I love this flavorful dish's make-ahead preparation. Guests love this Southwest-style dish with sour cream and fresh salsa.

½ pound pork or turkey sausage	4 slices bread
1 large onion, diced	6 large eggs
1–3 teaspoons hot pepper flakes	1 cup milk
	1 cup salsa
	1 cup shredded Cheddar cheese

Brown sausage and onions together. Add the hot pepper flakes. One teaspoon for mild, 3 for hot and spicy. Lightly spray an 7x11-inch baking dish with nonstick cooking spray. Line the baking dish with the bread slices. Sprinkle the sausage/onion mixture over the bread. Mix the eggs, milk, and salsa together. Pour over the bread slices. Top with the cheese. Cover with foil and refrigerate overnight.

At brunch or breakfast time, put casserole in a preheated 350° oven for 45 minutes. Take off the foil and heat for 10 more minutes. Remove from oven and let cool 10 minutes before serving. Serve with extra salsa, hot or mild, and sour cream. Enjoy!

Inn on the Rio's Favorite Recipes (New Mexico)

Megas

Surprise family and friends with this easy Tex-Mex breakfast.

5 tortillas, cut into ½-inch strips	2 tomatoes, chopped
Vegetable oil for frying	1 serrano chile, minced
2 chicken breast halves	½ white onion, chopped
1 small onion, quartered	3 tablespoons vegetable oil
½ clove garlic	4 eggs, beaten

Fry tortilla strips in hot oil until crisp. Boil chicken breasts, quartered onion, and garlic in water to cover for 20 minutes. Drain and dice the chicken breasts. Sauté tomatoes, serrano, and ½ onion in 3 tablespoons vegetable oil. Add tortilla strips and chicken. Add eggs and scramble. Serves 2.

Variation: Bake tortillas with Pam, use only 1 teaspoon vegetable oil to sauté vegetables, and substitute Egg Beaters.

Joe T. Garcia's, Fort Worth
Fort Worth is Cooking! (Texas II)

Breakfast Enchiladas

ENCHILADA SAUCE:

1 small onion, chopped
½ cup chopped green bell
  pepper

1½ tablespoons cooking oil
1 (15-ounce) can tomato sauce
1½ teaspoons chili powder

In a small skillet over medium heat, sauté onion and green pepper in oil until onion is limp. Stir in tomato sauce and chili powder. Reduce heat to low and simmer while the eggs are cooking.

5 eggs, beaten
2 tablespoons milk
¼ cup diced green chiles
Salt and pepper to taste

2 tablespoons butter or margarine
4 corn tortillas
¾ cup shredded Cheddar cheese

Preheat broiler. Combine eggs, milk, chiles, salt and pepper. In a skillet over medium-low heat, scramble egg mixture in melted butter. Cook until firm as desired. Dip tortillas 1 at a time into hot Enchilada Sauce until soft. Spoon ¼ of the eggs down center of each tortilla. Roll up and place, seam side down, in a single layer in a greased 10x6-inch glass baking dish. Bring remaining sauce to boil. Pour evenly over rolled tortillas, sprinkle with cheese. Broil about 4 inches from heat 2–3 minutes or until cheese melts. Serves 2.

Becky's Brunch & Breakfast Book (Texas)

Southwestern dishes, though referred to as "Tex-Mex" or "Mexican," actually reflect a blend of Hispanic and Indian cultures. There are four main ingredients in southwestern dishes—tortillas, pinto beans, cheese, and chiles.

Hot Cheese Grits

You simply cannot find a more southern dish than grits. Those Yankees who come down South turn up their noses at one of the best foods that ever originated in America. What would a slice of tender fried ham be without grits and redeye gravy? Some prefer grits with their breakfast eggs, because Mother always served them that way. And there is nothing better than a bowl of grits with melted butter and a touch of salt to start the day. There is quite an art to cooking grits so they aren't too watery and certainly not lumpy. The exact consistency may take a few practice cookings, but once you get the knack, you'll "Kiss My Grits!"

Grits have also become sophisticated. Here is Dorothy's recipe with sherry and green chiles.

2 cups quick grits	**2 eggs, beaten**
8 cups boiling water	**2 tablespoons sherry**
1 teaspoon salt	**1 teaspoon Lea & Perrins**
1½ sticks margarine	**Worcestershire**
8 ounces Kraft hot jalapeño	**1 teaspoon Tabasco**
cheese	**2 (12-ounce) cans green chiles,**
16 ounces Kraft garlic cheese	**chopped**

Slowly stir grits into boiling salted water. Turn heat off. Add margarine and cheese to grits mixture. Cool.

Add eggs, sherry, Lea & Perrins, Tabasco, and chiles. Spoon mixture into greased baking dish and bake 1 hour at 300°.

Note: This freezes well. Water will appear on top, but just remix and reheat. Superb with ham or chicken. Serves 30.

Recipe from Lamplighter Inn, Floydada
Texas Historic Inns Cookbook (Texas)

WIKIPEDIA.ORG

Old Tucson Studios is known as "Hollywood in the Desert." More than 200 movies, TV shows, commercials, and documentaries have been filmed there since it was built as a set for the movie *Arizona* in 1939. In addition to its historic role as a film location, Old Tucson Studios is southern Arizona's premier outdoor entertainment venue with a full array of live shows, thrilling stunts, Old West dramas, saloon musicals, and trail rides.

Golden Sandwiches

A pretty fruit cup would be a nice accompaniment.

8 slices bread
4 slices Swiss cheese
4 slices American cheese

4 slices ham
4 slices chicken breast
4 slices turkey

Make 4 sandwiches using bread, cheeses, ham, chicken, and turkey. Cut into fourths and secure with toothpicks.

BATTER:

1¼ cups ice water, divided
1 egg yolk, beaten
1½ cups self-rising flour

Dash of salt
1 egg white, beaten until stiff
Oil for frying

Add half of water to egg yolk. Stir in flour, salt, and add remaining water. Then fold in beaten egg white. Dip sandwiches into Batter. Deep-fry in hot oil until golden brown. Drain on paper towels. Serves 8.

Hullabaloo in the Kitchen

Apple Cinnamon Jelly

2¾ cups apple juice
5¾ cups sugar
4–6 large cinnamon sticks
  (broken into pieces)

1 box fruit pectin
½ teaspoon margarine or
  butter

Pour apple juice into 6- or 8-quart pot. Place sugar in a separate bowl; set aside. Into apple juice stir cinnamon sticks, fruit pectin, and margarine (to prevent foaming during cooking). Bring mixture to full rolling boil over high heat, stirring constantly. Quickly add sugar to juice and return to full rolling boil for 1 minute, stirring constantly. Remove from heat. Skim off any foam and remove cinnamon sticks. Pour into hot sterilized jars to within ⅛ inch of top. Add sterilized lids and process in boiling water bath for 10 minutes. Yields 4–5 (½-pint) jars.

Arizona State Fair Blue Ribbon Recipes (Arizona)

Prickly Pear Jelly

6½ cups prickly pear juice
2 packages Sure-Jell

½ cup lemon juice
9 cups sugar

Do not peel prickly pears. Wear gloves and rub spines off with gunny sack. Wash them well; it's not necessary for all spines to be removed. It's amazing how they disappear when cooked.

Put fully ripe fruit in kettle with a small amount of water, not more than 3 cups for an 8-quart kettle. Bring fruit to a boil, and mash with potato masher. Do not overcook. If pears are fully ripe, they will be fairly juicy. Drain through cloth.

Measure juice into large kettle and bring to boil. Add 2 packages of Sure-Jell. Boil hard 1 minute, a full rolling boil that cannot be stirred down. Add lemon juice and sugar. Bring to a hard boil, and let boil 1 full minute.

Be sure you measure exactly. If a more firm jelly is desired, omit ¼ cup of juice and add ½ cup sugar. Jelly will be a beautiful claret red and firm.

Chuck Wagon Cookin' (Arizona)

SOUPS, CHILIS, STEWS

KEITH ODOM

Radio astronomy is the study of celestial objects that emit radio waves. With radio astronomy, scientists can study astronomical phenomena that are often invisible in other portions of the electromagnetic spectrum. Probing the farthest reaches of the universe, the largest array of radio telescopes in the world is located at the National Radio Astronomy Observatory, located near Sorocco, New Mexico.

Taco Soup

2 pounds ground meat
1 onion, chopped
1 can chopped green chiles
1 can hominy or corn or both,
   undrained
2 cans pinto beans, undrained

3 cans tomatoes, undrained
1 package dry taco mix
1 package dry Hidden Valley
   Salad Dressing Mix
2½ cups water

Brown the ground meat and onion together. Drain. Add the remaining ingredients. Mix all together and simmer 30 minutes. Serves 12–15.

Our Best Home Cooking (New Mexico)

Taco Soup

1 pound lean ground beef
1 onion, chopped
1 envelope taco seasoning mix
1 (16-ounce) can pinto beans,
   undrained
1 (16-ounce) can kidney beans,
   undrained
1 (16-ounce) can golden
   hominy, undrained
1 (17-ounce) can cream-style
   corn

1 (14-ounce) can diced stewed
   tomatoes, undrained
1 (10-ounce) can diced
   tomatoes with chiles
   (optional)
1 envelope ranch-style
   dressing mix
Tortilla chips
1 cup (4-ounces) grated
   Cheddar or Monterey Jack
   cheese

Brown ground beef and chopped onion; drain. Add taco seasoning; mix thoroughly. Add without draining the cans of beans, hominy, corn, and tomatoes. Stir in the dry ranch dressing mix. Simmer over low heat until bubbly. Serve over tortilla chips and top with grated cheese. Serves 6–8.

Coastal Cuisine (Texas II)

Tortilla Soup

1 small onion, chopped
2 garlic cloves, mashed
1 (4-ounce) can green chiles, diced
2 tablespoons oil
1 (8-ounce) can stewed tomatoes
2 cups chicken broth
1 cup beef bouillon
1 teaspoon ground cumin
1 teaspoon chili powder
1 teaspoon salt
¼ teaspoon pepper
2 teaspoons Worcestershire
4 corn tortillas
Oil for frying tortillas
1 cup grated Monterey Jack or Cheddar cheese

Using a medium saucepan, sauté onion, garlic, and green chiles in oil until soft. Add tomatoes, chicken broth, and beef bouillon. Mix in spices and simmer for 1 hour.

Cut tortillas into quarters, then into ½-inch strips. Fry strips in hot oil until crisp and drain.

Add fried tortilla strips to soup and simmer 10 minutes. Ladle into bowls and top with shredded cheese. Serves 4.

Variation: If you are using ovenproof bowls for soup, place bowls under broiler for 4–5 minutes to melt cheese.

Taste & Tales From Texas . . . With Love (Texas)

Tortilla Soup
with Chicken and Lime

4 (5- to 6-inch) corn tortillas
2 teaspoons olive oil
2 (14½-ounce) cans low-salt
  chicken broth
2 cups water
¾ cup canned Mexican-style
  stewed tomatoes with juices
1 bay leaf
1 garlic clove, minced

¼ teaspoon ground cumin
⅛ teaspoon dried crushed red
  pepper
12 ounces precooked shredded
  chicken
2 green onions, sliced
¼ cup chopped fresh cilantro
2 tablespoons fresh lime juice
Salt and pepper

Preheat oven to 350°. Brush 1 side of tortillas with oil; cut in half. Stack halves and cut crosswise into ⅓-inch wide strips. Spread strips on nonstick baking sheet. Bake until light golden, about 15 minutes. Cool on baking sheet. Combine broth, water, tomatoes, bay leaf, garlic, cumin, and red pepper in saucepan; bring to boil. Reduce heat; simmer 5 minutes. Add chicken; simmer 5 minutes. Stir in green onions, cilantro, and lime juice. Season with salt and pepper. Ladle soup into bowls. Sprinkle with tortillas and serve. Makes 4 servings.

Favorite Recipes from the Foothills of Carefree, Arizona (Arizona)

The Carrizozo Malpais is one of the youngest and best-preserved lava fields in the continental United States. One hundred sixty-five feet deep at the thickest point, the formation is between two and five miles wide. The lava is similar to Hawaiian lava, jagged and rippled, and most of the lava field is a wilderness study area. The Valley of Fires Recreation Area provides access to the malpais on its east edge, about three miles west of Carrizozo, New Mexico.

Black Bean Soup

2 cups dried black beans, washed, soaked overnight and drained
1 cup diced ham
1 onion, chopped
1 carrot, chopped
2 stalks celery, chopped
3 jalapeño peppers, seeded and chopped
10 cups water
2 (14½-ounce) cans chicken broth
1 teaspoon salt
2 tablespoons snipped fresh cilantro
1 teaspoon oregano
1 teaspoon chili powder
1 teaspoon cayenne pepper
2 teaspoons cumin
1 (8-ounce) carton sour cream

In a large, heavy soup pot, place all ingredients except sour cream. Bring to a boil; turn heat down and simmer for about 2 hours or until beans are tender. Add more water as needed and stir occasionally; make sure there is enough water in pot to make soup consistency and not too thick. Place a few cups at a time in a food processor (using the steel blade) or the blender, and purée until smooth. Add sour cream and reheat soup. Serve in individual bowls.

Southwest Sizzler (Texas II)

Drunken Bean Soup

1 (16-ounce) package dried pinto beans (2½ cups)
3 cups water
1 slice bacon, cut into 8 pieces
2 teaspoons sugar
2 teaspoons salt
2 (12-ounce) cans beer
Shredded Cheddar cheese
1 cup shredded cooked roast beef
1 teaspoon chili powder
¼ teaspoon garlic powder
1 teaspoon ground cumin
1 (10-ounce) can tomatoes and green chiles, undrained
Salsa

Sort and wash beans; soak in Dutch oven covered with water by 2 inches for 8 hours. Drain beans and return to Dutch oven. Add 3 cups water; bring to a boil. Add bacon, sugar, and salt; cover, then reduce to simmer for 30 minutes. Stir in beer, meat, chili powder, garlic powder, and cumin. Cover and simmer 1 hour, stirring occasionally. Stir in tomatoes and green chiles; cover and simmer an additional 30 minutes. Serve with salsa and cheese. Yields 2 quarts.

Canyon Echoes (Texas II)

Red Bean and Sausage Soup

We stole the idea for this recipe from some friends who own a fine local restaurant, The Inn at Brushy Creek. I don't know who they stole it from. You steal it from us. (It's too good a thing not to keep going.)

1 cup diced onion	2 cups cooked red beans
3 cloves garlic, minced	1 tablespoon brown sugar
1 teaspoon olive oil	1 tablespoon vinegar
6 cups chicken or beef stock (or a mixture)	Freshly ground black pepper ½ pound sliced Carabeef* sausage
2 cups diced cabbage	
½ cup ketchup	
4 new potatoes, peeled and quartered	

Sauté onion and garlic in oil. Add stock, cabbage, ketchup, and new potatoes. Cook until potatoes are almost done. Add remaining ingredients and heat thoroughly. Yields 20 servings.

Cal: 97; Fat per 6-ounce serving: 1.8g.

*Carabeef is the trade name for naturally raised water buffalo which is ounce-for-ounce leaner than boneless, skinless chicken breast. It is available at whole foods markets. Any lean sausage may be substituted.

Lean Star Cuisine (Texas II)

Sunday Night Fireside Soup

1 pound sausage meat
4 cups water
2 (15¼-ounce) cans red kidney
  beans, drained
1 (1-pound 13-ounce) can
  tomatoes
1 onion, chopped
1 large bay leaf
½ clove garlic, minced

2 teaspoons salt
⅛ teaspoon black pepper
½ teaspoon thyme
⅛ teaspoon caraway seed
A pinch of crushed red pepper
1 cup peeled and diced raw
  potatoes
1 small green bell pepper, with
  seeds removed, chopped

Brown sausage meat in a skillet. Drain the sausage and crumble it. In a kettle, combine the sausage meat with the water, red kidney beans, tomatoes, onion, bay leaf, garlic, salt, black pepper, thyme, caraway seed, and red pepper. Simmer the mixture for 1 hour. Add the potatoes and green pepper. Simmer, covered, for another 20 minutes. Adjust seasonings and serve. Serves 8.

Gallery Buffet Soup Cookbook (Texas)

Make-a-Meal Soup

1 onion, chopped
1 tablespoon pure vegetable
  oil
1 pound smoked sausage,
  thinly sliced
3 cups water
2 chicken bouillon cubes
1 teaspoon salt
¼ teaspoon pepper
1 bay leaf
½ teaspoon thyme

3 carrots, chopped
3 celery stalks, chopped
¼ head cabbage, cut in 1-inch
  chunks
2 tablespoons uncooked rice
1 (8-ounce) can tomato sauce
1 (15-ounce) can kidney beans,
  drained
1 (28-ounce) can whole
  tomatoes

In a large saucepan, brown onion in oil until tender. Add remaining ingredients. Cover and simmer for 30 minutes. Makes 8 servings.

Our Best Home Cooking (New Mexico)

Corn Soup

This soup, with its south-of-the-border flavors, is popular throughout the Southwest. Served with tostadas and a green salad, it makes a complete meal.

3½ cups corn kernels,
  preferably fresh
1 cup chicken stock
2 tablespoons butter
2 cups milk
1 clove garlic, minced
1 teaspoon oregano

Salt and pepper
2 tablespoons canned green
  chiles, diced, drained
1 cup peeled, seeded, chopped
  tomatoes
1 cup cubed Monterey Jack
  cheese

Purée corn and stock in a blender or food processor. Place purée in a saucepan with butter. Stir and simmer 5 minutes. Add milk, garlic, oregano, salt and pepper; bring to a boil. Reduce heat, add chiles, and simmer 5 minutes. Divide tomatoes among 4 soup bowls. Remove soup from heat and add cheese. Stir until just melted. Ladle over tomatoes in bowls.

A Little Southwest Cookbook (New Mexico)

Mexican Corn Soup

4 cups fresh corn kernels
¼ cup chopped onion
2 tablespoons butter
2 tablespoons flour
Salt and pepper to taste
2 cups chicken broth

2 cups milk or cream
1 cup grated Cheddar cheese
1 (4-ounce) can green chiles,
  chopped (optional)
Tortilla chips
½ cup crisp bacon, crumbled

Sauté corn and onion in butter until tender. Add flour, salt and pepper; cook 1 minute. Gradually add broth, alternating with milk or cream, until thickened. Add Cheddar cheese and green chiles; do not overheat. Serve soup in individual bowls, stirring in 4 or 5 tortilla chips; garnish with crumbled bacon.

Lone Star Legacy (Texas II)

Chile-Corn Chowder

Thick and creamy, this hearty chowder will satisfy the hungriest appetite, especially when accompanied by hot muffins. You can freeze it, but it will not be as creamy when reheated.

4 cups vegetable stock
1 onion, chopped
2 tomatoes, chopped
2 potatoes, chopped
1 carrot, diced
1 stalk celery, minced
2–3 cloves garlic, minced
1 cup frozen or fresh corn, cut from the cob
½ cup arrowroot or cornstarch, dissolved in ½ cup soymilk or rice milk

¼ cup chopped mild chiles
½ teaspoon cumin powder
½ teaspoon chili powder
Cayenne or hot sauce, to taste
1 cup soymilk or rice milk
1 cup grated soy Cheddar or jalapeño Jack cheese (optional)
¼ cup minced fresh cilantro for garnish

In a large pot or soup kettle, combine all the ingredients except the soymilk or rice milk, cheese, and cilantro. Cook uncovered about 30 minutes, or until all of the vegetables are tender. Add the milk and cheese, and cook another 10 minutes, or until it begins to thicken. Yields 6 servings.

Variations: You can add bell peppers, mushrooms, zucchini or any other squash, and a half a cup of black or red beans.

Per serving: Calories 139; Protein 3g; Fat 1g; Carbohydrates 30g.

Flavors of the Southwest (Arizona)

Renowned artist Georgia O'Keeffe (November 15, 1887–March 6, 1986) is chiefly known for her paintings of flowers, rocks, shells, animal bones, and landscapes, which she often transformed into powerful abstract images. She fell in love with New Mexico on her first visit, moved there permanently in 1949, and remained there until her death at the age of 98. The Georgia O'Keeffe Museum in Santa Fe features the largest repository in the world of her work.

A Santa Fe Soup

1 avocado
8 ounces plain yogurt
1 (14½-ounce) can chicken
  broth, or homemade broth
1 clove garlic, pressed
12 sprigs cilantro, Chinese
  parsley, or regular parsley,
  chopped

Juice of ½ lemon
1 small green chile or jalapeño,
  chopped
Paprika

Put all ingredients in blender, excluding paprika. Blend well. Chill several hours. Serve with paprika sprinkled on top. Good served with cucumber sandwiches. This will keep for several days. Do not freeze. Serves 1–4.

Savoring the Southwest (New Mexico)

Caldo de Queso
(Potato-Cheese Soup)

6 large potatoes, peeled, cubed
1 medium to large onion,
  chopped
1 large clove garlic, chopped
1 tablespoon olive oil
½ quart chicken broth and
  ½ quart milk, or ½ quart of
  milk, ½ quart of water, and
  2 chicken bouillon cubes

3–4 fresh green chiles, peeled,
  seeded, and chopped (enough
  for ¾ cup), or 1 (6-ounce) can
  chopped chiles
½ pound shredded Cheddar
  cheese
Cilantro for garnish (optional)

Sauté potatoes, onion, and garlic in oil in a large soup pot. Cover ingredients with liquid, and simmer until tender, about 30 minutes. Toward end of the cooking time, add chiles. When serving, add a handful of cheese (to taste) to each bowl.

Note: Cheese may be added to the soup before serving; let it melt in the soup, if desired.

Corazón Contento (Arizona)

Mexican Potato Soup

Great on a cold day

3 slices bacon, diced
3 large potatoes, peeled and
  cubed
5 cups water
1 cup tomato sauce

¼ cup chopped onion
1½ teaspoons salt
1 (10-ounce) can green chiles,
  chopped
½ pound sharp cheese, grated

Brown bacon. Add potatoes and stir to coat. Add water, tomato sauce, onion, and salt. Reduce heat to simmer and cook 1 hour. Place chiles and cheese in bowls. Spoon hot soup over chiles and cheese to serve. Makes 6 servings.

The Wild Wild West (Texas II)

Onion Soup Gratinée

5 cups thinly sliced onions
5 tablespoons butter
1 tablespoon oil
1 teaspoon flour
1 teaspoon salt
1 teaspoon Dijon-style mustard

Pepper to taste
6 cups brown stock or beef broth
1 cup dry sherry
⅓ cup grated Parmesan cheese
⅓ cup grated Cheddar or
  Gruyère cheese

In a deep, heavy skillet, sauté the onions in the combined butter and oil for 30–40 minutes, or until well browned. Stir in flour, salt, mustard, and pepper. Cook an additional 2 minutes. Heat stock or broth and add to onions. Add sherry and cook over low heat, stirring well, until mixture comes to a boil. Simmer for 30 minutes. Transfer soup to an earthenware casserole and sprinkle with cheeses. Place casserole under preheated broiler for 3–4 minutes, until brown and bubbly. To serve, place one slice of Cheese Toast in each of six heated bowls. Divide soup among them.

CHEESE TOAST:

6 (½-inch) slices French bread
Softened butter

6 tablespoons grated Parmesan
  cheese

Spread each slice of bread with butter and sprinkle with 1 tablespoon of cheese. Toast at 325° until brown. Serves 6.

The Galveston Island Cookbook (Texas)

Peach Tree Chilled Avocado Soup

If I had to name our single most popular soup in the Tea Room, this would be the one. Our customers love it! It is one of our regular daily soups during the summer months.

4 medium ripe avocados,
   peeled and pitied
1 garlic clove, minced
4 green onions, chopped
5 tablespoons chopped fresh
   cilantro
1 tablespoon sliced pickled
   jalapeño with juice
½ teaspoon Tabasco

3 cups sour cream
1 cup buttermilk
8 cups chilled Swanson's
   chicken broth
Salt to taste
Garnish: Sour cream and
   finely minced green onions
   (green part only)

In a blender or food processor, combine avocados, garlic, green onions, cilantro, jalapeños with juice, and Tabasco. Process until smooth. Add sour cream and process again. Stir in buttermilk and chilled chicken broth. Taste for salt. Cover and refrigerate until very cold. Garnish with a dollop of sour cream and chopped green onions, green part only. Serves 12–14.

The Peach Tree Tea Room Cookbook (Texas II)

Bloody Mary Soup

2 tablespoons butter
1 medium onion, diced
3 stalks celery, diced
2 tablespoons tomato purée
1 tablespoon sugar
5 cups V-8 vegetable juice

1 tablespoon salt (optional)
2 teaspoons Worcestershire
¼ teaspoon pepper
1 tablespoon fresh lemon juice
4 ounces vodka

Melt butter in large saucepan. Sauté onion and celery in butter over medium heat. Add tomato purée and sugar. Cook for one minute. Add V-8 juice and simmer for 8 minutes. Stir in remaining ingredients. Strain and serve hot or well chilled. If using a food processor or blender, there is no need to strain.

Bon Appétit de Las Sandias (New Mexico)

Tomato and Red Bell Pepper Soup

To serve, place thin slices of avocado or pieces of cooked asparagus spears (or both) in the bottom of each bowl. Then, pour in the hot soup, and garnish with a teaspoon of crème fraîche and fresh sprig of basil or mint.

2 tablespoons oil
1 cup coarsely chopped onion
2 cups peeled, deseeded, and coarsely chopped fresh tomatoes, or 1 (1-pound) can Progresso Peeled Italian-Style Tomatoes with Basil
1½ cups low-sodium chicken broth
2 large red bell peppers, peeled and chopped

1 tablespoon chopped fresh garlic
½ cup light cream
½ cup 2% milk
⅓ cup low-sodium chicken broth (additional)
½ teaspoon light salt
½ teaspoon dried basil
8–10 drops Tabasco
Crème fraîche (optional)
Mint sprigs (optional)

In a large saucepan, heat oil over medium heat. Add onion and cook until tender. Add the tomatoes and cook for 10–15 minutes, stirring occasionally. Add the 1½ cups chicken broth, peppers, and garlic, and simmer for about 30 minutes. Transfer mixture into a food processor or electric blender and purée. Return the purée to the saucepan. Add remaining ingredients, and cook, stirring occasionally until hot. Garnish with a dab of crème fraîche and a sprig of fresh mint. Makes 4 (1-cup) servings.

Per serving. Cal 166; Prot 475g; Carb 12g; Fat 11 g; Chol 12mg; Fiber 1.23g; 60% Cal from Fat.

The 30-Minute Light Gourmet (Texas II)

Gazpacho

Serve this cooling summer classic with fresh hot tortillas, quesadillas, or crisp corn chips and guacamole.

1 medium white or yellow onion, diced

3 cloves garlic, pressed or minced

½ teaspoon salt

1 tablespoon extra virgin olive oil

5 cups vegetable stock, divided

9 ripe tomatoes, cored

2 cucumbers, trimmed and peeled

5 ripe tomatoes, finely diced

1 small hot green chile (jalapeño), seeded and minced

2 mild green chiles (Anaheim), or 1 green bell pepper, seeded and finely diced

1 red bell pepper, finely diced

2 tablespoons minced parsley

2 tablespoons minced cilantro

¼ cup lemon juice

2 tablespoons lime juice

Salt and black pepper to taste

Sauté the onion and garlic with the salt in the olive oil until the onion is very sweet and golden brown. Transfer this mixture to blender container, add 3 cups vegetable stock, and blend until fairly smooth. Pour into a large bowl. Place the 9 cored tomatoes, one cucumber, and 2 cups vegetable stock in the blender container and blend until almost smooth. (This may need to be done in 2 batches.) Add this mixture to the stock and onion liquid. Add the remaining diced and minced vegetables, herbs, and juices to the soup. Season to taste with salt and black pepper. Chill and serve. The Gazpacho should be cold, tangy, and spicy. It will keep, covered, in the refrigerator for up to 2 days. Serves 6–8.

Cooking at the Natural Cafe in Santa Fe (New Mexico)

Crab Bisque

Margaret Hughes and Harry Corless were American Regional Cuisine Winners with this recipe.

4 shallots, diced
1 clove garlic, minced
8 tablespoons butter
⅛ teaspoon thyme
6 tablespoons flour
2 cups cream
4 cups chicken stock

¼ teaspoon Dijon mustard
¼ teaspoon Worcestershire
1 pound crabmeat, picked over
** for shells**
Salt and pepper to taste
6 tablespoons chopped parsley

Sauté shallots and garlic in 2 tablespoons butter, until fragrant. Add thyme and remaining butter and blend. Add flour and cook the roux over moderate heat until very slightly colored.

Combine cream, stock, mustard, and Worcestershire and add in a stream to roux, stirring constantly. Add crabmeat. Bring to a simmer and cook for 7–8 minutes. Add salt, pepper, and parsley, and stir to blend.

March of Dimes Gourmet Gala Cookbook (Texas)

Tombstone, Arizona, "the town too tough to die," is most famous for the Gunfight at the OK Corral when the Earp brothers, Wyatt, Virgil, and Morgan, along with friend Doc Holliday, shot it out with the Clanton and McLaury Gang. Once a booming mining town, today Tombstone preserves the history and heritage of the "Wildest Town in the West!"

Shrimp and Chicken Gumbo

1 (2- to 3-pound) chicken, cooked,
  reserving stock (about 3 quarts)

Cook chicken in large stockpot until tender; reserve broth.

ROUX:

5 tablespoons oil or bacon   1 tablespoon Kitchen Bouquet
  drippings
4 tablespoons flour

Stirring constantly, cook oil and flour until dark golden. Add Kitchen Bouquet to make it darker.

6 small green onions with tops,   Dash of pepper
  chopped   Dash of Tabasco
1 medium onion, chopped   4 or 5 dashes Worcestershire
1 small green bell pepper,   2 pounds shrimp, cooked and
  chopped   deveined
4 stalks celery, chopped   ½ pound crabmeat (optional)
5 cups cut okra, fresh or frozen   Filé to taste
2 tablespoons salt, more or less
½–¾ teaspoon garlic powder,
  or 2 cloves garlic, pressed

Add first 4 ingredients to roux and stir and cook until wilted. Add this to chicken stock, bring to a boil, and add chicken which has been boned and cut into pieces. Add okra and season with salt, garlic, pepper, Tabasco, and Worcestershire. Simmer for a few minutes. Add shrimp and crabmeat, if desired. Serve over rice and add filé to taste. Serves 10–12.

Variataion: Sausage may be used instead of seafood.

Hospitality (Texas)

Rattlesnake Chili

No, there is no rattlesnake meat in this. It was named for the type of bean I used—rattlesnake beans—the first time I made this. Pintos, kidneys, black turtles, Anasazis, and teparies also work well.

3 cups cooked beans
1 onion, chopped
1 sweet red or green bell pepper,
   chopped
2 ears corn, cut from the cob, or
   1 (10-ounce) package frozen
   corn
3 tomatoes, chopped
1 (8-ounce) can tomato sauce
3–4 cloves garlic, minced
2 mild or hot chiles, roasted,
   peeled, and minced

2 tablespoons chili powder
1 tablespoon cumin powder
1 teaspoon epazote*
2 tablespoons minced fresh
   cilantro
Pinch of ground cloves
Salt or vegetable seasoning to
   taste
1 bottle beer (optional)
Juice of 1 lime

Mix all the ingredients together in a large pot (or crockpot), and cook about an hour or longer—the longer the better. Serve with cornbread or tortillas, and perhaps a little grated low-fat dairy or soy cheese. Enjoy! Yields 8 servings.

Variations: Add chopped zucchini or yellow squash, chopped cooked potatoes, or mushrooms. For something deliciously different, try serving this over a baked potato.

*Epazote: An herb native to Mexico commonly used in long-simmering dishes.

Per serving: Calories 149; Protein 6g; Fat 0g; Carbohydrates 30g.

Flavors of the Southwest (Arizona)

Chile con carne literally means "pepper with meat." Not an authentic Mexican dish, earliest accounts show it was sold on the square in San Antonio in the last decades of the nineteenth century. Lyndon Johnson suggested chili be named the state food of Texas—it now is.

Texas Chili

The smell of this chili cooking brought my family running.

3 pounds lean beef
¼ cup oil
6 cups water
2 bay leaves
6 tablespoons chili powder
1 tablespoon salt
10 cloves garlic, minced
1 teaspoon comino seeds
1 teaspoon crushed oregano
  leaves

½ teaspoon red pepper
¼ teaspoon pepper
1 tablespoon sugar
3 tablespoons sweet Hungarian
  paprika
1 tablespoon dried onion flakes
3 tablespoons flour
6 tablespoons cornmeal

In a 6-quart saucepan, sear beef (cubed or coarsely ground) in oil until beef color is gray, not brown. Add water, bay leaves, chili powder, salt, garlic, comino seeds, oregano, red pepper, pepper, sugar, paprika, and onion flakes. Simmer, covered, 2 hours. Cool. Refrigerate overnight so flavors will mellow.

Remove top layer of solidified fat. Reheat. With a little cold water make a paste of flour and cornmeal. Add paste to chili. To obtain a smooth texture, cook and stir 5–7 minutes after thickening has been added. Remove bay leaves before serving. Serves 6.

Cook 'em Horns (Texas)

A popular saying among self-proclaimed chili purists is, "If you know beans about chili, you know chili ain't got no beans." The concept that beans do not belong in chili may be further credited to the fact that most official chili cookoffs do not allow beans. In many cases, a chili will be disqualified if it contains beans, considered filler. Perhaps this is because beef was plentiful and cheap in cattle towns of the Southwest. As chili spread east into areas where beef was more expensive, however, chili made with beans became more prevalent.

Chili with Avocados

There are probably as many chili recipes as there are chili cooks. This version, without beans and served in avocado halves, is an informally elegant and festive main dish.

3 onions, coarsely chopped
4 cloves garlic, chopped
3 tablespoons vegetable oil
2 pounds beef round, cut in
small cubes
1 pound lean pork, cut in
small cubes
⅓ cup chili powder
1 tablespoon flour
1 large can Italian tomatoes,
cut up, with juice

3 bay leaves
1 tablespoon oregano
2 teaspoons ground cumin
1 tablespoon brown sugar
Salt
1 tablespoon red wine vinegar
1 cup pimento-stuffed green
olives, drained
3 avocados, peeled, halved

In a medium saucepan, sauté onions and garlic in oil until soft. Remove and set aside. Brown meat over high heat in same pan. Stir in onions, garlic, chili powder, flour, tomatoes, bay leaves, oregano, cumin, sugar, salt, and vinegar. Bring to a boil, lower heat, and simmer covered for 2 hours, stirring occasionally. Discard bay leaves. Stir in olives, correct seasoning, and serve over avocado halves.

A Little Southwest Cookbook (New Mexico)

Best-Ever Chili

9 pounds lean beef, chopped
3 quarts water
3 (16-ounce) cans tomatoes
6 medium onions, chopped
3 tablespoons sugar
1 tablespoon garlic powder
10 tablespoons chili powder

1 tablespoon cumin
1 tablespoon marjoram
9 tablespoons paprika
3 tablespoons salt
1 tablespoon black pepper
1 tablespoon cayenne pepper
6–12 tablespoons cornmeal

Brown beef lightly in large nonstick saucepan; drain. Add water, tomatoes, and onions. Simmer for 1–1½ hours. Add sugar, garlic powder, chili powder, cumin, marjoram, paprika, salt, black pepper, and cayenne pepper; mix well. Simmer for 45 minutes. Stir in cornmeal 1 tablespoon at a time, simmering until of desired consistency. Yields 30 servings.

Approx. Per Serving: Cal 325; Prot 27g; Carbo 10g: Fiber 2g; T Fat 20g; 55% Calories from Fat; Chol 89mg; Sod 818mg.

Gatherings (Texas II)

Sonoran Chicken Chili

1 tablespoon olive oil
½ cup chopped shallots
3 cloves garlic, minced
2 (14-ounce) cans chopped
  tomatoes with garlic, oregano,
  and basil
1 (14-ounce) can whole tomatoes,
  chopped
1 (14-ounce) can no-salt-added
  chicken broth
1 (4-ounce) can chopped green
  chiles

½ teaspoon oregano
½ teaspoon coriander
¼ teaspoon cumin
4 cups chopped cooked chicken
1 or 2 (16-ounce) cans white
  beans, drained
3 tablespoons freshly squeezed
  lime juice
¼ teaspoon pepper

Heat the olive oil in a large saucepan over medium-high heat. Add the shallots and garlic. Sauté until the shallots are soft. Add the seasoned tomatoes, undrained chopped tomatoes, broth, green chiles, oregano, coriander, and cumin. Bring to a boil. Reduce the heat. Simmer for 20 minutes. Add the chicken and beans; mix well. Cook until heated through. Add the lime juice and pepper; mix well. Garnish with shredded Cheddar cheese. Serves 8.

Reflections Under the Sun (Arizona)

French Stew

"The best stew I've ever tasted"

2 pounds round steak, cubed
6 carrots, peeled and thinly sliced
1 onion, sliced into rings
1 cup chopped celery
1 (4-ounce) can mushrooms,
    drained
1 (16-ounce) can tomatoes,
    drained
⅛ teaspoon pepper

⅛ teaspoon rosemary
⅛ teaspoon thyme
⅛ teaspoon marjoram
Salt to taste
2 slices bread, cubed
1 (10-ounce) package frozen green
    beans
½ cup red wine, heated

Combine first 12 ingredients in a Dutch oven; mix well. Bake at 250° for 3½ hours. Add beans; bake 30 minutes. Stir in wine just before serving. Yields 12–14 servings.

Flavor Favorites (Texas)

Caldillo

3 pounds cubed beef
1½ cups diced onions
3 cups tomatoes, diced
1½ cups green chile strips
½ cup beef stock

2 tablespoons salt
2 tablespoons pepper
2 teaspoons garlic salt
2 teaspoons cumin
2 pounds potatoes, peeled, cubed

Sauté beef and onions in bacon fat; add tomatoes, chile strips, stock, and seasonings. Cover and cook over low heat until meat is tender. Add cubed potatoes during last 30 minutes. Caldillo may be frozen after preparation. Makes 1 gallon.

The Pride of Texas (Texas)

Chuckwagon Beef Stew

This is a hearty cross between soup and stew. Depending on accompaniments, it can be lunch or a light dinner.

10 cups water
1 chicken bouillon packet
1 beef bouillon packet
3 cups tomato sauce
1 pound top sirloin, cut into
   1-inch cubes
1½ cups diced celery
1½ cups diced onions
1½ cups diced potatoes

1½ cups diced carrots
2 or 3 garlic cloves, minced
1½ cups diced tomatoes
1½ cups diced yellow squash
1½ cups diced green beans
1½ cups sliced mushrooms
1 tablespoon salt
1 teaspoon black pepper

In a large stockpot, combine water, bouillon, and tomato sauce. Add beef, celery, onions, potatoes, carrots, and garlic. Bring to a boil, lower heat, and simmer 1 hour. Add tomatoes, squash, beans, mushrooms, salt, and pepper, and simmer an additional 30 minutes.

Contributed by Rawhide Western Town and Steakhouse, Scottsdale
Arizona Chefs: Cooking at Home with 36 Arizona Chefs (Arizona)

Blue Corn Dumplings

1 cup blue corn flour
2 teaspoons baking powder
1 teaspoon salt

1 teaspoon bacon drippings, lard,
   or other shortening
⅓–½ cup milk

Mix (or sift) dry ingredients thoroughly in a mixing bowl. Cut in shortening and add enough milk to make a drop batter. Drop by spoonfuls on top of simmering stew. Cover kettle and steam dumplings for 15 minutes. Stew should be kept bubbling. Serves 4–6.

Hopi Cookery (Arizona)

The ground meal made from blue corn is nuttier in flavor, higher in protein, and lower in starch than the meal made from either white or yellow corn, and it produces a more fragile tortilla. The color of the kernel and the meal is gray-blue. If the kernel is popped, the popped corn is white.

Pueblo Stew

1 large onion, chopped
2 cloves garlic, minced
1½ tablespoons chili powder
2 teaspoons cumin seed
1 teaspoon dry oregano
2 tablespoons olive oil
1 each: zucchini, pattypan, and
   crooked neck squash, cut into
   1-inch chunks
1 (12-ounce) container tofu,
   cubed
1 (14-ounce) can golden hominy,
   drained

1 pound tomatoes, chopped
¼ pound green beans, cut into
   1-inch lengths
2 cans or 2 pounds cooked pinto
   beans
4 bouillon cubes
2 cups water
1 tablespoon cilantro
Garnish: Monterey Jack cheese
   and sour cream

In a 4- to 5- quart pan, cook onion, garlic, and spices in oil until onion starts to brown. Add squash, tofu, hominy, and tomatoes and cook about 5 minutes. Add green and pinto beans, bouillon, and water. Simmer uncovered about 30 minutes, until tender and until consistency is that of thick stew. Add minced cilantro and ladle into bowls. Garnish with additional cilantro, shredded Jack cheese, and sour cream. Serve with warm tortillas.

Portal's Best Little Cookbook (Arizona)

Green Chile Stew

Traditional in many homes.

2 pounds boneless pork, cut
  into 1-inch cubes
3 tablespoons all-purpose
  flour
2 tablespoons butter
1 cup chopped white onion
2 garlic cloves, minced
3 cups peeled, chopped ripe
  tomatoes

1 teaspoon salt
½ teaspoon dried-leaf oregano
¼ teaspoon ground cumin
20 fresh New Mexico chiles,
  roasted, peeled, seeded,
  deveined, and chopped

Toss pork with flour, to coat. In a 4-quart Dutch oven or heavy pot, heat butter and add pork cubes a few at a time. Stir to brown. Push to side of pot, and add onion and garlic; cook until onion is soft. Stir in browned pork. Add tomatoes, salt, oregano, and cumin. Cover and simmer one hour; add water as necessary and stir occasionally. Add chiles, and simmer 30 minutes; add water as necessary. Makes 4 servings.

Sassy Southwest Cooking (New Mexico)

SALADS

The San Antonio River Walk (Paseo del Rio) is a network of walkways along the banks of the San Antonio River. There's music and happenings around every corner as it winds and loops under bridges one level down from the automobile street. Lined by bars, shops, and restaurants, it is an enormously successful tourist attraction, enjoyable on foot or aboard a Rio San Antonio river taxi.

Stuffed Lettuce Salad

1 firm head of lettuce
½ cup grated Cheddar cheese
½ cup mayonnaise
¼ teaspoon curry powder

1 cup chopped ham
⅓ cup chopped celery
1 pimento, diced
⅛ cup snipped fresh parsley

Wash and drain a firm head of lettuce. At the core end cut a circle out. Continue cutting down to within ½ inch of the top of the head. Then hollow out. Blend Cheddar cheese, mayonnaise, and curry powder. Stir in ham, celery, pimento, and parsley. Pack mixture solidly into lettuce. Tie a string around lettuce to hold in place. Chill until firm. Serve in slices with French dressing. This recipe is nice for lunch. Serves 4–6.

A Different Taste of Paris (Texas)

Mexican Salad

1 large head lettuce, shredded
1 onion, chopped
1 or 2 tomatoes, chopped
1 pound hamburger meat
1 package taco seasoning

1 cup water
1 (10½-ounce) bag Fritos
Catalina dressing
Colby or Cheddar cheese
  (optional)

Combine lettuce, onion, and tomatoes in large salad bowl; set aside. Brown hamburger meat; drain; add taco seasoning mix and water. Let simmer and cook down. When done, add to salad mixture; add Fritos. Toss with Catalina dressing. Add grated cheese, if desired.

Recipes for Rain or Shine (New Mexico)

Chop Chop Salad

With garlic toast and dessert, the perfect light but satisfying dinner for a warm Arizona evening.

DRESSING:

1 cup oil
¼ cup balsamic vinegar
⅛ cup sun-dried tomatoes
⅛ cup snipped fresh basil

1 teaspoon chopped garlic
½ teaspoon sugar
Salt and pepper to taste

Blend all ingredients in food processor or blender.

2 cups mesclun salad mix (or
   your choice of lettuces)
½ pound salami, diced
½ pound mozzarella cheese,
   diced (reserve a few cubes)

4 canned artichoke hearts, diced
½ cup sliced black olives
½ cup chopped pepperocini
4 roma tomatoes, diced

Toss all ingredients with dressing to taste. Garnish with a few reserved mozzarella cubes.

Contributed by Cafe Saguaro, Scottsdale
Arizona Chefs: Cooking at Home with 36 Arizona Chefs (Arizona)

New Mexico Burning Salad

SALAD:

3 cups shredded lettuce
1 (15-ounce) can dark red
   kidney beans, drained
2 medium tomatoes, chopped

1 avocado, chopped
1 small zucchini, chopped
½ cup green chiles

DRESSING:

⅓ cup olive oil
½ cup lime juice

½ teaspoon cumin
½ teaspoon salt

Toss Salad ingredients in bowl. Mix Dressing ingredients and pour over Salad. Serve in bowls garnished with olives, cubed provolone cheese, and corn chips.

Cooking with Kiwanis (New Mexico)

Spinach Salad with Mango Chutney Dressing

My greatest salvation from entertaining failure came when I was a bride of three months and entertaining our first couple who had been married ten years. I was tossing the salad and the bowl fell to the floor—spilling all of the contents. With horror I looked at my female guest who looked critically at the floor, scooped up the salad and placed it back into the bowl. She responded, "The floor looks clean and you did say it was a tossed salad."

2 heads spinach, torn in bite-size
 pieces
4 green onions, sliced
½ can ripe olives, halved

Cracked pepper and salt
1 (4-ounce) can Mandarin orange
 slices, drained

Combine ingredients and serve with Mango Chutney Salad Dressing.

MANGO CHUTNEY SALAD DRESSING:

17 ounces mango chutney
2 teaspoons minced garlic
1½ tablespoons stone-ground
 mustard

1 cup red wine vinegar
1 cup vegetable oil
Raisins (optional)

Chop chutney in blender or food processor. Blend in garlic, mustard, and vinegar. Add oil. Let stand overnight. Serve dressing over spinach. Makes 3 cups.

A Doctor's Prescription for Gourmet Cooking (Texas)

GARY TYLER

The title of "oldest house in the United States of America built by a European" is controversially claimed by the owners of a structure located at 215 East De Vargas Street on the eastern side of Old Santa Fe Trail in Santa Fe, New Mexico, within the Barrio De Analco Historic District. The house was supposedly built around 1646. The house has been through the administration of numerous governments including the Spanish, Mexican, Territorial, statehood. Many ghost stories, including tales of ghostly apparitions, are associated with the structure.

Spinach Salad with Bacon Dressing

1½ pounds tender fresh spinach leaves, washed, torn

½ cup Bacon Dressing
2 eggs, hard-boiled, shredded

In a salad bowl, toss spinach with Bacon Dressing until leaves are well coated. Divide in salad plates and top each with shredded egg.

BACON DRESSING:

1 slice bacon, very crisp, cooled and blotted
1½ teaspoons red wine vinegar
½ teaspoon hickory smoked salt

¼ teaspoon dry mustard
1 tablespoon water
5 tablespoons vegetable oil

Crumble the crisp bacon and add it to the vinegar in a jar with a tight lid. Add the hickory smoked salt and dry mustard. Mix until the salt is dissolved. Add water and oil. Cover jar tightly and shake vigorously for 30 seconds. Store covered in refrigerator. Makes ¼–½ cup. Yields 4–6 servings.

La Piñata (Texas)

Mexican Cole Slaw

6 cups shredded red and green cabbage
3 tablespoons chopped cilantro or parsley
1 red bell pepper, thinly sliced
1 red onion, thinly sliced
1 (4-ounce) can chopped green chiles, drained

Juice of 2 limes
2 cloves garlic, minced
¼ cup white wine vinegar
1 tablespoon sugar
½ teaspoon salt
¼ teaspoon Tabasco
¼ cup water
⅓ cup olive oil

Place cabbage, cilantro, red pepper, onion, and chiles in a glass bowl. In a jar with a tight-fitting lid, combine the lime juice, garlic, vinegar, sugar, salt, Tabasco, water, and oil. Shake well. Pour dressing over the slaw and toss to coat well. Marinate refrigerated, tightly covered, with plastic wrap, for at least 12 hours, tossing frequently. Drain and serve well chilled. The salad can be made up to 3 days in advance, but drain it after 2 days and keep it tightly covered.

Bon Appétit de Las Sandias (New Mexico)

Copper Pennies

2 pounds carrots, sliced
  crosswise
1 small onion, finely chopped
1 medium bell pepper, finely
  chopped
3 ribs celery, finely chopped
1 cup tomato soup, undiluted

1 cup sugar
¼ cup oil
¾ cup apple cider vinegar
1 tablespoon dry mustard
1 tablespoon Worcestershire
Lettuce

Cook sliced carrots in salted water until fork-tender. Add chopped onion, bell pepper, and celery to the drained carrots. Set aside. Mix and bring to a boil soup, sugar, oil, vinegar, mustard, and Worcestershire. Pour this hot mixture over above vegetables. Refrigerate overnight. Serve on lettuce. Serves 10–12.

Central Texas Style (Texas II)

24-Hour Vegetable Salad

10–15 fresh mushrooms,
  sliced
¼ cup chopped green onions
2 cucumbers, peeled and sliced
¼ cup chopped fresh parsley
1 large green bell pepper, sliced
3 large tomatoes, cut into
  wedges

6 ounces Swiss cheese, cut into
  thin strips
1 (6-ounce) can whole pitted
  black olives
½ teaspoon garlic salt
½ teaspoon salt
¾ cup Italian salad dressing

In a large deep glass bowl, layer first 8 ingredients in order given; top with drained olives. Add garlic salt and salt to the salad dressing, stir and pour over top of salad. Cover and refrigerate for at least 12 hours, better if it stays 24 hours. Toss and serve. Serves 6.

Savoring the Southwest (New Mexico)

Squash Salad

5 medium squash (yellow, green
   or mixed), thinly sliced
½ cup thinly sliced onion
½ cup chopped celery
½ cup chopped green bell pepper
1 clove garlic, crushed (or garlic
   powder)

2 tablespoons wine vinegar
¾ cup sugar (or less)
1 teaspoon salt
½ teaspoon pepper
⅓ cup oil
⅔ cup cider vinegar

Combine squash, onion, celery and pepper; toss lightly. Combine all other ingredients; stir well. Spoon over vegetables. Chill 12 hours, stirring occasionally.

Note: Sugar substitute can be used instead of sugar.

The Pride of Texas (Texas)

Broccoli Salad Supreme

4 cups chopped raw broccoli
1 cup chopped celery
¼ cup chopped green onions
1 cup seedless green grapes
1 cup seedless red grapes
⅓ cup sugar

1 cup good quality mayonnaise
1 tablespoon red wine vinegar
½ pound bacon, fried crisp
   and crumbled
⅔ cup sliced or slivered almonds,
   toasted

Toss together the vegetables and grapes in a large salad bowl. Mix the sugar, mayonnaise, and vinegar in a separate small bowl to make dressing; pour dressing over vegetables and grapes and stir gently to allow dressing to coat evenly. Refrigerate overnight before serving, if time allows, for flavor to mix. Just before serving, add crumbled bacon and toasted almonds. Serves 10–12.

Amazing Graces (Texas II)

Texas Tabbouleh

Steve Southern, chef of Huntington's in the Westin Hotel Galleria in Dallas, developed this variation on the traditional bulgur salad.

¾ cup bulgur
1 cup freshly squeezed orange
  juice
⅔ cup chopped tomatoes
⅔ cup chopped cucumber
1 tablespoon tequila (optional)

1 jalapeño pepper, seeded
  and diced
1 heaping teaspoon chopped
  cilantro
Salt to taste

Place bulgur in bowl and mix with orange juice; let sit for 30 minutes. Add tomatoes, cucumbers, tequila, jalapeño, chopped cilantro, and salt. Mix well. Refrigerate at least 1 hour. Serves 4.

Gourmet Grains, Beans, and Rice (Texas II)

Colorful Black Bean Salad

2 (15-ounce) cans black beans,
  drained, rinsed
1 (11-ounce) can corn kernels,
  drained
1 medium red bell pepper,
  chopped
1 bunch green onions, chopped
¼ cup chopped red onion
3 cloves garlic, minced

2 teaspoons chopped fresh basil
1½ teaspoons salt
1 teaspoon sugar
1 teaspoon pepper
⅓ cup red wine vinegar
¼ cup light olive oil
5–6 red or green bell peppers or
  tomatoes, halved, seeded

Combine the black beans, corn, red pepper, green onions, red onion, garlic, and basil in a bowl; mix well. Combine the salt, sugar, pepper, wine vinegar, and olive oil in a small bowl. Whisk until well mixed. Pour over the black bean mixture; toss to mix well. Spoon into the bell peppers or tomatoes. Serve immediately. Serves 10–12.

Reflections Under the Sun (Arizona)

Linda Martin's "Eyes of Texas" Salad

Black-Eyed Pea Festival Grand Champion, 1982.

1½ cups black-eyed peas, drained
1 cup chicken, boned and chopped
¼ cup chopped celery
½ teaspoon salt

1 cup cooked rice
¼ cup chopped onion
¼ cup mayonnaise
1 teaspoon pepper
Dash of hot sauce

Blend above ingredients and pack in mold. Let set for ½ hour. Ice with Topping.

TOPPING:

1 avocado, mashed
½ cup sour cream
1 teaspoon garlic salt
½ cup mayonnaise

½ teaspoon Worcestershire
¼ teaspoon salt
½ teaspoon lemon juice

Eats: A Folk History of Texas Foods (Texas II)

Fantastic Cold Green Bean Salad

½ cup olive oil
⅛ cup white wine vinegar
1½ tablespoons lemon juice
¼ teaspoon paprika
¼ teaspoon dry mustard
1½ teaspoons dill weed
Salt and pepper to taste

½ cup mayonnaise
4 tablespoons sour cream
¼ cup blue cheese
2 (1-pound) cans green beans (cut or whole)
2 bunches green onions, chopped
1½–2 cucumbers, sliced

Make a dressing from the olive oil, white wine vinegar, lemon juice, paprika, dry mustard, dill weed, salt and pepper. Add the mayonnaise, sour cream, and blue cheese to the above mixture. Pour over beans and marinate two hours before serving. Add the green onions and cucumber and toss lightly. Serves 6–8.

Entertaining at Aldredge House (Texas)

Tiny Green Beans and Baby Red Potatoes in Salsa Vinaigrette

What was once the bounty of early spring in the Southwest can now be enjoyed all year. Prepared this way, a pair of favorite vegetables have a Tex-Mex tang and can accompany a wide variety of southwestern menus. You can vary the type of salsa here to suit your palate and the other dishes in your meal.

15 tiny red potatoes, well scrubbed and with a ½-inch belt of skin removed
1½ pounds fresh small green beans, rinsed with stems removed, leaving tips
1 cup water

¼ cup white vinegar
¼ cup extra virgin olive oil, preferably Spanish
½ cup fresh salsa, or to taste
8 fluffy red lettuce leaves, rinsed
16 thin strips of red bell pepper

In a saucepan, bring water about one inch deep to a boil. Add the potatoes and green beans and cover. Simmer about 5 minutes, or until the potatoes are just tender, not mushy. (Peek once or twice to be sure the water has not evaporated.) Combine the vinegar, oil, and salsa. When the vegetables are just done (do not overcook!), drain excess liquid, cover, and allow to dry out on the surface over a low flame—about 5 minutes.

Toss with the vinaigrette; keep tossing every 15 minutes or so until the vegetables have absorbed most of the liquid. After about an hour, place the lettuce leaves on individual plates, then arrange the green beans and potatoes in an attractive pattern. Garnish with a crisscross of bell pepper strips; chill before serving. Yields 8 servings.

Fiestas for Four Seasons (New Mexico)

Arizona frequently has the nation's hottest and coldest temperatures on the same day. The mean temperature is 75° average in the desert to 45° in the high country, but it usually gets a lot meaner in the summer, often over 110°!

Cynthia's Jalapeño Potato Salad

In Fredericksburg, we have a Wild Game Dinner annually. We developed this recipe especially for this occasion and it turned out to be a real hit! Since then, we have fixed it often and it always gets raves from the men! It is great with barbecue and baked beans.

10 cups peeled, cubed, and
  boiled potatoes (about 5
  pounds)
8 boiled eggs, coarsely
  chopped
10 ribs celery, diced
10 green onions, chopped
1 large yellow onion, diced
3–4 cups good quality
  mayonnaise

½ cup chopped pickled
  jalapeños
2 tablespoons juice from
  jalapeños
¼ cup chopped parsley
2 teaspoons comino
1 tablespoon black pepper
1 tablespoon salt

In large bowl, combine potatoes, eggs, celery, and both onions. Combine remaining ingredients and add to potato mixture. Mix well and chill several hours or overnight. Serves 24.

The Patch Tree Tea Room Cookbook (Texas II)

Right-in-the-Skillet Potato Salad

2 pounds potatoes
6 slices bacon
¼ cup bacon drippings
1½ tablespoons flour
1 cup water
⅓ cup vinegar
1¾ teaspoons salt

⅛ teaspoon pepper
1 tablespoon sugar
1 cup chopped celery
1 head romaine, broken
1 medium onion, chopped
6 radishes, sliced thin
2 teaspoons celery seed

1. Cook potatoes in jackets; peel and slice.
2. Cook bacon, drain, and crumble. Set aside. Add flour to bacon drippings in skillet; add water, stirring until smooth; add vinegar, salt, pepper, and sugar.
3. Cook sauce over low heat until thickened.
4. Add 1 layer each of potato, then celery, romaine, and onion, repeating until all are used. Pour on sauce.
5. Toss the salad with spatula taking care not to break potato slices. Sprinkle radishes, bacon, and celery seed over top. Keep warm while serving. Serves 6–8.

Morning, Noon and Night Cookbook (Texas)

A Truly Different Chicken Salad

Chicken salad recipes are usually good, but this one is so different from the rest that it is now our favorite.

VINAIGRETTE DRESSING:

½ teaspoon dried parsley
¼ teaspoon basil
¼ teaspoon dried chives
¾ teaspoon salt
½ teaspoon pepper

1 clove garlic, crushed
1 teaspoon dry mustard
¼ cup white wine vinegar
½ cup olive oil
¼ cup oil

Mix all of the ingredients by shaking in a jar. Chill. Shake well before serving.

SALAD:

8 chicken breast halves, skin
   removed
1 tablespoon lemon juice
½ teaspoon salt
¾ cup Vinaigrette Dressing
1 cup mayonnaise

2 teaspoons chopped fresh
   tarragon, or 1 teaspoon dried
1 lemon rind, grated
1 bunch of lettuce, red-tip, curly
   leaf, etc.

Put the chicken breasts into a glass baking dish or pan in a single layer. Mix the lemon juice and salt and pour over the chicken. Cover and bake for 30 minutes at 400°. Cool and cut chicken into small, bite-sized pieces. Marinate it in the Vinaigrette Dressing for about 3 hours at room temperature. Mix the mayonnaise, tarragon, and lemon rind. Combine with the drained chicken pieces. Chill. When ready to serve, put salad on large lettuce leaves. Serves 8.

Of Magnolia and Mesquite (Texas)

Texas has desert, mountains, plains, forests, lakes, hills, beaches . . . no wonder people are so entranced with its world-in-a-state landscape. Author Mary Lasswell describes it as such: "I am forced to conclude that God made Texas on his day off, for pure entertainment, just to prove what diversity could be crammed into one section of earth by a really top hand."

Grilled Chicken with Macadamia Nuts

1 pound skinless, boneless
  chicken breasts, cut into
  bite-size pieces
1 cup roughly chopped honey
  roasted macadamia nuts

¼ cup chopped green onions
½ cup fresh orange sections
2 tablespoons finely diced or
  julienned red bell pepper

Grill chicken, or bake in a 350° oven for 20 minutes, until chicken is no longer pink. Cool. In a medium salad bowl, combine cooled chicken, nuts, green onions, orange sections, and bell pepper. Serve with Ginger Chili Vinaigrette. Serves 4–6.

GINGER CHILI VINAIGRETTE:

½ teaspoon fresh, minced
  ginger
¾ teaspoon chopped chipotle
  pepper
¼ teaspoon chopped onion
¼ teaspoon chopped garlic
1½ teaspoons chopped pimentos
Pinch of salt

Pinch of black pepper
1 tablespoon chopped fresh
  parsley
1 tablespoon pasteurized egg
  substitute
¼ cup tarragon vinegar
¼ cup fresh orange juice
½ cup corn oil

In a blender, combine ginger, chipotle pepper, onion, garlic, pimentos, salt, pepper, parsley, egg substitute, vinegar, and orange juice. Blend well. Slowly add oil, blending until well-combined. Chill before serving. Makes about 1 cup.

By Request (Arizona)

My Favorite Chicken Salad

6 large chicken breasts
1 large carrot, sliced
1 small onion, chopped
1 stalk celery, chopped
½ teaspoon dill
1 teaspoon salt
½ teaspoon pepper
½ teaspoon basil
1 cup blanched almonds
2 tablespoons butter

1 cup chopped celery
1 cup green grapes, seeded and
  halved
⅓ bottle capers
3 eggs, hard-boiled and chopped
12 olives, slivered
2 cups mayonnaise
2 tablespoons cream
Salt and pepper to taste
Lettuce leaves

Boil chicken breasts with carrot, onion, celery, dill, salt, pepper, and basil. Then allow to simmer until chicken is tender. Refrigerate chicken in broth overnight.

Brown almonds in butter. Debone and skin chicken; cut in generous size squares and add chopped celery, grapes, almonds, capers, eggs, and olives. Blend mayonnaise with cream. Add salt and pepper to taste. Mix lightly with chicken mixture and serve on lettuce leaves.

Par Excellence (Arizona)

Shrimp Filled Avocado Shells

1 avocado, halved and seeded
Fresh lemon or lime juice
½ cup cooked small shrimp
¼ cup minced water chestnuts
2 green onions, minced

2–3 tablespoons mayonnaise
½–1 teaspoon curry powder to
  taste
Salt and freshly ground pepper
Lettuce leaves

Sprinkle cut edges of avocado with lemon or lime juice. Combine all remaining ingredients except lettuce and toss lightly. Mound in avocado halves. Set each on lettuce-lined plate. Cover and chill until ready to serve. Serves 2.

Spindletop International Cooks (Texas)

Shrimp and Napa Cabbage Salad with Roasted Peanuts

DRESSING:

½ cup rice wine
⅓ cup peanut oil

2 tablespoons chile oil
2 tablespoons sugar

In mixing bowl, whisk together all ingredients.

SALAD:

1 head Napa cabbage, cleaned and sliced crosswise in thin ribbons
1 large carrot, peeled and thinly julienned
1 cup cilantro leaves

¼ pound pancetta*, fried crisp and crumbled
1 pound shrimp, peeled, deveined, and cooked
Dressing to taste
½ cup roasted peanuts

Toss cabbage, carrot, cilantro, bacon, shrimp, and Dressing together about 20 minutes before serving. Garnish with peanuts.

*Italian bacon, available at Italian delis and specialty stores

Contributed by Kingfisher, Tucson
Arizona Chefs: Cooking at Home with 36 Arizona Chefs (Arizona)

GWEN McFEE

Built in 1816, El Santuario de Chimayó, a Roman Catholic church in Chimayó, New Mexico, has a reputation as a healing site; believers claim that dirt from a back room of the church can heal physical and spiritual ills. It has become known as the "Lourdes of America," and attracts close to 300,000 visitors a year, including up to 30,000 during Holy Week (the week before Easter). The sanctuary was designated a National Historic Landmark in 1970.

Tossed Fajita Salad

EACH SALAD:

3–4 ounces beef loin, thinly sliced

1 teaspoon vegetable oil

Salt and freshly ground pepper

¼ cup green bell pepper, cut in thin strips

¼ cup red bell pepper, cut in thin strips

¼ cup yellow bell pepper, cut in thin strips

1–2 green onions, sliced (with some green tops)

⅓ cup sliced and drained water chestnuts

Dressing

About a handful (maybe more) romaine lettuce

Salt and freshly ground pepper

Crisped tortilla strips

To prepare meat, remove fat from beef loin and cut it into narrow 2- to 2½-inch strips. Use a heavy skillet to heat oil and stir-fry meat strips 1 or 2 minutes, just long enough for redness to disappear. Season with salt and pepper to taste. Remove to covered storage container.

Add prepared bell peppers, onions, and water chestnuts to meat strips. Toss with sufficient amount of Dressing to match individual taste and enough to slightly marinate salad ingredients. Chill at least 15 minutes but no longer than 30 minutes before serving. When ready to eat, break romaine into bite-size pieces and toss with other ingredients, including tortilla strips. Season to taste and present on chilled plate or in shallow bowl.

DRESSING:

½ cup light oil (such as imported sunflower)

2 teaspoons white wine

3 tablespoons Oriental seasoned (sweet) rice vinegar

Make Dressing by mixing all ingredients with a whisk to thoroughly blend. (It will keep indefinitely when refrigerated.) Makes ¾ cup.

Gourmet Gringo (Arizona)

Margarita Chicken Pasta Salad

DRESSING:

¼ cup olive oil or vegetable oil
¼ cup sour cream
3 tablespoons fresh lime juice
1 (4.5-ounce) can chopped green
   chiles

½ cup fresh orange juice
2 teaspoons sugar
1 teaspoon cumin
⅛ teaspoon salt
3 teaspoons tequila (if desired)

In blender container, combine Dressing ingredients. Blend 30 seconds or until well blended.

4 cups uncooked rainbow rotini
   (spiral pasta)
1 pound skinned, boned chicken,
   cut in strips or pieces for frying
1 (1.25-ounce) package taco
   seasoning mix

1 tablespoon olive oil
1 (11-ounce) can Mexicorn,
   drained
1 (15-ounce) can black beans,
   drained and rinsed

Cook pasta as directed on package. Drain and rinse in cold water. In resealable food storage plastic bag, combine chicken and taco seasoning mix; shake to coat. In large nonstick skillet, heat 1 tablespoon oil over medium-hot heat. Add chicken; cook and stir 8-10 minutes or until golden brown and no longer pink. Remove from heat. In large serving bowl, combine cooked rotini, corn, beans, and Dressing. Toss to coat. Fold in cooked chicken. Serve warm or cold. Makes 8 servings.

Kingman Welcome Wagon Club Cookbook (Arizona)

Colossal Cave, outside of Tucson, Arizona, is one of the largest dry caverns (formations do not form) in the world; explorers have yet to find its end. Although there are an estimated 39 miles of cave tunnels, it took over two years to map just two miles of passageway where tours penetrate six stories deep into the cave.

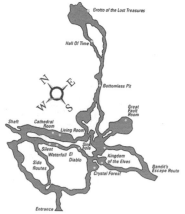

Fresh Fruit Salad
with Spicy Avocado Dressing

SALAD:

1 large mango, peeled and
  sliced
3 apricots, peeled and
  quartered
3 plums, peeled and
  quartered

2 cups strawberries, halved
1 small bunch green grapes,
  washed and stemmed
1 pound mixed lettuces

AVOCADO DRESSING:

½ medium avocado, peeled
  and mashed
½ cup plain yogurt
1 tablespoon honey, or to
  taste
2 scallions, minced (white part
  only)
½ teaspoon lemon zest
¼ teaspoon orange zest

⅛ teaspoon salt
¼ teaspoon ground cumin
⅛ teaspoon freshly ground
  black pepper
½ teaspoon minced Fresno or
  red jalapeño chile
2 tablespoons light cream or to
  taste

Whisk the dressing ingredients together in a medium bowl, or mix in a blender, if you prefer. Adjust seasoning to taste, and drizzle over mixed fresh fruits and greens. Serves 6–8.

Note: The Avocado Dressing also goes well with cold chicken or turkey; and, if you omit the honey and add half a minced garlic clove, it partners beautifully with cold shrimp or scallops, or a bowl of summer vegetables.

Red Chile Bible (New Mexico)

KEITH ODOM

Fabulous '50s food and period decor make Route 66 Diner a must-eat for visitors to Albuquerque, New Mexico. Sit at the soda fountain or in a comfy booth, play the jukebox, and enjoy nostalgic foods just like they used to be. On Central Avenue (old Route 66), here's where you can still "get your kicks on Route 66."

Alligator Pear Salad

The term "alligator pear" is a regional name for avocados. Alligator pears were probably so called because the peel resembles the hide of an alligator and they are somewhat pear shaped. One family member recalls as a child the name "alligator pear" brought romantic and dramatic possibilities to the imagination that "avocado" just never could match.

2 ripe alligator pears
1 teaspoon olive oil
½ teaspoon salt
¼ teaspoon sugar
Juice of ½ lemon

½ teaspoon onion juice
　(optional)
Few dashes hot red pepper
　sauce (optional)
Paprika

Mash pears fine with olive oil, salt, sugar, and lemon juice (onion juice and pepper sauce, if desired). Place on top of tomato slice in center of lettuce cup and serve with mayonnaise topped with paprika.

Perfectly Splendid (Texas II)

Sedona Christmas Salad

This old-fashioned salad somehow seems right at home in the "new age" world of today's Sedona.

1 cup unpeeled and diced red
　apples
1 cup unpeeled and diced green
　apples
1 cup pineapple chunks
½ cup diced celery
½ cup grated carrots
1 cup golden raisins

1 cup mayonnaise
½ cup dry white wine
1 teaspoon crushed dried mint
　leaves
1 cup chopped pecans
1 cup grated sharp Cheddar
　cheese

Place the fruits, vegetables, and raisins in a salad bowl. Mix together mayonnaise, wine, and mint leaves. Pour over the fruit mixture and toss lightly. Add pecans and cheese, and lightly toss again. Serves 6–8.

Christmas in Arizona Cook Book (Arizona)

Apple Salad

This is an 1860 recipe.

Chop together 4 large ripe apples, 1 cup of celery, and 1 cup of nuts. Make a boiled dressing as follows: Yolk of 2 eggs and 1 teaspoon mustard, 1 teaspoon salt, 2 teaspoons sugar, ¼ teaspoon pepper, 2 tablespoons butter, 1 cup of sweet cream, and the whites of 2 eggs beaten stiff. Add to the apple mixture.

A Pinch of This and A Handful of That (Texas II)

Andre's Lime Salad

20 regular size marshmallows
2 cups water
1 small package lime Jell-O
1 (15-ounce) can crushed
   pineapple

1 cup grated Cheddar cheese
1 cup chopped pecans
½ pint whipped cream

Melt marshmallows in hot water. Add Jell-O and stir until dissolved. Set in refrigerator until partially set. Add other ingredients, adding whipped cream last. Fold in well. Pour into lightly oiled mold and let set.

A Taste of Victoria (Texas)

Gazpacho Salad

2 envelopes plain gelatin
2 cups tomato juice
¼ cup red wine vinegar
1 teaspoon salt
2–3 drops Tabasco
2 tomatoes, diced
1 green bell pepper, diced

¼ cup sliced green onions
1 small can pitted ripe olives
1 cucumber, peeled, seeded, and
   diced
16 large butter lettuce leaves
8 teaspoons nonfat mayonnaise

Sprinkle gelatin over tomato juice to soften. Place over low heat and stir until dissolved. Remove from heat and stir in vinegar, salt, and Tabasco. Cool until slightly thickened. Fold in tomatoes, green pepper, onions, olives, and cucumber. Place in sprayed or oiled ring mold. Chill several hours. Unmold on butter lettuce. Decorate with mayonnaise. Serves 8.

Bon Appétit (Arizona)

Molded Gazpacho Salad with Avocado Cream

This recipe is particularly popular with men.

GAZPACHO SALAD:

2 envelopes gelatin
4½ cups tomato juice, divided
¼ cup wine vinegar
1 clove garlic, crushed
2 teaspoons salt
¼ teaspoon pepper
Dash of cayenne pepper
2 large tomatoes, peeled, chopped, and drained

½ cup finely chopped green onions
¾ cup finely chopped green bell pepper
¾ cup peeled, finely chopped cucumber, drained
¼ cup finely chopped pimento
Parsley

Soften gelatin in 1 cup tomato juice for 5 minutes. Heat until mixture simmers and gelatin is dissolved. Remove from heat and add remaining tomato juice, vinegar, garlic, salt, pepper, and cayenne. Chill until mixture begins to set. Fold in tomatoes, onions, green pepper, cucumber, and pimento. Pour into a greased 6-cup ring mold. Chill about 3 hours or until firm. Unmold salad, garnish with parsley, and serve with Avocado Cream. Serves 6–8.

AVOCADO CREAM:

⅓ cup mashed avocado
½ cup sour cream

½ teaspoon salt
Dash of cayenne pepper

Combine ingredients and blend well.

Flavors (Texas)

Creamy Gazpacho Salad

A great discovery!

1 can tomato soup
1 envelope plain gelatin
¼ cup cold water
1 (8-ounce) package cream
  cheese, softened
½ cup chopped celery
½ cup chopped bell pepper

1 tablespoon finely chopped
  onion
1 teaspoon lemon juice
½ cup chopped pecans
1 cup mayonnaise
⅓ cup sliced green olives

Heat soup, gelatin, and water; blend. Add cream cheese and stir constantly while leaving on medium heat. Blend well. Cool and add remaining ingredients. Pour mixture into a mold or a 9x9-inch glass baking dish and let set overnight.

Cut into squares to serve. Serves 8.

Note: To make a main dish, add 1 cup cooked shrimp.

A Little Taste of Texas (Texas II)

Dijon Vinaigrette

If we had any sense we would keep this recipe as a trade secret; it's the most popular dressing at the resort by far, and deservedly so. Too good, really, not to share. You may substitute dried leaf basil for the fresh (halve the quantity and use more parsley) but it won't be quite the same. Use chives, thyme, and other fresh herbs also.

2 cloves garlic
¼ cup parsley sprigs, packed
¼ cup basil leaves, packed
½ teaspoon cracked black
  pepper

1 cup Dijon mustard
1 cup balsamic vinegar
2 cups tomato juice
2 tablespoons honey

Drop garlic into food processor or blender while motor is running. Add fresh herbs and process until finely chopped. Add the remaining ingredients and mix only until blended. Chill. It keeps well in the refrigerator for a week. Yields 4 cups.

Cal: 7; Fat per tablespoon: .2g.

Lean Star Cuisine (Texas II)

VEGETABLES

MESA CONVENTION AND VISITORS BUREAU

Goldfield, one of several ghost towns throughout Arizona, was once a booming mine town. The gold discovered in 1892 was one of the richest strikes at that time, yielding more than three million dollars worth of gold.

Sloppy Josés

As good as or better than any Sloppy Joes you've ever tasted. Please don't let the amount of ingredients intimidate you; it's very simple. Serve with lots of napkins.

2 cups diced onions
1 cup diced red bell peppers
1 cup diced green bell peppers
3 cups chopped tomatoes
2 teaspoons extra virgin olive oil
4–5 cloves garlic, minced
2 cups textured vegetable protein
   granules, hydrated in 1¾ cups
   boiling water
2 cups tomato purée

1½ tablespoons tamari
¼ cup lemon or lime juice
1 tablespoon chili powder
1 tablespoon cumin
2 teaspoons dry mustard
Pinch of cayenne
Pinch of cloves
Pinch of cinnamon
1 tablespoon sorghum or
   unsulfured molasses (optional)

In a large, heavy skillet, sauté the onions, peppers, and tomatoes in the oil over low heat until tender. Add the garlic and sauté another 2–3 minutes. Add the rest of the ingredients, cover, and cook over medium-low heat 20–30 minutes. Uncover and cook another 10 minutes, or until the mixture is thick and the flavors have married well. Serve on whole-grain rolls with lettuce, tomato slices, and pickles or cucumber slices. Enjoy! Yields 8 servings.

VARIATIONS:

Substitute tempeh, tofu, or another variety of textured vegetable protein.

Shiitake mushrooms or diced zucchini are good additions. Add to the onions, peppers, and tomatoes.

A touch of orange juice may sound strange, but try adding it with or instead of lemon or lime juice. Chopped fresh cilantro adds an exotic touch.

Per serving: Calories 139; Protein 12g; Fat 1g; Carbohydrates 19g.

Flavors of the Southwest (Arizona)

Vegetable Enchilada

A Sunday brunch pleaser.

6 cups assorted vegetables, cut into small pieces (zucchini, broccoli, carrots, cauliflower, onion, etc.)

2 tablespoons vegetable oil

⅛ teaspoon chili powder, or to taste

¼ teaspoon cumin

Salt and pepper to taste

1 cup grated Cheddar cheese, divided

1 cup grated Jack cheese, divided

12 flour tortillas

1 jar chile salsa

Cook veggies in oil until crisp-tender. Add spices and ½ of each cheese. When cheese melts, fill tortillas with mixture and roll closed. Place filled tortillas in baking dish and spoon salsa and remainder of cheese over the enchiladas. Bake at 350° until hot. Serves 6.

A Fork in the Road (New Mexico)

Vegetable Chalupa

Zucchini, sliced in rounds

Onion, chopped coarse

Mushrooms, cut lengthwise

Celery, cut crosswise

Olive oil

Corn tortillas

Sour cream

Fresh ripe tomatoes, chopped

Very ripe avocado, sliced

Cheddar cheese, grated

Picante sauce

Braise equal amounts zucchini, onion, mushrooms, and celery in small amount of olive oil until onion is clear. Brown tortillas in a dry skillet for about 15 seconds per side. Put each tortilla on a dinner plate. Pile on the braised vegetables. Top with a dollop of sour cream, tomatoes, avocado, and cheese. Run under the broiler until bubbly. Serve with picante sauce.

The Only Texas Cookbook (Texas)

Vegetable Paella

This paella is very easy to assemble. The flavors of the fresh vegetables are so pronounced even non-vegetarians will rave.

1 cup olive oil	**2 cups cauliflower florets**
2 leeks, white part only, chopped	**½ pound shelled green peas**
4 onions, chopped	**5 cups vegetable stock [about 3**
4 cloves garlic, chopped	** (13¾-ounce) cans]**
4 small tomatoes, chopped	**Salt and pepper to taste**
8 fresh artichoke hearts	**4 teaspoons chopped fresh**
4 red bell peppers, roasted,	** cilantro**
** peeled, and julienned**	**1 pound short-grain rice**

In a casserole (preferably an earthenware casserole) over low heat, heat the oil. Add half of the leeks, onions, garlic, and tomatoes. Cook for 2 minutes. Add artichoke hearts, bell peppers, cauliflower, and peas. Add half of the vegetable stock and cook on low heat for 10 minutes; season with salt and pepper. Add the remainder of the leeks, onions, tomatoes, garlic, all the cilantro, the rice, and the rest of the stock, and blend. Cook for another 20 minutes or so until rice is done. Add more stock, if needed. Serves 6–8.

The Wigwam Resort, Litchfield Park, Arizona
Vegetarian Southwest (Arizona)

The Sonoran Desert, Arizona, is the only place in the world where saguaro cactuses grow. Saguaro National Park has the largest concentration of the cactus. The park was established to protect the unique organ pipe cactus and its Sonoran Desert habitat. The area supports over 30 other species of cactuses as well as a multitude of wildlife.

Company Beans

¼ pound ground beef
1 cup chopped onion
1 (15-ounce) can garbanzo beans,
  drained
1 (15-ounce) can kidney beans,
  drained
1 (15-ounce) can pork and beans,
  drained

¾ cup brown sugar
¼ cup ketchup
¼ cup barbecue sauce
2 teaspoons vinegar
1 teaspoon brown mustard

Brown ground beef with onions. Add garbanzo beans, kidney beans, pork and beans, brown sugar, ketchup, barbecue sauce, vinegar, and brown mustard. Bake in 3-quart casserole at 350° for 1 hour. Can also be put in a crockpot and cooked on LOW for 3 hours. Add bacon, if desired.

Favorites for All Seasons (Arizona)

Frijoles Mexicana
(Mexican Refried Beans)

Make day prior to serving.

2 cups frijoles (Mexican beans,
  or use pinto beans)
5 cups water
4 tablespoons lard, divided

1 tablespoon chopped onion
½ cup tomato purée
Chili powder (optional)

Soak beans overnight and cook, covered, in 5 cups of water for 1½ hours, or until very tender. Drain (and save liquid). Heat 2 tablespoons of the lard in frying pan, add beans, and fry over low heat about 10 minutes, mashing them with a fork. Add water in which the beans were cooked a little at a time, stirring constantly. Keep over low flame until the water has evaporated. Cool and place in a refrigerator until the following day.

Melt the other 2 tablespoons of lard in a large skillet. Fry onion for a few minutes; add tomato purée and chili powder, if desired. When onion is tender, add fried beans and cook until beans are very hot. Serves 6.

From My Apron Pocket (Texas)

Mayan Ranch Barbecue Beans

For over 50 years, the Mayan Ranch in Bandera, Texas, has given visitors the opportunity to be cowboys. This hill country dude ranch serves up the best of the West with old-fashioned barbecue dinners. They say this recipe isn't too sweet like baked beans, but just right for eating with brisket.

2 (23-ounce) cans ranch-style
  beans
1 onion, chopped and sautéed
  until tender
1 link Opa-brand sausage

2 tablespoons prepared
  mustard
½ cup maple syrup
½ cup picante sauce

Combine beans, onion, sausage, mustard, and maple syrup in a glass baking dish or pan. Top with picante sauce. Bake in a 350° oven for 1½ hours. Serves 10–12.

Note: Beans can also be cooked in an iron skillet outside until onions are tender.

Texas Barbecue (Texas II)

Bart's Barbecue Green Beans

A real crowd pleaser.

6 slices bacon, diced
1 onion, chopped
4 (1-pound) cans cut green
  beans, drained

1 cup firmly packed brown
  sugar
1 cup ketchup

Cook bacon and onion together in medium-size skillet over medium heat until bacon is crisp. Remove with slotted spoon and place in ungreased 2-quart baking dish. Add green beans. Mix brown sugar and ketchup in medium-size bowl. Fold into green beans. Bake covered at 250° for 3 hours. Serves 6–8.

Recipes from the Cotton Patch (New Mexico)

Frosted Green Beans

This is a wonderful addition to a special meal.

6 tablespoons white vinegar	8 hard-boiled eggs, chopped
¾ cup salad or olive oil	6 tablespoons mayonnaise
Salt and pepper to taste	4 teaspoons vinegar
2 pounds canned green beans, whole or cut, drained	2 teaspoons prepared mustard
1 large onion, minced	8 slices bacon, cooked and crumbled

Make a marinade of 6 tablespoons vinegar, oil, salt and pepper. Add drained beans and onion. Marinate several hours or several days in refrigerator.

In a bowl, combine eggs, mayonnaise, 4 teaspoons vinegar, mustard, and salt and pepper to taste. Refrigerate and allow flavor to develop. To serve, drain beans and onion. Place on chilled platter. Top with egg salad. Sprinkle bacon over all.

A Different Taste of Paris (Texas)

Tangy Carrots

Grand with roast beef, steak, grilled calves' liver, etc.

12 carrots	Juice of ½ lemon
1 onion, chopped	½ cup seasoned bread crumbs
5 tablespoons horseradish	3 tablespoons butter
1 cup Hellman's mayonnaise	½ cup carrot liquid
Salt and pepper to taste	

Slice carrots in approximately ¾-inch pieces. Cook in water until barely tender. Reserve ½ cup liquid. Place carrots 1 layer deep in a shallow casserole. Mix all other ingredients except the bread crumbs and butter and pour over the carrots. Cover with bread crumbs and dot with butter. Bake at 375° for 20 minutes.

A Different Taste of Paris (Texas)

Sweet-Sour Cabbage

(From Mother's Apron Pocket)

1 large cabbage head,
    shredded (5 cups)
3 or 4 slices of bacon, fried
2 tablespoons brown sugar
2 tablespoons flour

½ cup water
⅓ cup vinegar
Salt and pepper to taste
1 small onion, minced (optional)

Cook cabbage in a quart of water for 5 minutes. Fry bacon, crumble, and set aside. Add sugar and flour to the bacon drippings; blend. Add water, vinegar, and seasonings to taste. Cook until thickened. Add the cooked and drained cabbage to the sweet-sour sauce. Toss with bacon and onion. Heat thoroughly and serve. Serves 6.

From My Apron Pocket (Texas)

Chimayó Corn Pudding

1½ cups creamed corn
1 cup yellow cornmeal
1 cup (2 sticks) butter, melted
¾ cup buttermilk
2 medium onions, chopped
2 eggs, beaten

½ teaspoon baking soda
2 cups grated sharp Cheddar
    cheese
1 (4-ounce) can green chiles,
    drained

Preheat oven to 350°. Grease a 9-inch square baking pan. Combine first 7 ingredients and mix well. Turn half the batter into the greased pan; cover evenly with half the cheese, all the chiles, then remaining cheese. Top with remaining batter. Bake 1 hour. Let cool 15 minutes before serving. This is a spicy side dish that's sure to become a family favorite . . . delish served with any and all Bar-B-Q. Makes 8–12 servings.

Collectibles III (Texas II)

Corn Casserole

1 (15½-ounce) can creamed corn
1 (15½-ounce) can whole-kernel
  corn, drained
1 cup grated sharp Cheddar
  cheese
1 cup cracker crumbs
½ cup grated onion
1 (2-ounce) jar pimentos
1 egg

⅔ cup evaporated milk
½ cup butter or margarine,
  melted
1 teaspoon salt
1½ teaspoons pepper
1 tablespoon sugar
½ teaspoon cayenne
½ cup chopped bell pepper
Paprika

Mix all ingredients together, except paprika, in order given, stirring well. Pour into slightly oiled casserole, sprinkle with paprika, and bake at 400° approximately 1 hour. Serves 12.

Ready to Serve (Texas)

Green Chile Corn Casserole

1 box Jiffy Corn Muffin Mix
2 eggs
½ stick butter or margarine,
  softened
⅔ cup milk
1 (4-ounce) can chopped
  green chiles, undrained

4 ounces Cheddar or Jack
  cheese, grated (optional)
¼ teaspoon ground cumin
1 (15½-ounce) can whole-kernel
  corn, drained
1 (15½-ounce) can creamed corn

Mix all ingredients together with an electric mixer to incorporate margarine, adding corn last. Bake at 350° in your favorite, slightly greased, 2-quart baking dish for one hour or until set.

Families Cooking Together (New Mexico)

Mexican Corn Pudding

1 (16-ounce) can creamed corn
2 eggs, beaten
1 can tamales, shucked and
  cut up
2 tablespoons butter

1 (4-ounce) can chopped ripe
  olives
½ cup (or more) grated Cheddar
  cheese

Combine corn, eggs, and tamales; dot with butter. Mix gently; put in greased casserole. Bake at 350° for approximately 45 minutes. Remove from oven; add olives and sprinkle cheese on top. Return to oven until cheese melts. Serve while hot. Makes a nice supper dish with a salad. Serves 4.

Enjoy! (Texas)

Hominy Casserole

2 large cans hominy (drain 1 can)
1 can diced green chiles
5 small green onions, chopped

1 (16-ounce) carton sour cream
½ cup grated cheese

Mix together everything except grated cheese. Top with grated cheese and bake at 350° for 35 minutes.

Lion's Club of Globe Cookbook (Arizona)

Sunday Potatoes

The more onion soup, the more flavor.

3 potatoes, sliced
Salt and pepper to taste

2 tablespoons dry onion soup mix
1 stick butter

Butter a medium casserole and layer potatoes. Sprinkle with salt, pepper, and onion soup. Slice 1 stick butter on top. Cover and bake in 325° oven for 1 hour. Yields 4 servings.

Calf Fries to Caviar (Texas)

Swedish Green Potatoes

"This is best if made up and refrigerated, then baked the next day," says Janis Frieder, wife of ASU basketball coach Bill Frieder. "I serve it with grilled tenderloin, fresh asparagus, and a salad. Everyone loves it."

8 large potatoes, peeled and
  cut into 1-inch pieces
¾ cup sour cream
1 teaspoon sugar
4 tablespoons butter
2 teaspoons salt

¼ teaspoon pepper
2 tablespoons snipped dill
1 (10-ounce) package frozen
  chopped spinach, cooked and
  well drained
1 cup shredded Cheddar cheese

In a large pot, boil, drain, and mash potatoes. Add sour cream, sugar, and butter, and beat until fluffy. Add remaining ingredients. Preheat oven to 400°. Place potatoes in a greased baking dish. Bake 30 minutes or until bubbly. Serves 8.

The Arizona Celebrity Cookbook (Arizona)

Mexican Hash Browns

5 slices bacon
3-4 tablespoons oil
4 medium potatoes, peeled
  and cut into ¼-inch slices
2 tablespoons margarine
1 medium onion chopped

¼ cup chopped green bell pepper
1 clove garlic, crushed
2 tablespoons chopped pimentos
¼ teaspoon salt
Pepper to taste

Cook bacon in a large skillet until crisp; drain on paper towels. Add oil to bacon grease if not enough to cook potatoes, if not now, oil may be needed while potatoes are cooking. Heat skillet over medium heat; when hot, add potatoes and cook until golden brown. Drain potatoes on paper towels. Melt margarine in skillet; add onion, green pepper, and garlic. Sauté until tender. Stir in potatoes, crumbled bacon and pimentos. Sprinkle with salt and pepper. Toss to combine. Serve immediately.

Not Just Bacon & Eggs (Texas II)

Roasted Scarlet Potatoes

1½ pounds (2 large) baking
  potatoes, scrubbed
2 tablespoons canola oil
½ teaspoon sweet paprika
1 teaspoon Chimayó chili
  powder

⅛ teaspoon ground cumin
¼ teaspoon dried Mexican
  oregano
Salt and freshly ground pepper
  to taste

Preheat the oven to 375°. Cut the potatoes in half crosswise, then cut each half into 4 wedges. In a heavy, cast-iron skillet, heat the oil to moderately hot and stir in paprika, chili powder, and cumin. After 30 seconds, add the potato wedges, sprinkle with oregano, and salt and pepper to taste, and toss the potatoes in the oil and spices to coat. Transfer the skillet to the hot oven and roast the potatoes about 40 minutes, turning occasionally, until tender and browned. Serves 4.

Red Chile Bible (New Mexico)

A Change from Baked Potatoes

And such a tasty change!

4 tablespoons margarine
4 tablespoons bacon drippings
6 potatoes, peeled and cubed
1 small onion, sliced in rings

6 green onions, sliced, including
  tops
Seasoned salt
Cracked pepper

Preheat oven to 350°. Melt margarine and bacon drippings in 9x13-inch glass baking dish while oven is preheating. Mix potatoes and onions with margarine and bacon drippings to coat. Season to taste. Bake in oven for 45 minutes to 1 hour, stirring occasionally. Serves 6–8.

Delicioso! (Texas II)

Mashed Potato Soufflé

4–6 potatoes, peeled and cut
1 (8-ounce) package cream
  cheese, softened
1 egg

1 cup light cream
Salt and pepper to taste
Tabasco to taste
¼ cup chopped scallions

Boil potatoes until tender. Drain. While still hot, whip potatoes with cream cheese, egg, and cream. Season to taste with salt, pepper, and Tabasco. Fold in scallions. Pour into buttered casserole dish, leaving 2–3 inches at the top for "puffing." Bake at 350° for 45 minutes. Serves 6.

Note: Soufflé can be assembled and refrigerated until baking time.

Purple Sage and Other Pleasures (Arizona)

Twice Baked Chile Potatoes

3 large white baking potatoes
1 tablespoon olive oil
6 tablespoons butter, divided
¼ cup minced yellow onions
2 cloves garlic, minced
3 green chiles, roasted, peeled,
  seeded, and chopped

Salt to taste
1 teaspoon freshly ground black
  pepper
¼ cup milk
Parmesan cheese
Paprika

Preheat oven to 400°. Wash, scrub, and dry the potatoes; coat lightly with oil. Bake for one hour or until the potatoes are done.

Heat 2 tablespoons of the butter in a frying pan; sauté onion and garlic until onions are soft. Add green chiles, salt, and pepper to the pan and cook over low heat, until the chiles are warmed through.

Cut potatoes in half lengthwise and scoop out the pulp, being careful not to cut through the skin of the potato. Mix potato pulp with the chile and onion mixture. Stir in the 4 remaining tablespoons of butter and the milk, and spoon the pulp back into the potato shells. Sprinkle with Parmesan cheese and paprika, return to the oven, and heat at 300° for 15–20 minutes or until the potatoes are warmed through. Serves 6.

Billy the Kid Cook Book (New Mexico)

Sweet Potato and Apple Casserole

3 medium sweet potatoes,
  sliced
2 large apples, sliced
2 cups small (miniature)
  marshmallows
¾ cup sugar

1 teaspoon salt
1 teaspoon cinnamon
2 tablespoons cornstarch
½ cup water
4 tablespoons butter

Spread half of the potatoes in a 3-quart casserole. Add apples and marshmallows; repeat layers. Mix sugar, salt, and cinnamon. Sprinkle over mixture. Dissolve cornstarch in water. Pour over mixture. Dot with butter. Cover and bake at 350° for one hour.

Our Best Home Cooking (New Mexico)

Sweet Potato Bake
with Pecan Topping

The pecan tree was so loved by Texas Governor James Hogg that his last request was that a pecan tree be planted at the head of his grave and a walnut tree at the foot, and that when these trees bore, the nuts be given to the people of Texas to plant to make "Texas a land of trees." A few years later, the State Legislature voted to make the beautiful pecan the state tree.

3 cups cooked and mashed
  sweet potatoes
¼ cup milk
⅓ cup butter, melted

1 teaspoon vanilla
2 eggs, beaten
½ teaspoon salt

Mix mashed sweet potatoes, milk, butter, vanilla, eggs, and salt. Spoon into an oiled 1½-quart casserole.

TOPPING:

1 cup chopped pecans
1 cup brown sugar
3 tablespoons flour

⅓ cup butter, melted
1 cup flaked coconut (optional)

Combine Topping ingredients and sprinkle over sweet potatoes. Bake at 375° for 25 minutes. Serves 6.

Tastes & Tales From Texas . . . With Love (Texas)

Apple Mallow Yam Yums

2 apples, sliced
½ cup chopped pecans
½ cup brown sugar, packed
½ teaspoon cinnamon

2 (16-ounce) cans yams
¼ cup butter
2 cups miniature marshmallows

Toss apples, nuts, brown sugar, and cinnamon together. Alternate layers of apples and yams in a buttered casserole. Dot with butter. Bake at 350° for 35–40 minutes. Sprinkle marshmallows over all and broil until lightly brown. Serves 6–8.

Delicioso! (Texas II)

Eggplant Mexicano

5 slices bacon, chopped
1 onion, chopped
2 fresh tomatoes, chopped
2 jalapeños, seeded and
  chopped
½ cup chicken broth
½ cup dry white wine

1 teaspoon salt
½ teaspoon freshly ground
  black pepper
2 medium eggplants, peeled and
  cut into cubes, divided
1 cup shredded colby cheese,
  divided

Preheat oven to 325°. Fry the bacon; remove from pan and reserve. Sauté onion in the bacon drippings. Add the tomatoes, jalapeños, chicken broth, wine, salt, and pepper. Line the bottom of a glass casserole dish with half of the eggplant, spoon half of the tomato mixture over eggplant, then sprinkle with half of the cheese and bacon. Repeat process, ending with the cheese. Bake for 45 minutes, or until the eggplant is done and the cheese is melted and lightly browned. Serves 4–6.

Billy the Kid Cook Book (New Mexico)

Henry McCarty (reportedly November 23, 1859–July 14, 1881), better known as Billy the Kid, was a 19th-century American frontier outlaw and gunman who participated in the Lincoln County War. According to legend, he killed over twenty men, but he is generally accepted to have killed four. He was relatively unknown during his own lifetime, but was catapulted into legend the year after his death when his killer, Sheriff Pat Garrett, along with co-author M.A. "Ash" Upson, published a sensationalistic biography titled The Authentic Life of Billy, the Kid. Since then, he has grown into a symbolic figure of the American Old West.

Unbelievably Eggplant
(Microwave)

Even eggplant haters love it this way.

1 (1½-pound) eggplant, peeled
    and cut into ½-inch cubes
⅓ cup chopped onion
Margarine
3 tablespoons flour
1½ cups milk
1 cup shredded sharp Cheddar
    cheese (4 ounces)

¼ teaspoon pepper
1 (2¼-ounce) can sliced ripe
    olives, drained
1 cup dry herb stuffing mix (such
    as Pepperidge Farm)

Place eggplant and onion in a 2-quart glass batter bowl. Cover and microwave on HIGH 8 minutes, stirring after 4 minutes. Drain. Transfer to a 1½-quart round casserole.

Place 3 tablespoons margarine in same glass bowl. Microwave on HIGH 30 seconds, or until melted. Blend in flour using a wire whisk. Whisk in milk. Microwave on HIGH 2 minutes; stir with whisk. Microwave on HIGH 2 minutes, or until mixture begins to boil; whisk. Stir in cheese until melted. Add pepper.

Stir in reserved eggplant and onions, and half the can of olives. Pour half of eggplant mixture into casserole. Sprinkle with half of stuffing. Add remaining eggplant mixture and top with remainder of stuffing. Garnish with remaining olives and dot with margarine. Microwave on 70% (MEDIUM-HIGH) 6 minutes, or until heated through. Makes 4–6 servings.

Micro Quick! (Texas)

Billy Bob's Texas in Fort Worth is the largest honky tonk in the world. Located in the historic Fort Worth Stockyards with 127,000 square feet of space (which is nearly 3 acres inside and 20 acres of parking) for entertainment and events, Billy Bob's has 32 individual bar stations, country music's biggest stars, Live Pro Bull Riding, and a Texas-size dance floor for everyone to enjoy. It's no wonder that Billy Bob's Texas has been named Country Music Club of the Year five times by the Academy of Country Music.

Lynn's Squash and Cheese Bake

3 medium yellow squash,
  trimmed and sliced thin
6 tablespoons butter, divided
1 (10-ounce) package fresh
  spinach, washed and trimmed
2 cups cream-style cottage
  cheese

1½ cups coarsely crumbled Ritz
  crackers
¼ teaspoon oregano
¼ teaspoon basil
¼ teaspoon parsley
3 medium tomatoes, sliced
6 slices provolone cheese

Sauté squash slightly in 2 tablespoons butter. Remove from skillet and set aside. Repeat with spinach in 2 tablespoons butter. Mix cottage cheese, crackers, and herbs in bowl. Spray 8x8-inch baking dish with cooking spray. Put squash in dish, layer ½ of cheese mixture over the squash, then spinach, and the remainder of the cheese mixture. Top with tomato slices. Place the provolone cheese slices in checkerboard fashion. Bake at 375° for 30 minutes. Serves 6.

Kids in the Kitchen (Arizona)

Royal Squash

2 pounds yellow squash
1 large onion, diced
1 can cream of chicken soup
1 small carton sour cream
1 carrot, grated

Dash of garlic salt
1 stick margarine
1 package Pepperidge Farm Herb
  Dressing

Boil the squash and onion together in a small amount of water until tender. Drain well and combine with the soup, sour cream, carrot, and garlic salt. Set aside. Melt the margarine and add the dressing; mix well. Spread half of the mixture over the bottom of a casserole. Cover with the squash. Spread on the other half of the dressing. Bake at 350° for about 30 minutes, until bubbly. Serves 10-12.

The Galveston Island Cookbook (Texas)

Chile Cheese Squash

Squash was one of the earliest crops grown by the first inhabitants of the Sedona area.

1 pound squash (zucchini, summer, or yellow), cut in ¼-inch pieces
½ cup mayonnaise (not salad dressing)
1 (4-ounce) can diced green chiles
½ cup grated Cheddar cheese
½ cup bread crumbs

Cook squash until just tender. Drain well. Return to saucepan; stir in remaining ingredients. Serve hot. Serves 4.

Sedona Cook Book (Arizona)

Stuffed Zucchini

8 medium (6-inch) zucchini
1 tablespoon salt, dissolved in a large bowl of water
1 heaping cup ground lamb
1 cup short-grain white rice, well washed and drained
1½ teaspoons plus a pinch of salt, divided
¼ teaspoon pepper
¾ teaspoon cinnamon
2 tablespoons butter, room temperature
1 (6-ounce) can tomato paste, divided
1 (16-ounce) can crushed tomatoes

Wash zucchini and cut off stalk ends. Hollow out interiors, taking care not to pierce sides or ends of squash. Place cored zucchini in salted water.

Combine lamb, rice, 1½ teaspoons salt, pepper, cinnamon, butter, and a few spoonfuls of the tomato paste in a large bowl, mixing by hand.

Drain zucchini. Fill each one with lamb mixture, leaving ⅓ space free for expansion during cooking. Place stuffed zucchini in rows in a large pot. In a small bowl, mix tomatoes and remaining paste, and pour over squash. Add water to cover zucchini and sprinkle with a pinch of salt.

Place a plate upside down on top of stuffed zucchini. Cover with pot lid and cook on low heat about 1 hour or until rice is done. Serves 4.

Recipe by newscaster Hugh Downs, Scottsdale
The Arizona Celebrity Cookbook (Arizona)

Zucchini with Sour Cream

Captivating.

3 medium zucchini
½ cup sour cream or more
2 tablespoons soft butter
2 tablespoons grated cheese
Salt and pepper to taste

Paprika
1 tablespoon chopped chives
¼ cup buttered bread crumbs
Additional grated cheese

Slice washed, unpeeled zucchini into thin rounds; simmer, covered, in a small amount of water for 6–8 minutes, shaking the pan frequently. Drain. Combine sour cream, butter, 2 tablespoons grated cheese, salt, pepper, and paprika; stir over low heat to melt cheese. Remove from heat and mix in chives; toss lightly with zucchini. Place in a buttered 1½-quart flat baking dish; top with crumbs and sprinkle with additional cheese. Bake in a preheated 375° oven for about 10 minutes. Can be prepared ahead and refrigerated, but increase the baking time to 30 minutes. Serves 6.

Crème of the Crop (Texas)

Zucchini Boats

3 plump zucchini
1 clove garlic
½ cup chopped onion
6 tablespoons butter, divided
2 tomatoes, chopped
1 (4-ounce) can green chiles,
  chopped

¾ cup bread crumbs
¼ cup grated Parmesan cheese
Salt and pepper to taste
1 tablespoon chopped parsley

Wash zucchini and cut in half lengthwise. Scoop out shells and reserve pulp. Sauté garlic and onion in 3 tablespoons butter until onion is transparent. Remove garlic clove. Add zucchini pulp, tomatoes, and chiles to sautéed onion and mix well. Fill shells with mixture. Melt remaining butter and mix with bread crumbs, cheese, salt, pepper, and parsley. Heap each zucchini boat with bread crumb mixture. Cover and bake in buttered baking dish at 350° for 30 minutes.

Fiesta Mexicana (New Mexico)

Vera Cruz Tomatoes

3 strips bacon
¼ cup chopped onion
8 ounces fresh spinach, snipped
½ cup dairy sour cream
Dash of bottled hot pepper
  sauce

4 medium tomatoes
Salt to taste
½ cup (2 ounces) shredded
  mozzarella cheese

Cook bacon until crisp; drain, reserving 2 tablespoons drippings. Crumble bacon and set aside. Cook onion in reserved drippings till tender. Stir in spinach. Cook, covered, till tender, 3–5 minutes. Remove from heat. Stir in sour cream, bacon, and pepper sauce. Cut tops from tomatoes. Remove centers, leaving thick shells. Salt shells; fill with spinach mixture. Place in 8x8x2-inch baking dish. Bake in 375° oven for 20–25 minutes. Top with shredded cheese; bake 2–3 minutes more or till melted. Makes 4 servings.

Square House Museum Cookbook (Texas)

Summer Tomatoes

6–8 tomatoes

DRESSING:

½ teaspoon dried oregano
2 teaspoons dried basil, or 2
  tablespoons shredded fresh
  basil
½ teaspoon minced garlic

½ teaspoon salt
1 teaspoon sugar
2 green onions, finely diced
2 tablespoons finely diced red
  onions

Blanch tomatoes and peel skins. Blend Dressing ingredients. Pour Dressing over whole tomatoes and marinate overnight. Serve in a large bowl garnished with fresh parsley and basil. No further dressing is necessary. Makes 6–8 servings.

Pass it on... Slice and drizzle with balsamic vinegar and olive oil and sprinkle with bits of mozzarella cheese.

Pass it On... (Texas II)

Spinach-Tomato Bake

10–12 ounces fresh spinach
2 tablespoons lemon juice
4 tablespoons sour cream
1 (3-ounce) can broiled-in-
butter mushrooms

3 fresh tomatoes, peeled and
thinly sliced
Salt and pepper
Parmesan cheese

Chop spinach in blender or with scissors. Mix with lemon juice, sour cream, and mushrooms. Season with salt and pepper. Place in buttered casserole and cover with tomato slices. Dust with salt and pepper and a thick layer of Parmesan cheese. Bake at 300° until brown and bubbly, about 15 minutes. Serves 4–6.

Houston Junior League Cookbook (Texas II)

Southwestern Spinach

2 (10-ounce) packages frozen,
chopped spinach
2 tablespoons chopped onion
4 tablespoons butter or
margarine
2 tablespoons flour
½ cup evaporated milk
½ cup spinach cooking water

½ teaspoon black pepper
¾ teaspoon celery salt
¾ teaspoon garlic salt
1 cup grated sharp cheese
1 teaspoon Worcestershire
1 (4-ounce) can chopped green
chiles
Buttered bread crumbs

Preheat oven to 350°. Cook the spinach according to the package directions. Drain, reserving ½ cup liquid. Sauté the onion in butter until soft. Blend in the flour. Slowly add the milk and spinach water stirring constantly to avoid lumps. Cook until smooth and thickened. Add the remaining ingredients except the bread crumbs. Pour into a 9-inch square baking dish and top with the bread crumbs. Bake 25 minutes. Serves 6–8.

Green Chile Bible (New Mexico)

Broccoli Delight

2 (16-ounce) packages frozen
  broccoli, cooked and drained
1 can cream of mushroom soup
2 bunches chopped green onions

1 small can sliced water chestnuts,
  drained
2 cups grated Cheddar cheese
1 cup slivered almonds

Mix all ingredients together. Bake in a lightly greased casserole dish at 350° for 30 minutes.

Cooking with Cops (Arizona)

Walnut Broccoli

So good, you hardly know it's broccoli.

3 (10-ounce) packages frozen
  chopped broccoli
½ cup butter
4 tablespoons flour
1½ teaspoons instant chicken
  bouillon, or 2 bouillon cubes

2 cups milk
1 (8-ounce) package commercial
  cornbread stuffing mix
1 cup chopped walnuts

Cook broccoli according to package directions. Drain and place in a greased 9 x 13-inch baking dish. In saucepan, melt butter, add flour, and stir to blend. Add chicken bouillon and milk, stirring constantly. Cook until smooth and thick. Pour over the broccoli. Prepare the cornbread stuffing mix according to package directions, using lowest amount of water. Add walnuts and spread over the broccoli mixture. Bake at 350° for 30 minutes. Pecans or almonds may be used instead of walnuts. Yields 12 servings.

Cook 'Em Horns: The Quickbook (Texas II)

You can still mosey through Judge Roy Bean's Jersey Lilly bar, courtroom, billiard parlor, and jail in Langtry, Texas, sixty miles from Del Rio. In 1885, Judge Roy Bean was 'The Law West of the Pecos" in a county three times the size of Rhode Island and ten times as tough.

Asparagus Stir Fry

1 bunch asparagus (15–20
  spears)
2 tablespoons olive oil

1 clove garlic, minced (optional)
Lemon pepper to taste

Clean asparagus and cut off 1 inch of bottom. Cut spears into 2-inch pieces. Heat oil in a stir-fry pan; add asparagus and garlic, and stir until crisp tender. Sprinkle with lemon pepper and serve. You will never serve it steamed again!

Hospice Hospitality (Arizona)

Greens

About a peck of greens are enough for a mess for a gathering of six folks. Almost any sort can be used. We've had the best of luck with dandelions, chicory, mustard or turnip greens. All greens should be carefully examined, and the tough ones thrown out. Thoroughly wash through several waters until they are entirely free from sand. Adding a handful of salt to each pan of water while washing the greens will free them of insects and worms.

When ready to boil the greens, put them into a large pot half full of boiling water with a handful of salt, and boil them until the stalks are tender—anywhere from 5–20 minutes. Remember that over-long boiling wastes the tender nature of the leaves and lessens both the flavor and nourishment of the dish.

As soon as they are tender, drain them in a colander, chop them a little and return them to the fire. Season them with salt, pepper, and butter. The greens should be served as soon as they are hot.

As mentioned early on in this receipt, this serves 6 people, but could well serve 60. Just add a little more of everything in its measure.

Jane Long's Brazoria Inn (Texas II)

Artichoke Casserole

This dish is a tradition with all holiday meals. The only disagreement is who gets to bring it! We rarely have leftovers, and when we do, they don't last long.

1 (14-ounce) can artichoke
  hearts, drained and quartered
3 hard-cooked eggs, sliced
½ cup pimento-stuffed
  green olives, sliced
¼ cup sliced water chestnuts

1 (10¾-ounce) can cream of
  mushroom soup, undiluted
¼ cup milk
½ cup buttered bread crumbs
½ cup (2 ounces) grated
  Cheddar cheese

Layer artichoke hearts, eggs, olives, and water chestnuts in greased 9x9x2-inch baking dish. Blend soup and milk together. Pour over ingredients in casserole dish. Top with bread crumbs and cheese. Bake, uncovered, at 350° for 25–30 minutes or until bubbly and browned. Serves 8.

Per ½-cup serving: Cal 144; Prot 6.55g; Carb 10.8g; Fat 9g; Chol 88.4mg; Sod 646mg.

Changing Thymes (Texas II)

French-Fried Onion Rings

Onion rings fried in peanut oil taste better than those fried in shortening and they have less cholesterol.

6 medium Spanish onions,
  thinly sliced
1 cup milk
1 cup buttermilk

1 egg, beaten
1 cup all-purpose flour
2–3 cups peanut oil
Salt to taste

Separate onion slices into rings. Combine milk, buttermilk, and egg in a medium mixing bowl. Add onion rings and refrigerate for 30 minutes. Spread flour on a plate. Heat oil to 375° in a medium saucepan or deep-fat fryer. Remove onion rings from milk mixture and dip one at a time into flour. Fry in hot oil until golden brown. Cook no more than 8–10 rings at one time to prevent oil from cooling below 375°. Remove from oil, drain on paper towels, and sprinkle with salt. Yields 6–8 servings.

More Tastes & Tales (Texas II)

Creamy Baked 1015 Onions

Texas 1015 onions are wonderfully mild, sweet onions grown in the Rio Grande Valley. Their name comes from the date the onions are planted, October 15th. Because the days are short during the growing season, the onions have less acidity than those grown in the long, hot days of summer. In taste tests of the Texas 1015, the Vidalia onion of Georgia and the Walla-Walla of Washington, the Texas onion wins again and again. Onions are usually used to enhance other flavors, but this dish makes the onion the culinary star.

4 large Texas 1015 onions
2 tablespoons margarine,
  divided
2 garlic cloves, minced
1 cup chicken broth
1 packet Lipton's Cream of
  Chicken Cup-a-Soup Mix

¼ cup grated Parmesan cheese
2 teaspoons sodium-reduced
  soy sauce
½ teaspoon black pepper
½ cup seasoned bread crumbs

Peel and slice the onions. Separate some of the slices into rings. Reserve 1 tablespoon of margarine for the topping. Place 1 tablespoon of margarine, the garlic, the chicken broth and the contents of the packet of soup mix in a large saucepan; stir. Add the onion rings and simmer until tender.

Transfer the onion rings to a 2-quart casserole leaving some of the broth mixture in the pan. Mix the Parmesan cheese, soy sauce, and pepper with the broth mixture and pour over the onions. Melt the reserved margarine and mix with the bread crumbs. Sprinkle the bread crumb mixture over the top of the onion mixture and bake at 350° for 30 minutes. Serves 6.

4.2 grams fat per serving.

New Tastes of Texas (Texas II)

Onion Pie

"Out of this world!"

2 cups chopped onions
1 cup butter
2 eggs, yolks and whites beaten separately
½ cup cream or Milnot

Salt and cayenne pepper to taste
1 cup dry white wine
2 (9-inch) prepared pastry shells*

Sauté onions in butter until limp, but not browned. Cool. Preheat oven to 350°. Stir egg yolks, cream, salt, cayenne, and wine into onions. Fold beaten egg whites into onion mixture. Fill pie shells and bake 30 minutes. Serves 12 generously, or serve 6 and freeze one. Serve as a starch with steaks or roast beef. Serve hot or cold as a luncheon dish.

*I like to precondition the crust by brushing with egg white and baking for 8–10 minutes in a 400° oven. Crust should be cool before mixture is poured in and baked.

Collectibles II (Texas)

PASTA, RICE, ETC.

KEITH ODOM

The International UFO Museum and Research Center in Roswell, New Mexico, is fast becoming the clearing house for information related to UFOs and their phenomenon. The founders were participants in the Roswell Incident of 1947.

Chicken Tequila Fettuccine

1 pound spinach fettuccine
½ cup chopped fresh cilantro,
  divided
2 tablespoons minced garlic
2 tablespoons minced jalapeños
3 tablespoons butter, divided
½ cup chicken stock
2 tablespoons gold tequila
2 tablespoons lime juice
3 tablespoons soy sauce
1¼ pounds chicken breasts,
  diced
¼ medium red onion, thinly sliced
½ medium red bell pepper
½ medium green bell pepper
1½ cups heavy cream

Cook pasta al dente according to package. Cook ⅓ cup cilantro, garlic, and jalapeños in 2 tablespoons butter over medium heat for 5 minutes. Add stock, tequila, and lime juice. Bring mixture to a boil and cook till paste-like; set aside. Pour soy sauce over diced chicken; set aside for 5 minutes. Meanwhile, cook onion and peppers with remaining butter till limp. Add chicken and soy sauce, then add reserved tequila/lime paste and cream. Boil sauce till chicken is cooked through, and sauce is thick. Serve sauce over fettuccine on serving dishes. Serve with cilantro and jalapeños as garnish. Makes 4–6 servings.

Pleasures from the Good Earth (Arizona)

Spyros Pasta

1 small red onion, chopped
2 cloves garlic, chopped
2 ounces wild mushrooms
  (oyster, portobello), sliced
1 tablespoon olive oil
2 ounces sun-dried tomatoes,
  reconstituted according to
  package directions
¼ cup white wine
½ cup chicken stock
½ cup chopped fresh spinach
2⅔ tablespoons chopped fresh
  basil
¼ cup plus 2 tablespoons grated
  Parmesan cheese
Salt and pepper to taste
8 ounces linguine, cooked

Sauté onion, garlic, and mushrooms in olive oil. Add sun-dried tomatoes. Add white wine to deglaze, scraping any particles from the pan, and reduce until almost dry. Add chicken stock, spinach, basil, cheese, and salt and pepper to taste. Toss with linguine to serve. Serves 4.

Approximate values per serving: Cal 310; Fat 7g; Chol 6mg; Carbo 48g; Sod 530mg; Cal from Fat 21%.

By Request (Arizona)

Chicken Spaghetti
"Carole Curlee Special"

BROTH:

1 (3- to 4-pound) chicken
Salt to taste
Water to cover

1 onion
2 stalks celery

Boil chicken in salted water to cover with onion and celery till tender. Cool to handle; bone chicken, reserving broth.

1 large onion, chopped
3 ribs celery, sliced
1 carrot, grated (optional)
3 tablespoons margarine
2 cans cream of chicken soup
1 can or more saved broth or
  evaporated milk
1¾ cups grated Cheddar
  cheese, divided
1 teaspoon chili powder

Salt and pepper to taste
½ teaspoon garlic salt
1 small jar pimentos, chopped
1 small can sliced
  mushrooms (optional)
3–4 chicken bouillon cubes
  (optional)
1 (12-ounce) package
  spaghetti, cooked

Sauté onion, celery, and carrot in margarine. Add soup and broth (or milk). Add 1 cup grated cheese to the sauce mixture and heat. Also, add chili powder, salt, pepper, garlic salt, pimentos, and mushrooms. Add the boned chicken. Taste for seasoning; can add chicken bouillon cubes for more flavor. Toss the sauce with cooked spaghetti. Put a ladle of extra sauce on top for eye appeal, and toss ¾ cup grated cheese on top. Either refrigerate until later, or cook at 325° for 25 minutes or until bubbly and hot. You can add a little more liquid if you want thinner sauce. This is super! Serves 8.

A Casually Catered Affair (Texas II)

Southwestern Risotto

Can be served as a main meal with a green salad.

½ cup chopped onion
2 cloves garlic, crushed
2 tablespoons butter or
  margarine, melted
1 cup medium-grain rice,
  uncooked
½ cup dry white wine
6 cups chicken broth, divided
½ cup whipping cream
2 medium tomatoes, seeded
  and chopped

1 jalapeño pepper, seeded
  and minced
½ cup sliced green onions
½ cup grated Parmesan
  cheese
3 tablespoons minced cilantro
Garnish: fresh cilantro
  sprigs, cubed tomatoes

Cook onion and garlic in butter in a large skillet or saucepan over medium heat, stirring constantly, until tender. Add rice; cook 2–3 minutes, stirring frequently with a wooden spoon. Add wine and cook, uncovered, until liquid is absorbed. Add one cup broth; cook, stirring constantly, over medium-high heat 5 minutes or until broth is absorbed. Add remaining broth, 1 cup at a time, cooking and stirring constantly until each cup is absorbed, 25–30 minutes. (Rice will be tender and have a creamy consistency.)

Stir in whipping cream and next 5 ingredients. Cook 2 minutes. Garnish with cilantro and tomatoes. Serves 6.

Texas Sampler (Texas II)

Chilaquiles

2 medium onions, chopped
1 clove garlic, minced finely
2 cans mild, chopped green
  chiles
2 cans stewed tomatoes
2 stalks fresh celery, chopped
Fresh cilantro sprig (optional)

Salt and pepper to taste
1 dozen tortillas, quartered and
  softened in hot oil
2 pounds grated Monterey Jack
  cheese
3 cups sour cream for garnish

Simmer all ingredients except tortillas and cheese. Salt and pepper to taste. Heat oil; dip pieces of quartered tortilla in hot oil until softened. Layer tortillas, sauce, and cheese to top of a 9x13-inch casserole dish. Place in oven at 350° for 15–20 minutes to heat thoroughly and melt cheese. Cut through like a cobbler and serve with sour cream on top. A wonderful brunch dish! (Can be prepared ahead of time and refrigerated up to 2 days. Heat at 350° for 1 hour to serve.) Serves 10–12.

Spindletop International Cooks (Texas)

The Lyndon B. Johnson Space Center (JSC) is the National Aeronautics and Space Administration's center for human spaceflight activities. The center, originally known as the Manned Spacecraft Center, opened in 1963. On February 19, 1973, the center was renamed in honor of the late U.S. president and Texas native, Lyndon B. Johnson. The center consists of a complex of 100 buildings on 1,620 acres located in the Bay Area of southeast Houston, Texas. JSC is home to the U.S. astronaut corps and is responsible for training astronauts from both the United States and its international partners. JSC is one of ten major NASA field centers.

Green Enchiladas
with Spicy Sauce

ENCHILADAS:

1 dozen corn tortillas
½ cup oil
2 cups shredded Monterey Jack
  cheese
¾ cup chopped onion
¼ cup butter or margarine

¼ cup flour
2 cups chicken broth
1 cup sour cream
1 (4-ounce) can jalapeño peppers,
  seeded and chopped

Cook tortillas, one at a time, in hot oil in skillet for 15 seconds on each side. (Do not overcook or tortillas will not roll.) Place 2 tablespoons of the cheese and 1 tablespoon of the onion on each tortilla; roll up. Place seam side down in baking dish. Melt butter or margarine in another saucepan; blend in flour. Add chicken broth; cook, stirring constantly, until mixture thickens and bubbles. Stir in sour cream and peppers; cook until heated through, but do not boil. Pour over tortillas. Bake at 425° for 20 minutes. Sprinkle remaining cheese on top; return to oven for 5 minutes or until cheese melts. Serve with Spicy Sauce. Serves 6.

SPICY SAUCE:

1 medium tomato, finely chopped
½ cup finely chopped onion
2 jalapeño peppers with seeds,
  finely chopped

¼ cup tomato juice
½ teaspoon salt

Combine all ingredients.

Enjoy! (Texas)

Spanish Rice

A Mexican dinner would not be complete without this dish.

1 cup rice
2 tablespoons oil
1 onion, chopped
2 cloves garlic, minced
1 (16-ounce) can stewed
tomatoes, chopped

1 (14-ounce) beef broth
Salt and pepper
½ teaspoon cumin powder

Place rice, oil, onion, and garlic in skillet and brown. Add tomatoes, beef broth, salt and pepper, and cumin. Cover and simmer 20 minutes or until tender and juice is absorbed.

'Cross the Border (Texas II)

BARNEY McKEE

Four Corners Monument is the only point in the United States where four states touch: Utah, Colorado, New Mexico, and Arizona (clockwise in photo).

Crazy Crust Pizza

BATTER:

1 cup flour
1 teaspoon salt
1 teaspoon Italian seasoning or
  leaf oregano

⅛ teaspoon pepper
2 eggs
⅔ cup milk

TOPPING:

1½ pounds ground beef, or 1 cup
  thinly sliced pepperoni
¼ cup chopped onion
1 (4-ounce) can mushrooms
  (optional)

1 cup pizza sauce or Hunt's Herb
  Sauce
1 cup shredded mozzarella
  cheese

In medium skillet, brown ground beef, seasoning to taste with salt and pepper. (No need to brown pepperoni, if used.) Drain well. Set aside. Lightly grease and dust with flour 12- or 14-inch pizza pan or 15x10-inch jellyroll pan. Prepare Batter. Combine flour, salt, Italian seasoning, pepper, eggs, and milk. Mix until smooth. Pour Batter into pan, tilting pan so batter covers bottom. Arrange Topping of meat, onion, and mushrooms over batter. Bake on low rack in oven at 425° for 25–30 minutes until pizza is deep golden brown. Remove from oven. Drizzle with pizza sauce and sprinkle with cheese. Return to oven for 10–15 minutes. Serves 3 or 4.

The Blue Denim Gourmet (Texas)

GWEN McKEE

The Albuquerque International Balloon Fiesta is a yearly balloon fiesta that takes place in Albuquerque, New Mexico, during early October. It is a nine-day event, and has around 750 balloons, the largest hot air balloon festival in the world. In addition, it is widely considered the most photographed event in the world. Tourists can hire a balloon ride most anytime of the year, as Gwen and friends did here, landing smoothly in a cul-de-sac!

Quiche

3 cups shredded potatoes	Salt and pepper to taste
3 tablespoons oil	

Mix potatoes with oil, salt and pepper and spread in bottom and sides of 9x13-inch greased pan; bake at 375° for 10–15 minutes until it starts to brown. Set aside.

MIX:

½ pound crisp bacon or diced ham, or both	2 (4-ounce) cans green chiles, diced
1½ cups grated Swiss or Cheddar cheese	½ teaspoon salt
	½ teaspoon cayenne pepper
1 cup cottage cheese	¼ cup butter, melted
1 cup Monterey or Gruyère cheese	6 large eggs, well beaten

After potatoes are brown, mix all other ingredients together. Pour over potatoes and bake until knife or toothpick comes out clean. Bake at 375° for 45–55 minutes. This can be baked ahead of time and just warmed in the microwave for 1–2 minutes. Keeps well in fridge for a week.

Lion's Club of Globe Cookbook (Arizona)

Beef Tortilla Pizza

1 pound ground beef	4 teaspoons olive oil
1 medium onion, chopped	1 medium tomato, chopped
1 teaspoon oregano	Mexican toppings: cilantro, sliced olives, 1 cup Jack cheese, etc.
1 teaspoon ground cumin	
1 teaspoon salt	
4 large flour tortillas	

Sauté beef with chopped onion. Pour off drippings. Sprinkle with oregano, cumin, and salt. Place tortillas on two large baking sheets. Lightly brush tortillas with olive oil. Bake in preheated 400° oven for 3 minutes. Remove from oven and top tortillas with beef mixture, then divide tomato and desired Mexican toppings over beef-covered tortillas. Bake at 400° for 12–14 minutes more. (If doing all 4 tortillas at once, rearrange baking sheets halfway through baking time.)

Bon Appétit de Las Sandias (New Mexico)

Yucatán Quiche

CRUST:

¾–1 cup safflower oil   7–8 corn tortillas

In a medium-size skillet, heat the safflower oil. Dip each tortilla briefly to soften and seal, then press between paper towels.

Spray a 9-inch pie pan with a nonstick vegetable coating and then line with the prepared tortillas, overlapping them, extending about ½ inch over the pan edge.

FILLING:

2 eggs

2 cups half-and-half or cream

½ teaspoon salt

2 cups (about 8 ounces) shredded Monterey Jack cheese

1 cup refried beans

½ pound sausage, cooked and drained

2 tablespoons mild green chiles, diced

In a small bowl, combine the eggs, half-and-half or cream, and salt. Set aside.

Sprinkle half the cheese over the tortillas, followed by the beans, sausage, chiles, and then the egg mixture. Evenly distribute the remaining cheese over the top. Bake in a preheated 350° oven for 30 minutes or until firm. Yields 6 servings.

GARNISH:

1 avocado, sliced   Snipped cilantro leaves

1 tomato, sliced

Garnish the baked quiche with avocado and tomato slices. Place cilantro leaves over the top. Serve warm.

Creative Mexican Cooking (Texas)

Larry McMurtry's novel *Lonesome Dove* was reportedly based on the Charles Goodnight/Oliver Loving trail rides in and around Weatherford, Texas. Goodnight's 600-mile return by wagon to Parker County with Loving's body helped make the McMurtry novel a best seller and a favorite television drama. Loving is buried in the old Greenwood Cemetery in Weatherford.

Pancho Villa's Favorite Quiche

¼ cup chopped onion
1 tablespoon oil
1 pie shell (can be pre-made kind)
3 eggs
1 cup evaporated milk
½ teaspoon (or more if you like it) ground cumin

1½ cups grated Jack cheese (although Mormon cheese from Chihuahua works best)
1 cup grated mild Cheddar cheese
1 (4-ounce) can chopped green chiles

Preheat oven to 325°. Sauté onion in oil. Line quiche or pie pan with pie crust. Brush crust with beaten egg white, then lightly beat remaining eggs with onion and other ingredients. Pour into pie crust. Form a collar around the edge of the pie crust by crimping aluminum foil (this keeps edges from burning). Bake at 325° for 40 minutes, or until knife inserted in center comes out clean. Makes 4 generous servings or 8 cocktail-size servings.

Padre Kino's Favorite Meatloaf (Arizona)

Chile Pie

Not really a "pie," this is more like a quiche without a crust. Delectable as a main dish for lunch, it could also make a light supper. And how about doubling the recipe, making it in a rectangular baking dish, and cutting in small squares to serve at a party?

4–6 whole green chiles
1 cup grated Jack or longhorn cheese
4 eggs

1 cup scalded half-and-half or
1 cup evaporated milk
½ teaspoon garlic salt

Line a buttered 8- or 9-inch pie pan with chiles (fresh, canned, or frozen). Sprinkle with the cheese. Beat eggs and combine with half-and-half and garlic salt. Pour over cheese. Bake at 325° for about 40 minutes or until the custard has set. Cut in wedges and serve. Serves 4.

The Best from New Mexico Kitchens (New Mexico)

Pepper Relish

This is delicious when served over beans and peas.

4 cups chopped green bell pepper
4 cups chopped sweet red pepper
4 cups chopped onions
4 cups chopped celery
¼ cup salt
3 cups sugar
3 cups vinegar

Cover peppers, onions, and celery with boiling water. Drain after 5 minutes and add the rest of the ingredients. Boil rapidly for 10 minutes. Pour into sterilized jars and seal.

The Honey Island Boarding House, Honey Island
Boardin' in the Thicket (Texas II)

Richardson Woman's Club Pickles

We started selling these at bake sales in 1958!

1 gallon whole dill or sour pickles
5 pounds sugar
3 tablespoons mustard seed
8 sticks cinnamon
1 teaspoon allspice
3 tablespoons celery seed
3 tablespoons whole cloves
8 cloves garlic
4 jalapeño pods (optional)

Drain and discard juice from pickles. Cut into ¾-inch thick slices and place in a 2-gallon crock. (Don't use aluminum!) Pour sugar and spices over pickle slices. After 24 hours stir with wooden or stainless steel spoon. Then stir 2 or 3 times daily. They are ready to eat after the third day. May be left in crock (covered) or put into four 1-quart jars and sealed.

Note: There will be lots of juice left when pickles are gone. Don't throw it away! It's wonderful for basting a baked ham. Also gives a delightful flavor to tuna or chicken salad. (Put some pickles in the salad, too!)

The Texas Experience (Texas II)

MEATS

Bull Riding is one of the main events of the North Texas State Fair, which also features a parade, carnival, live music, games, barbecue cook-off, and more. Held annually for more than eighty years, this nine-day event is one of the longest running events of its type in the Lone Star State.

Tacos, Shed Style

To many a visitor to New Mexico, The Shed in Santa Fe epitomizes all the mouthwatering attributes of New Mexico cooking at its finest. And there are those who say if you haven't had lunch at The Shed, you haven't been to Santa Fe.

1 pound lean ground beef	1 pound longhorn cheese,
1 cup homemade chile sauce or	grated
canned enchilada sauce	Chopped lettuce
12 blue corn tortillas	Chopped onions
Cooking oil	Chopped tomatoes

Brown the ground beef in a heavy skillet and drain off all grease. Mix in the chile sauce. Fry tortilla quickly in hot oil until they are limp. Drain. Allowing 2 to a plate (use oven-safe plates), place 2 tablespoons of the meat mixture on each tortilla. Add a spoonful of the cheese, lettuce, onions, and tomatoes to each. Fold tortilla over and sprinkle with more grated cheese. Place in 425° oven until the cheese melts. Serves 6.

The Best from New Mexico Kitchens (New Mexico)

Real Mexican Tacos

2 pounds round steak	¼ teaspoon salt
1½ onions, chopped	2 tablespoons shortening
3 garlic cloves, chopped	1 (8-ounce) can tomato sauce
1 tablespoon green chiles	18 corn tortillas
1 bell pepper, sliced	Tomato chunks, shredded lettuce,
⅛ teaspoon cumin	grated cheese

Boil meat until well done, reserving stock. Grind meat in grinder. Mix ground beef, onions, garlic, chiles, pepper, cumin, and salt in skillet with shortening over low heat. Add tomato sauce and stock (1–1½ cups). Cook down for 1 hour. Fry corn tortillas and fill with meat mixture. Garnish with tomato chunks, shredded lettuce and grated cheese.

Cowboy Cookin' (Arizona)

Tacos

1 pound ground beef
1 onion, chopped finely
1 pod garlic, chopped finely
2 small jalapeño peppers, chopped
1 can Ro-Tel tomatoes and chiles (or 1 large fresh tomato peeled and grated for pulp)
2 teaspoons cumin
1 teaspoon Lawry's seasoned pepper
1 package chalupa shells
1 package Lawry's taco seasoning mix (optional)
1 cup grated Cheddar cheese
1 cup shredded lettuce
½ cup chopped, fresh tomatoes

Mix beef, onion, garlic, pepper, tomatoes, cumin, and seasoned pepper; cook until beef is done. Add Lawry's seasoned mix, if it is being used, when meat is almost done. Heat taco shells in oven and fill at the last minute with meat mixture. Add grated cheese and top with lettuce and tomatoes. Serves 4.

A wonderful idea for a party is to put all ingredients out and let each person fix their own taco to their liking! Add sour cream to your list of condiments.

Cuckoo Too (Texas)

Beef Burritos
(Rolled Sandwiches)

1 cup refried beans
8 (10-inch) flour tortillas
2 cups shredded cooked beef
1 cup grated Cheddar cheese
2 cups shredded lettuce
2 tomatoes, chopped

Spread 2 tablespoons beans on each tortilla; cover with ¼ cup beef. Top with cheese, lettuce, and tomatoes. Fold one end of warm tortilla over filling; roll. To heat, omit lettuce and tomatoes, wrap in foil and heat in preheated 350° oven for 15 minutes, or wrap loosely in plastic wrap and cook in microwave for 30 seconds.

Variation: Try beans and cheese. Cooked chicken. Ground beef with taco seasoning. Or eggs with sausage or bacon.

'Cross the Border (Texas II)

Picadillo

Picadillo is wonderful served over plain boiled rice, but in the Southwest, it is more often a stuffing for tacos, tamales, chicken, or best of all—green chiles.

½ pound ground beef
½ pound ground pork
1 cup chopped onion
2 cloves garlic, minced
1 cup chopped canned
    tomatoes
1 tablespoon vinegar
Pinch of sugar
½ teaspoon ground cinnamon
Pinch of ground cloves

¼ teaspoon ground cumin
1 teaspoon salt
1 bay leaf
3 drops Tabasco
½ cup seedless raisins
½ cup chopped green olives
    (optional)
½ cup blanched, slivered
    almonds

Stir meats in a frying pan over high heat. When they begin to release fat, add onion and garlic. As the meat starts to brown, pour off fat and add all other ingredients except raisins, olives, and almonds. Simmer, covered, 30 minutes. Add water or stock if necessary, but not too much, for when done, the picadillo should be moist but not soupy. Finally, add raisins, olives, and almonds and cook 10 more minutes. Serves 4.

The Aficionado's Southwestern Cooking (New Mexico)

Chile Relleno Bake

½ pound hamburger
½ pound chorizo or pork
    sausage
1 cup chopped onion
2 cloves garlic, minced
2 (4-ounce) cans whole green
    chiles, divided

2 cups shredded Cheddar, divided
4 eggs
¼ cup flour
1½ cups milk
½ teaspoon salt
Tabasco

Brown beef and sausage. Add onion and garlic; cook till transparent. Drain. Line greased 9x9-inch pan with one can drained and seeded chiles. Top with 1½ cups cheese. Add meat mixture; top with remaining chiles. Beat eggs and flour till smooth; add milk, salt, and Tabasco. Blend well and pour over casserole. Bake 60 minutes at 350° uncovered. Remove from oven; sprinkle with remaining cheese. Let stand for 5 minutes before serving.

Pleasures from the Good Earth (Arizona)

Green Chile Stroganoff

1 medium onion, chopped
1 (4-ounce) can mushrooms,
  sliced
¼ cup butter or margarine
Garlic to taste
2 pounds lean beef, cubed and
  rolled in flour

2 cups water
2 beef bouillon cubes
1 (4-ounce) can chopped green
  chiles
1 cup sour cream
1 (8-ounce) package noodles

Sauté the onion and mushrooms in butter with the garlic. Brown the cubed beef in this mixture. Drain off the excess fat. Add the water and bouillon cubes. Cover and simmer 2 hours. Add the green chiles and simmer 10 more minutes. Remove from the heat and stir in the sour cream. Cook the noodles according to the package directions. Serve the stroganoff over the noodles. Serves 4.

Green Chile Bible (New Mexico)

Easy Enchilada Casserole

2 pounds ground beef
1 onion, chopped
1 stick margarine
1 (8-ounce) can taco sauce
1 (15-ounce) can enchilada sauce
1 (10¾-ounce) can cream of
  mushroom soup

1 (10¾-ounce) can cream of
  chicken soup
1 package corn tortillas
2 cups grated Cheddar cheese

Brown ground beef. Sauté onion in the margarine. Add sauces and soups to the onion and meat mixture. Layer the meat mixture and tortillas in a large casserole (9x13-inch) and top with grated cheese. Bake at 350° for approximately 30 minutes.

Tortillas can be torn into fourths and added to the meat mixture instead of layering. Bake as above.

For microwave, cover with plastic wrap and cook 15 minutes on roast.

La Piñata (Texas)

Ranch Hand Mexican Pie

Enough prepared mashed
  potatoes for 4 servings
1 egg, slightly beaten
¼ cup sliced green onions
  (with tops)
1 pound ground beef
½ cup chopped onion
1 (8-ounce) can tomato sauce
¼ cup sliced ripe olives

2–3 teaspoons chili powder (to
  taste)
¼ teaspoon salt
¼ teaspoon garlic powder
1 cup shredded Cheddar or
  Monterey Jack cheese
Garnish: sour cream, green
  bell pepper, tomato,
  avocado

Heat oven to 425°. Grease 9-inch pie plate. Place mashed potatoes in a bowl; stir in egg and green onions. Spread and press potato mixture evenly against bottom and side of pie plate. Bake 20–25 minutes or until light brown. Cook ground beef and chopped onion in 10-inch skillet, stirring occasionally, until beef is brown; drain thoroughly. Stir in remaining ingredients except cheese. Cover and cook over low heat 5 minutes, stirring occasionally. Spoon into shell; sprinkle with cheese. Bake 2–3 minutes or until cheese is melted. If desired, garnish with sour cream, green bell pepper, tomato, and avocado. Serves 4.

Down-Home Texas Cooking (Texas II)

KEITH ODOM

Carlsbad Caverns, in southeastern New Mexico, has been described as the 8th Wonder of the World. It contains 83 separate caves, including the nation's deepest limestone cave—1,597 feet—and third longest. The temperature is a constant 56 degrees. Besides the beauty of the glistening formations in the cave chambers, there are spirals of bats that exit the cave nightly from May through October.

Texas Tamale Pie

1 pound hamburger
1 medium onion, chopped
1 (16-ounce) can tomatoes
1 (8-ounce) can tomato sauce
1 (14½-ounce) can red kidney
   beans

1 package frozen succotash
1 small package corn muffin mix
Salt, pepper and chili powder to
   taste

Brown hamburger and onion in a small amount of oil. Add tomatoes and tomato sauce. Simmer. Add kidney beans and succotash. Cook 10 minutes. Season to taste. Mash a few of the kidney beans against side of skillet for thickening. Pour into casserole. Mix corn muffin mix according to directions on package, adding extra milk so it is thinner than usual. Spoon on top of hamburger mixture. Bake at 375° until cornbread is done, 25–30 minutes. Serves 6.

San Antonio Cookbook II (Texas)

Frito Pie

1 pound ground beef
1 package taco seasoning
2 cans chili (hot or mild
   according to your taste)

1 package Fritos (dip size)
1 medium-size onion, chopped
3 cups grated cheese (Mexican
   three cheeses or Cheddar)

Preheat oven to 400°. Prepare meat according to directions on taco mix packet. Heat chili in saucepan. Spray a large casserole dish or stoneware dish with nonstick cooking spray and layer ingredients in the following order: layer of Fritos, lightly mashed to settle, layer of prepared meat. Sprinkle onion over layer and spoon chili over layer. Cover layer with cheese. Repeat layering until all ingredients are added (usually 2 or 3 layers). The Fritos should be soaked, but firm and crisp at serving. Bake covered for 20 minutes. Serve with salad, avocados, and salsa.

Note: Moisture is the key to this dish. Do not cook the meat too dry and a ¼ cup water in the chili will add enough moisture.

Dishes from the Deep (Arizona)

Cheeseburger Pie

1 pound ground beef	¼ cup chopped green bell pepper
½ teaspoon ground oregano	¾ teaspoon salt
½ cup crushed soda crackers	¼ teaspoon pepper
1 (8-ounce) can tomato sauce	Pastry for 1 (9-inch) one-crust
¼ cup chopped onion	pie, unbaked

Brown meat. Drain. Stir in remaining ingredients and pour into pastry shell.

CHEESE TOPPING:

1 egg, beaten	½ teaspoon Worcestershire
¼ cup milk	2 cups grated Cheddar cheese
½ teaspoon salt	
½ teaspoon dry mustard	

Combine egg and milk. Stir in seasonings and cheese. Spread topping evenly over filling. Cover edge of pie crust with 2- to 3-inch strip of aluminum foil to prevent excessive browning. Remove foil the last 15 minutes of baking. Bake in 425° oven for 30 minutes. Serves 6–8.

Amarillo Junior League Cookbook (Texas)

E Z Shepherd's Pie

1 onion, chopped	4 tablespoons margarine
3 pounds ground beef	4 cans peas or corn, drained
2 cups instant potato flakes	Salt and pepper to taste
2 cups milk	12 slices Cheddar cheese

Brown onion in 14-inch Dutch oven. Add beef and brown. Drain excess grease off. Mix potato flakes, milk, and margarine according to package directions. Let stand for 1 minute. Spread peas evenly on top of meat mixture. Spread potatoes on top. Season to taste. Place lid on oven and cook 30 minutes with 12 coals on top and 18 coals on bottom (or in 350° oven). Top with cheese and cook for 10 additional minutes.

Dutch Oven and Campfire Cookbook (Arizona)

Padre Kino's Favorite Meatloaf

2 cups chopped onions
2 tablespoons oil
2 pounds extra lean, double
 ground beef
1 pound lean chorizo
1 cup seasoned bread crumbs
 (Italian)
½ cup beef bouillon

2 eggs, lightly beaten
⅔ cup grated Cheddar cheese
1 teaspoon pepper
1 tablespoon salt
2 teaspoons thyme
2 teaspoons paprika
1 teaspoon allspice
1 teaspoon crushed, dried oregano

Preheat oven to 350°. Sauté onions in oil. Mix with other ingredients well. Shape into a loaf (not too high) and bake in a large pan at 350° for 1½ hours. If your oven runs hot, shape a tin foil tent over it to keep it moist. Serves 10.

Padre Kino's Favorite Meatloaf (Arizona)

KEITH ODOM

Shiprock, the most prominent landmark in northwestern New Mexico (near Four Corners, USA,) is a towering rock formation rising an impressive 1,700 feet from the plain. The peak and surrounding land are of great religious and historical significance to the Navajo people. Climbing Shiprock has been illegal since 1970.

Six Layer Dinner

3 peeled, sliced raw potatoes	3 cups sliced raw carrots
½ cup chopped green bell pepper	1 pound hamburger, cooked and crumbled
½ cup chopped onion	1 (8-ounce) can tomato sauce
¾ cup uncooked rice	1 (8-ounce) can water

Layer in order given in a buttered rectangular baking dish. Cover and bake 1½ hours at 350°. Serves 4–6.

Rehoboth Christian School Cookbook (New Mexico)

Mary Ann's Magnifico Meatballs and Spaghetti Sauce

SPAGHETTI SAUCE:

¾ cup chopped onion	1 clove garlic, minced
3 tablespoons olive oil	2 (6-ounce) cans tomato paste
1 cup water	2 (1-pound) cans tomatoes
1 tablespoon sugar	1½ teaspoons salt
1½ teaspoons crushed oregano	½ teaspoon pepper
1 bay leaf (optional)	

Sauté onion in oil until tender; stir in remaining ingredients. Simmer uncovered 30 minutes. Add Meatballs; cook 30 minutes longer.

MEATBALLS:

4 slices dry bread	1 teaspoon salt
2 eggs	½ cup grated Parmesan or Romano cheese
2 tablespoons chopped parsley	1 teaspoon crushed oregano or basil
1 clove garlic, minced	2 tablespoons olive oil
1 pound ground beef	
Dash of pepper	

Soak bread in water 2 or 3 minutes; squeeze out moisture. Combine bread with remaining ingredients except oil, mixing well. Form small balls (about 20). Brown slowly in hot oil. Add to Spaghetti Sauce; cook 30 minutes. Serve over hot spaghetti.

First Baptist Favorites (Arizona)

Beaver Street Burgers

2 cups boiling water
2/3 cup sun-dried tomatoes
4 pounds beef chuck or ground
  chuck
2 tablespoons finely chopped
  fresh basil leaves
2 tablespoons minced fresh
  garlic

2 teaspoons kosher salt
1 tablespoon freshly ground black
  pepper
8 slices Havarti cheese
8 leaves romaine lettuce
8 slices red onion
8 French rolls

Pour about 2 cups boiling water over the dried tomatoes to reconstitute. Cover and soak until the tomatoes are soft, about 30 minutes. Drain off the remaining water, reserving 2 tablespoons of the tomato "liquor," and chop tomatoes.

If using beef chuck roast, cut meat into 1-inch strips. Grind in a meat grinder using the biggest hole grinder plate (3/8-inch).

Preheat a grill.

In a medium bowl, combine the ground chuck or ground beef, basil, garlic, reconstituted tomatoes, salt, pepper, and sun-dried tomato liquor. Combine well and grind, using the smallest hole on the grinder plate, and form into 8 patties.

Grill over hot coals to desired doneness and serve with sliced Havarti cheese, Basil Pesto Mayonnaise, lettuce, onion slices, and crusty French rolls. Serves 8.

BASIL PESTO MAYONNAISE:
1/4 cup mayonnaise   2 tablespoons basil pesto

Combine mayonnaise and pesto well. Makes 1/4 cup.

Approximate values per serving: Cal 887; Fat 61g; Chol 168mg; Carbo 36g; Sod 1,219mg; Cal from Fat 62%.

By Request (Arizona)

Jalapa Hamburgers

Jalapeños are named after Jalapa, the capital of Veracruz, Mexico. The jalapeños coupled with the tequila give these hamburgers a great lift.

2 pounds ground beef
1 teaspoon Worcestershire
¼ cup tortilla chips, finely crushed

1 teaspoon Dijon mustard
1 jalapeño, chopped
½ teaspoon ground black pepper
¼ cup tequila

Mix all ingredients together and form into equal-sized patties. Grill over charcoal, fry, or broil until done to taste. Serve on Mexican rolls or in pita bread. Serves 4–6.

The Tequila Cook Book (New Mexico)

Party Tenderloin

1 (4-pound) beef tenderloin
½ teaspoon Lawry's seasoning
½ teaspoon garlic salt
½ teaspoon coarse black pepper

½ teaspoon salt
2 slices bacon, cut in 4 pieces each (optional)
3 green onions, diced

Rub meat with all seasonings and press into meat. Place in shallow roasting pan and broil on both sides until brown and crispy. Arrange bacon pieces on top of meat. Press diced green onions on top of tenderloin and bake at 400° for 35 minutes for rare. (Place slices of meat under broiler for a few minutes for those who prefer medium doneness.) Remove meat to serving platter and lightly cover to keep warm. Add small amount of water to pan drippings for au jus and season to taste. Serves 8.

Ready to Serve (Texas)

Gourmet Pot Roast

1 (3- to 4-pound) beef pot roast
1 tablespoon olive oil
3 (4-inch) pieces celery
1 large carrot, cut in chunks
1 large onion, quartered
½ teaspoon rosemary
½ teaspoon thyme

1 slice bacon, cut in 5 or 6 pieces
⅓ cup Burgundy wine
½ cup water
2 bay leaves
1½ teaspoons salt
¼ teaspoon pepper
1 teaspoon flour

In Dutch oven, brown roast in oil. In skillet or saucepan, cook celery, carrot, onion, rosemary, thyme, and bacon pieces, stirring constantly and until onion is golden. Add to meat. Add wine, water, bay leaves, salt, and pepper. Cover and simmer 2½ hours. Thicken liquid with flour blended with a little cold water or wine. Cook 30 minutes longer. Strain liquid, discarding vegetables and bay leaves. Serve gravy with sliced roast. Serves 6.

Ready to Serve (Texas)

New Mexico Pot Roast

1 (3- to 3½-pound) boneless
  chuck roast
½ cup all-purpose flour
1 teaspoon paprika
½ teaspoon ground black
  pepper
1 teaspoon garlic salt
2 teaspoons red chili powder,
  divided

2 tablespoons butter
1 cup water
1 cup dry red wine
4 ounces chopped green chiles
  (fresh or canned)
1 clove garlic, peeled, cut in half
2 bay leaves, broken in half

Rinse meat and pat dry with paper towel. Mix flour, paprika, pepper, garlic salt, and 1 teaspoon red chili powder in a plastic or paper bag. Shake meat in the bag to coat it. Melt butter in a Dutch oven or ovenproof dish. Sear roast on all sides over high heat. Remove from heat; add water, wine, green chiles, garlic, bay leaves, and remaining 1 teaspoon red chili powder. Cover and bake in 350° oven for 2½–3 hours, or until meat tests very tender. Remove bay leaves before serving. Serves 4–6.

New Mexico Cook Book (New Mexico)

Siesta Roast n' Beans

Sleep while it cooks.

1 (3- to 4-pound) roast
2 cups pinto beans, uncooked
1 can green chiles, chopped
1 can tomatoes

1 onion, chopped
1 can tomato sauce
Water
Salt and pepper to taste

Place roast in a large pan. Place pinto beans, green chiles, tomatoes, onion, and tomato sauce on top of roast. Cover entire contents with water. Place in 250° oven covered with lid. Cook at least 12 hours. (May cook longer). Season with salt and pepper. Serve with salad, cornbread, and a dessert for a complete meal.

'Cross the Border (Texas II)

Babette's Carnitas

Use two forks to shred this deliciously moist, tender meat.

1 (3- to 4-pound) beef chuck
  roast
1 (7-ounce) can chopped
  green chiles
2 tablespoons chili powder
½ teaspoon oregano

½ teaspoon cumin
1 clove garlic, minced
Salt to taste
Tortillas
Guacamole
Salsa

On a large piece of heavy-duty foil, place roast. In small bowl, combine green chiles, chili powder, oregano, cumin, garlic, and salt. Spread mixture on top surface of the beef roast. Wrap in foil and seal securely. Place in ovenproof dish and bake for 3½–4 hours at 300°. Cook longer if necessary. (The meat should be so tender that it will fall apart.) For each serving, spoon meat into hot tortilla. Serve with guacamole and salsa. Yields 4–6 servings.

More Calf Fries to Caviar (Texas II)

Barbara Harris' Chicken Fried Steak

2½ pounds round steak,
  tenderized and cut into 6
  equal pieces
2 cups buttermilk, in a pie
  plate

2 cups flour, in separate plate
Vegetable shortening, for
  frying

Dip each steak in buttermilk; dredge in flour; repeat process. Cook in deep fryer at 350° until golden brown, about 4–5 minutes. Serve immediately, drowned in wonderful creamy gravy! Serves 6.

Great Flavors of Texas (Texas II)

Tyrone Steak

Although the area around Silver City and Tyrone was known for its mining, ranching was also important to the region. On the ranch, steak was often just cooked in a little lard in a cast-iron skillet. Here is a different, easy and very tasty way to prepare a cut of meat that might not be tender enough just grilled or broiled.

4 tablespoons all-purpose
  flour
2 teaspoons ground red chile,
  divided
1 teaspoon ground black
  pepper
1 boneless round steak (2 to
  2½ pounds and about 1 inch
  thick)

3 tablespoons cooking oil
1 large onion, peeled and
  chopped
1 clove garlic, finely chopped
1 cup crushed tomatoes
1 tablespoon vinegar
Water to cover

Mix flour with one teaspoon of the ground chile and the black pepper. Dredge steak in the flour mixture. Heat the oil in a heavy skillet or Dutch oven (cast-iron works best) and sauté the chopped onion and garlic until onions are soft. Add steak to the pan and sear on both sides. Add tomatoes, vinegar, the remaining ground chile and enough water to cover the meat. Cover the pan, reduce heat and cook over low heat for 1½ hours or until the meat is tender. Serves 4–6.

Billy the Kid Cook Book (New Mexico)

Carne con Papas
(Potato-Beef Hash)

3–4 medium potatoes, cubed
3 tablespoons cooking oil
1 tablespoon salt
½ pounds chuck steak,
  cubed

1 teaspoon mixed spices
  (peppercorns and cumin)
2 cloves garlic
1 can whole tomatoes
3 cups water

Brown potatoes in oil and add salt. Add beef cubes to browned potatoes. Stir, cover, and simmer for 20 minutes. Grind spices and garlic and add a little water to mortar. Add spices, tomatoes, and water to meat and potatoes. Simmer 20 minutes.

South Texas Mexican Cook Book (Texas II)

Bírria
(Shredded Beef)

This Mexican beef is often served at weddings. In preparation, my dad would dig a hole in the back yard, line it with rocks, and light a fire. The meat with all its seasonings would be placed in a cast-iron Dutch oven and the lid put on firmly. When the coals were red hot and glowing, Dad would place the pan on the coals and cover the entire hole with a piece of tin. Then he would cover the tin lid with mud to seal it, and would leave the meat to cook overnight. Some of the old-timers would wrap the beef in banana leaves and wet burlap instead of using a Dutch oven.

4–5 pounds chuck roast or flank
  steak
2 bay leaves
2 large cloves garlic
1 can beer

2 jalapeños, seeds and veins
  removed
1 teaspoon oregano
1 large onion, sliced

Put all ingredients into a Dutch oven or other heavy pan with a lid, and cook in oven at 300° for 4–6 hours. Beef is ready when it is so tender it falls apart when pulled with a fork. Put the meat in a bowl and shred it while it's still warm. Remove the bay leaves from the beef juice, and store in the refrigerator for a few hours until the fat congeals on the surface. Remove the congealed fat, then warm the remaining juice and serve as a light sauce to accompany your bírria.

This dish is usually served with Spanish rice, charro beans, finely shredded cabbage or lettuce, and tortillas of choice. Serves 8–12.

Corazón Contento (Arizona)

Southwestern Stuffed Flank Steak

1 (2-pound) flank steak, well trimmed

Cut steak on 3 sides to make a pocket, and fold open to lie flat. Pound until flat and tenderized.

MARINADE:

1 cup dry red wine	**1 tablespoon red chili powder**
2 tablespoons olive oil	**¼ cup minced onion**
2 cloves garlic, minced	**½ teaspoon red pepper**
1 teaspoon cumin	** flakes**

Combine Marinade ingredients, then place steak in a glass dish or a Ziploc bag with Marinade. Leave in refrigerator for a minimum of 2 hours.

STUFFING:

2 tablespoons olive oil	**3 cloves garlic, minced**
½ cup chopped red bell pepper	**1½ cup cornbread stuffing mix**
½ cup chopped green bell	**½ teaspoon cayenne pepper**
** pepper**	**⅓ cup water**
⅓ chopped onion	

Heat oil in skillet over medium heat. Add peppers, onion, and garlic. Sauté, stirring constantly for 5 minutes, or until tender-crisp. Add stuffing mix, cayenne pepper, and water. Blend.

Remove steak from Marinade and pat dry. Discard Marinade. Cover steak with Stuffing mixture and roll up, jellyroll style. Secure the flap with toothpicks or skewers, or tie with kitchen twine. Bake in a preheated 400° oven for 50 minutes. Transfer to a carving board, tent with foil, and let stand 10 minutes. Carve into 1- or 1½-inch slices. Serves 6.

Bon Appétit de Las Sandias (New Mexico)

Pepper Steak

¼ cup oil
1 clove garlic, crushed
1 teaspoon salt
1 teaspoon ginger
½ teaspoon pepper
1½ pounds sirloin, cut in thin
   strips
2 large green peppers, sliced
4 green onions, cut into 1-inch
   pieces

2 large onions, sliced
¼ cup cold water
¼ cup soy sauce
1 tablespoon cornstarch
½ teaspoon sugar
½ cup beef bouillon
1 (6-ounce) can water chestnuts,
   sliced
Cooked rice

In hot oil, sauté garlic, salt, ginger and pepper until garlic is golden. Add meat and brown 2 minutes. Remove meat. Add green pepper and onions. Cook 3 minutes. Mix water with cornstarch and add to mixture. Return meat to pan and add all remaining ingredients. Simmer until thick. Serve over hot rice. Serves 6.

Amarillo Junior League Cookbook (Texas)

Bronc Rider Beef Strips

2 pounds beef sirloin (cut in
   strips)
¼ cup plus 1 tablespoon soy
   sauce, divided
1½ teaspoons sugar
½ medium onion, chopped

1 teaspoon garlic powder
2 tablespoons sliced ginger
1 teaspoon chili powder
2 tablespoons cooking oil
1½ tablespoons toasted sesame
   seeds

Marinate sirloin by combining ¼ cup soy sauce, sugar, onion, garlic powder, ginger, chili powder, and beef sirloin. Let set in refrigerator, covered, 1 hour. Drain meat and brown in oil in skillet. Remove from pan and coat with remaining soy sauce and sesame seeds. Serves 6.

Cowboy Cookin' (Arizona)

Barbecued Brisket

1 (8- to 10-pound) beef brisket
1 cup dry white wine
1 cup water

2 tablespoons dried minced
onions

Put brisket in a baking pan with wine, water, and onions. Cover with tin foil and bake in 250° oven overnight (10–12 hours), or until meat is tender. Let meat stand while you make the Sauce. (The meat is easier to slice when slightly cooled.)

SAUCE:

1 (14-ounce) bottle ketchup
¾ cup light brown sugar
½ cup red wine vinegar
1½ cups water
½ cup lemon juice
¼ cup prepared mustard
2 tablespoons Worcestershire
1 tablespoon light soy sauce

2 cloves garlic, run through a
garlic press
1 teaspoon ground black pepper
½ cup chopped green chile
1 medium-size yellow onion,
minced
1 tablespoon chopped cilantro
Tabasco to taste

Mix all ingredients together in a saucepan and simmer over medium heat for 30 minutes. Slice brisket, pour sauce over slices, and heat in 325° oven for 30 minutes. Serves 12–15.

New Mexico Cook Book (New Mexico)

Brisket Rub

This recipe comes from Fritz's Capitol City Catering of Austin. When these people cook, they really cook. The following recipe makes enough rub for 21 briskets. Don't despair, though; the leftover rub stores well.

1 cup sugar
1 cup salt
½ cup chili powder

¼ cup garlic powder
½ cup black pepper

Combine all ingredients and store in a tightly covered container. Rub 2½ tablespoons of mixture onto brisket prior to cooking. Makes about 3½ cups.

Texas Barbecue (Texas II)

Deluxe Cherry Brisket

Make two days ahead of time.

1 (5-pound) brisket
Soy sauce to taste
Worcestershire to taste
1 package Lipton Onion Soup Mix

Rosemary
Caraway seeds
Celery seeds
1 (21-ounce) can cherry pie filling

Season brisket with soy sauce and Worcestershire. Sprinkle soup mix on brisket; add rosemary, caraway seeds, and celery seeds. Marinate 2 days.

Wrap brisket and seasonings in 2 layers of aluminum foil and bake 4 hours at 325°. Let cool before unwrapping. Pour gravy into one container and place meat in another; refrigerate.

Scrape off all seasonings and slice cold meat. Put gravy in bottom of pan and put slices on top of gravy. Pour cherry pie filling over meat and bake in 350° oven for 30–45 minutes. Yields 6–8 servings.

Rare Collection (Texas)

Posole

1 (20-ounce) package frozen
  posole, or 1 (3-quart) can
  hominy
4–5 pounds pork shoulder roast
6 chicken bouillon cubes
2 medium onions, coarsely
  chopped

2 teaspoons sweet basil
1 teaspoon cilantro
3 cloves fresh garlic, crushed
4 tablespoons mild red chili
  powder (more or less, according
  to taste)
Salt to taste

Place posole (hominy) in large heavy stockpot and add 2 quarts water. Cover with lid. Simmer SLOWLY for about 2 hours, adding water as needed. (If using canned hominy, you just need to heat it.) Cut large pieces of pork off the bone and add both to pot. Add chicken bouillon, onions, sweet basil, cilantro, and garlic. Continue to simmer SLOWLY for 3–4 hours, until pork is tender and falling off bone and posole is tender. Remove pork bone and pork meat from pot. Pick meat off bone and shred all the pork and place back in the stockpot. Add the red chili powder and salt to taste. Make a paste of cornstarch and water to thicken slightly. Serve with warm flour tortillas. Serves 8–10 hearty appetites.

Portal's Best Little Cookbook (Arizona)

Posole

1 pork loin roast, about
  3 pounds
5 cups water
3 cups chicken broth
2 cups chopped onions
2 teaspoons salt
1 whole chicken, about
  2½ pounds
1½ tablespoons bacon grease

2 garlic cloves, crushed
1½ tablespoons chili powder
½ teaspoon paprika
2 (16-ounce) cans white hominy,
  drained
Chopped white onions, sliced
  radishes, sliced avocado, and
  lime wedges (garnish)

In a large Dutch oven, place pork roast and water. Bring to a boil. Add onions and salt. Reduce heat, cover, and simmer gently for 30 minutes. Add chicken and bring to a boil; reduce heat, cover, and simmer for 45 minutes. Remove pork and chicken from broth and allow to cool. Cover and refrigerate broth. Cut pork and chicken meat into small pieces and discard bones.

In skillet, heat bacon grease; add garlic, chili powder, and paprika; stir just until blended. Add small amount of broth and stir. Add mixture and hominy to broth and bring to a boil. Reduce heat, cover, and simmer gently for 30 minutes; add pork and chicken pieces and simmer until meat is thoroughly heated, about 15 minutes. Serve in individual bowls with garnishes as side dishes. Makes 8 servings.

Sassy Southwest Cooking (New Mexico)

WIKIMEDIA.COM

The ancient village of Oraibi, located on the Third Mesa of the Hopi Indian Reservation in Arizona, is the oldest continuously inhabited community in the country; the community began around 1100 AD. Ácoma Pueblo, New Mexico, also called Sky City because it sits atop a 357-foot mesa, was founded about the same time. Mesas are the flat-topped mountains found in the desert.

Chalupa

3 pounds pork loin roast or
  boneless shoulder
1 pound pinto beans
2 cloves garlic, chopped
2 tablespoons chili powder
1 tablespoon ground cumin
1 teaspoon oregano
1 (7-ounce) can chopped green
  chiles

3 teaspoons salt or to taste
Fritos
Grated cheese
Shredded lettuce
Onions
Diced tomatoes
Diced avocados
Salsa to taste

In a large pot, put pork roast, pinto beans, garlic, chili powder, cumin, oregano, chopped chiles, and salt. Cover with water; cook for 6 hours or until beans are tender. Remove roast and all fat and bone. Shred meat. Put meat back in bean mixture; cook for 1 hour longer without lid to thicken. Serve over Fritos with grated cheese, shredded lettuce, onions, diced tomatoes, diced avocados, and salsa to taste. Leftover chalupa can be used for burritos, dip, or cheese crisp.

Par Excellence (Arizona)

Tequila Marinated Pork Tenderloins

2 (1-pound) pork tenderloins
4 cloves garlic, thickly sliced

MARINADE:
1 cup tequila
2 teaspoons salt
1½ cups vegetable oil

3 tablespoons chopped fresh
  rosemary

1 tablespoon black pepper
¼ cup fresh lime juice

Make several 1-inch deep slits in the tenderloins. Stuff the slits with garlic and rosemary. Combine the Marinade ingredients and marinate the tenderloins 8–10 hours, or overnight, turning occasionally.

Prepare charcoal grill. (Recommend adding some mesquite chips that have been soaked in water.) When coals are white hot, put the tenderloins on the grill and cook 15–20 minutes, turning to grill evenly. Serves 4–6.

Duck Creek Collection (Texas II)

Pork Loin Roast for Four with Cinnamon Applesauce and Roasted Potatoes

PORK LOIN ROAST FOR FOUR:

2 pounds boneless pork loin roast
1 sprig rosemary
1 sprig thyme

1 clove garlic (reduced to paste)
Salt and pepper to taste

Preheat oven to 500°. Rub roast with herbs and seasonings. Place in a roasting pan with fat side up and cook for 20 minutes. Reduce heat to 350° and cook for 30–40 minutes or until internal temperature is 160°. Continually baste roast with excess pork juices while cooking to maintain moistness.

CINNAMON APPLESAUCE FOR FOUR:

4 Golden Delicious apples
1 cinnamon stick

¼ cup sugar
¼ cup water

Peel and core apples, then cut into medium-sized pieces. Add apples and cinnamon stick to sugar and water and bring to a boil. Reduce to a simmer for 15–20 minutes or until apples are very soft. Remove cinnamon stick and process apples through a food mill. Then return to stove and simmer for another 5 minutes, adding water to desired consistency.

HERB ROASTED POTATOES FOR FOUR:

4 Yukon Gold potatoes
1 tablespoon olive oil
½ tablespoon rosemary leaves
½ tablespoon chopped fresh parsley

½ tablespoon chopped fresh basil
½ tablespoon chopped fresh chives
Salt and pepper to taste

Preheat oven to 350°. Quarter potatoes lengthwise. Combine oil and herbs in mixing bowl and rub potatoes until evenly coated. Bake for 45 minutes or until soft when pierced with fork.

License to Cook Arizona Style (Arizona)

Pork Chop Skillet Dinner

4 pork chops
1 tablespoon shortening
4 tablespoons rice, uncooked
4 slices onion

4 slices green bell pepper
1 (16-ounce) can tomatoes
1 teaspoon salt
½ teaspoon pepper

Brown chops in medium skillet in heated shortening. Pour off excess fat. On each chop, place a tablespoon of rice, a slice of onion and green pepper, and a portion of tomatoes. Add seasonings and cover with liquid from tomatoes. Cover. Cook over low heat until chops are tender, about 1 hour. Serves 4.

Dishes from the Deep (Arizona)

Chimayó Red Chile

1 pound coarsely ground pork
  (optional)
1 large onion, chopped
3 cloves garlic, chopped

2–3 tablespoons flour
2 teaspoons salt
⅔ cup red chili powder
3 cups chicken/vegetable stock

Sauté the pork, onion, and garlic. (If not using meat, use 1 teaspoon canola oil or olive oil.) Add the flour and salt and stir. Add the chili powder and continue to stir for 2–3 minutes. Add the liquid and cook for 20 minutes. Serve alone, over fried potatoes, or as a sauce for burritos and enchiladas.

Inn on the Rio's Favorite Recipes (New Mexico)

STEPHEN LEA/WIKIMEDIA.ORG

Kitt Peak National Observatory in the Quinlan Mountains of the Arizona-Sonoran Desert has the world's greatest concentration of telescopes for stellar, solar, and planetary research.

Sausage con Queso

A dandy lunch dish when served over heated large round tostados.

2 pounds hot pork sausage
2 pounds Velveeta cheese, cubed
1 cup evaporated milk
1 (.7-ounce) package Good
    Seasons garlic salad dressing
    mix

1 (.7-ounce) package Good
    Seasons bleu cheese salad
    dressing mix

Brown sausage well and drain thoroughly. Melt cheese with the milk in the top of a double boiler; stir in salad dressing mixes and meat. To reheat, add additional evaporated milk. Serve with warm tostados. Fills a standard chafing dish.

Crème of the Crop (Texas)

Ham and Scalloped Potatoes with Green Chile

3 cups cooked cubed ham
3 green onions, chopped
½ cup diced green chiles
6 medium-size potatoes,
    peeled, thinly sliced
3 tablespoons butter
3 tablespoons all-purpose flour

2 cups milk
1 teaspoon dried mustard
1 teaspoon salt
1 teaspoon ground black pepper
¼ cup unseasoned bread crumbs
2 teaspoons paprika

Mix together ham, onions, and chiles. Put a layer of sliced potatoes in a well-buttered baking dish and sprinkle some of the ham-and-chile mixture over them. Repeat until sliced potatoes and ham and chile mixture are all used.

Melt butter in a frying pan; whisk in flour and then slowly pour in milk, whisking constantly until mixture is smooth and starts to thicken. Whisk in mustard, salt, and pepper, and then pour over potato mixture. Top with bread crumbs, sprinkle paprika on top, cover, and bake in a 375° oven for one hour. Uncover and bake for 30 more minutes or until potatoes are done. Serves 4.

New Mexico Cook Book (New Mexico)

Lamb Noisettes Janos

DUXELLES:

12 ounces domestic mushrooms
6 ounces shallots
1½ cups dry white wine

Salt and freshly ground pepper to
taste

In food processor fitted with a stainless-steel blade, finely chop mushrooms and shallots. Transfer to a medium saucepan. Add wine, salt and pepper, bring to a boil, and reduce until liquid has almost evaporated. Set aside.

LAMB:

1 boneless lamb loin (1½
  pounds)
Salt and freshly ground pepper
  to taste

Clarified butter for sautéing
1½ cups mousseline sauce*

Preheat oven to 375°. Sprinkle lamb with salt and pepper. Coat a sauté pan with clarified butter and when pan is very hot, sear lamb on all sides. It should be well browned.

Slice lamb into 16 equal slices, or noisettes. Place in one layer on a cookie pan and mound Duxelles onto each slice. Cook in oven for 5 minutes, or until meat is medium-rare.

Preheat broiler. Top each noisette with mousseline sauce and place pan 2 inches under broiler. Broil until mousseline is nicely browned. Divide noisettes among 4 warm dinner plates and serve. Serves 4.

*Mousseline sauce is simply hollandaise that has been lightened and enriched by the addition of whipped cream.

Janos: Recipes and Tales from a Southwest Restaurant (Arizona)

Apricot-Prune Stuffed Lamb

½ cup apricots, dried or fresh
½ cup prunes, raisins, or
  double amount of apricots
¾ cup rice
½ cup chopped celery
½ cup chopped onion
¼ cup chopped pecans or
  almonds

½ teaspoon salt
1½ cups water (use 1 cup if
  apricots are fresh)
1 (5-pound) boneless lamb
  shoulder roast

Cut apricots and prunes into small pieces (watch for and discard pits). Combine all ingredients except lamb. Simmer, covered, 15–20 minutes or until all water is absorbed. Cool slightly, just enough to handle.

Preheat oven to 325° (slow oven). Unroll lamb shoulder. Sprinkle with salt. Spread stuffing over lamb shoulder, roll and tie (with kitchen twine). Place lamb, fat side up, on a rack in a shallow pan. Roast, uncovered, until internal temperature reaches 180° (3–3½ hours). Makes 10–15 servings.

The Joy of Sharing (New Mexico)

Chicken Fried Venison

I have known this way of cooking venison since I was very young and have taught many people to cook the meat this way.

2 pounds meat (may be nice
  slices ¼ inch thick, or the
  small bits you get when
  trimming out hocks) and then
  beat flat with board
13 ounces evaporated milk

Salt
Pepper
Flour
Garlic powder (optional)
Onion powder (optional)

Put the meat in a large bowl with the evaporated milk and enough water to completely cover the meat. Allow to stand for 1 hour. Take the meat out, drain only slightly, and then season to taste and roll in the flour. Drop into hot grease (375°) and fry until brown. Do not overcook or the meat will become dry and tough. Serve with gravy made from the flour and some of the milk left over and good hot bread.

Recipe by Bertie Varner, Y.O. Ranch
Texas Celebrity Cookbook (Texas)

Burgundy Venison Steak Tips

The best of the best. You must try venison in a rich deep-colored sauce.

3 tablespoons oil
2 pounds venison steak, cut in
  small cubes
2–3 tablespoons dry onion
  soup mix
3 beef bouillon cubes

2 cups water
1 cup Burgundy wine
1 cup fresh mushrooms, or
  1 (4-ounce) can, drained
3 cups cooked rice

In large Dutch oven or heavy pot, heat oil; brown venison. Add remaining ingredients except mushrooms and rice. Cover and simmer for about one hour. Add mushrooms the last 5 minutes. Serve over rice. Makes 6 servings.

Sassy Southwest Cooking (New Mexico)

Venison Sausage and Rice Supreme

1 pound deer sausage
½ cup diced onion
1 cup chopped celery
1 (3-ounce) can mushrooms
½ cup toasted almonds

1 can water chestnuts
1½ packages chicken noodle
  soup (dehydrated kind)
2½ cups hot water
3 cups cooked rice

Cook rice as directed on package. Rinse and drain water chestnuts and set aside. Slit skin on deer sausage and crumble into skillet. Brown, stirring frequently.

Remove meat and sauté onion and celery in drippings. Add mushrooms, almonds, water chestnuts, soup, hot water, cooked rice, and cooked sausage. Mix all together and place in a lightly greased 1½-quart casserole. Cover and cook for 45 minutes to 1 hour at 350°.

Wild-n-Tame Fish-n-Game (Texas)

Noreen's Barbeque Sauce

2 (26-ounce) bottles Heinz
  ketchup
1 (10-ounce) bottle
  Worcestershire
¾ cup (packed) McCormick's
  dry mustard
¼ cup vinegar (pour in
  ketchup bottle to rinse)
3 cups water (use to rinse
  both ketchup bottles)
⅓ cup dark brown sugar, packed
⅓ cup sorghum molasses
2 cups water (use to rinse out
  molasses)
2 medium onions (quarter and
  drop in sauce)
6 medium garlic cloves (quarter
  and drop in sauce)
¼ cup oil
1 teaspoon salt

Pour all ingredients into large (approximately 6-quart) kettle with cover. Use water and vinegar to rinse out ketchup bottles and molasses measuring cup. Cook slowly at 225°–250° with cover on for 2 hours, then take off cover. Stir occasionally, adjusting seasonings to taste.

After sauce has thickened as desired, strain into jars, removing onions and garlic. Sauce will keep several weeks or longer if refrigerated, if not used sooner.

Hint: Perfect on pork backbone or ribs: Place 4 pounds lean backbone or ribs in glass casserole; salt both sides. Slice 1 or 2 big onions and place on top. Lay several stalks of celery on top of the onions. Cover with 2 cups Noreen's Barbecue Sauce. Bake 3 hours in 250° oven. Turn and cook 3 more hours. Heat the sauce and serve with meat. Eat all you can and freeze the rest for later.

Through Our Kitchen Door (Texas)

Though Lyndon B. Johnson made barbecue quite famous in Texas with his huge political occasions, "barbacoa" actually came from Spain via the West Indies. "Barbecue" can refer to the food that is prepared, the grill it is cooked on, or the event at which it is served.

Texas Tech Barbecue Sauce

This recipe was recorded on the feed bin at the west end of the dairy barn there on the campus. It was used at all Aggie steak feeds back then. It was copied in 1948.

1 pint vinegar	1 teaspoon cloves
1 quart cooking oil	45 ounces prepared mustard
16 ounces seasoned salt	2 teaspoons allspice
27½ ounces lemon juice	3 bottles Worcestershire
1 teaspoon cinnamon	1 teaspoon red pepper

Mix all ingredients together. Makes a large amount.

Raider Recipes (Texas II)

Jalapeño Jelly

This is definitely a meat jelly, not a breakfast jelly. It is used as a complement for turkey and dressing, fajitas, and most any kind of meat. A dab of jelly added to cheese spread on a cracker makes a quick and tasty hors d'oeuvre.

1 pound green bell peppers	1¼ cups white vinegar
¼ pound fresh jalapeños	⅓ cup lemon juice
5½ cups sugar	1 (6-ounce) bottle of Certo

Grind green peppers and jalapeños in a food grinder. (If a grinder is unavailable, it is possible to chop it up in a blender.) Add sugar and vinegar. Bring to a boil for 5 minutes, stirring constantly. Add ⅓ cup lemon juice; bring to a boil. Add bottle of Certo and bring to a rolling boil for one minute. (A rolling boil is when no amount of stirring can make the boiling subside.) Pour into hot, sterile jelly jars. Wait 2 weeks before using. Makes 7 (½-pint) glasses.

Note: If you would like the jelly to have a green color, add about 3 drops of yellow food coloring and 2 drops of blue. You can just add green coloring instead, but the yellow and blue give a more attractive tint.

My mother never made jalapeño jelly, but I gave her a jar each Christmas and other times I visited her. This makes an excellent little gift for friends and neighbors at Christmastime.

Mrs. Blackwell's Heart of Texas Cookbook (Texas)

POULTRY

Monument Valley, a Navajo Nation tribal park in northern Arizona, as seen through the Tear Drop window. The stark sandstone buttes of Monument Valley rise a thousand feet above the valley floor. The valley is accessible from U.S. Highway 163.

CHRIS COE ARIZONA OFFICE OF TOURISM

Rip's Barbecued Chicken (Texas Style)

1 (5-ounce) bottle Worcestershire
5 ounces water (halfway
  between ½ and ¾ cup)
5 ounces vinegar
2 tablespoons margarine
2–3 slices uncooked bacon,
  chopped
½ teaspoon salt
½ teaspoon black pepper
½ teaspoon celery salt
½ tablespoon prepared
  mustard
Grated rind of ½ lemon
1–2 dashes Tabasco
1–2 cloves garlic, crushed
3–4 chickens, about 1½
  pounds each

Combine first 12 ingredients and simmer for 30 minutes. In the meantime split chickens in half and season with salt and pepper. Place chickens on hot grill, skin down, and brown on both sides, turning occasionally (takes about 15 minutes). Baste first with oily part of sauce that has floated to top. Continue basting and turning over gentle coals until done. Chickens will be tender and a deep rich brown (takes about 45 minutes). Serves 6–8.

M. D. Anderson Volunteers Cooking for Fun (Texas II)

King Ranch or Mexican Chicken

1 dozen tortillas
Chicken broth
1 cup diced onions
1 can green pepper, diced
1 can cream of mushroom
  soup
1 can cream of chicken soup
1 tablespoon chili powder
1 (2- to 3-pound) fryer, cooked
  and diced
¾ pound Cheddar cheese,
  grated
1 can Ro-Tel tomatoes and
  green chiles, or 1 can tomato
  soup mixed with 1 tablespoon
  chili powder

Line large baking dish with layer of tortillas. Sprinkle with chicken broth. Sauté onions and green pepper and add soups and chili powder. Pour layer of soup mixture over tortillas, then layer chicken, then layer cheese. Repeat layers. Pour over the Ro-Tel tomatoes or the tomato soup with chili powder. If a milder taste is desired, you may use ½ can Ro-Tel tomatoes and ½ can plain tomatoes. Bake 1 hour in 350° oven. Serve with vegetable salad and Mexican rice or beans.

Decades of Mason County Cooking (Texas II)

Spanish Chicken Casserole with Saffron Rice

1 (3- to 3½-pound) frying chicken
Salted water
1 cup (or more) chicken stock
¼ teaspoon saffron
1 cup raw long-grain rice
2 onions, 1 chopped and 1 cut in rings

2 green bell peppers, 1 chopped and 1 cut in rings
2 cups chopped fresh tomatoes
Salt and freshly ground pepper
2 tablespoons coarsely chopped cilantro

Preheat oven to 350°. Clean and cut up chicken, removing all fat. Give chicken a cleansing bath in salt water for 15 minutes. Drain on paper towels. Use a large casserole or flat baking pan to bake chicken 45 minutes to an hour, until browned (turn pieces at least once). Remove half of chicken to plate and pour off excess fat. Add saffron to chicken stock and mix thoroughly, then add to pan. Scrape bottom and sides of pan to loosen any brownings, and mix with stock.

Add rice to bottom of pan around chicken, then a layer of chopped onion and chopped bell peppers. Return the rest of chicken pieces to dish. Layer tomatoes over chicken. Then add onion and bell pepper rings on top. Salt and pepper to taste; sprinkle with cilantro.

Cover tightly and bake 1 hour and 15 minutes, until rice has browned sufficiently. Let rest short time before serving. Serves 6.

Gourmet Gringo (Arizona)

With over 823,000 acres, the King Ranch is the largest in the United States and covers all or part of six south Texas counties. The ranch was founded in 1853 by Captain Richard King and Gideon K. Lewis and was designated a National Historic Landmark in 1961. In addition to cattle, King Ranch raises quarter horses, cutting horses, and thoroughbreds.

Chicken and Dumplings

1 large chicken   Water
Salt and pepper to taste

Place the seasoned chicken in a large pot, adding enough water to cover. Bring to a boil. Cover pot, reduce the heat, and simmer the chicken until tender. Remove the chicken from the broth and cool. Reserve the broth. Bone the chicken, cut the meat into pieces, and set aside.

DUMPLINGS:

1½ teaspoons salt   1¼ cups sweet milk, room
3 teaspoons baking powder   temperature
6 tablespoons butter, melted   3¾ cups flour

Mix all ingredients in order listed and divide the dough in half. Roll half the dough very thin on a well-floured surface. Cut the dough into short strips. Set aside. Roll out and cut the remaining dough. Drop the dumpling strips into the boiling chicken broth. Cover, reduce heat, and simmer for approximately 40 minutes. Add chicken pieces the last 15 minutes. Add thickening to the broth if needed.

The Cariker Hotel, Kountze
Boardin' in the Thicket (Texas II)

Texas Quick Chicken and Dumplings

1 large chicken, or 4 large breasts   1 dozen flour tortillas
    and 6 thighs   Salt and pepper to taste

Boil chicken in pot with plenty of water. Debone chicken and return to broth. Bring back to a boil and add flour tortillas while water is boiling. (Tortillas should be cut in wide strips about 2 inches long. You should get 8 dumplings per tortilla.) Reduce heat and cover pot. Cook slowly for about 10 minutes.

"I'm Glad I Ate When I Did, 'Cause I'm Not Hungry Now" (Texas)

The Best Grilled Chicken

Make extra and you'll have a great portable lunch the next day.

3 pounds chicken parts, with
   skin and bones

2 cups Tim's Soy Magic
   Marinade

Soak chicken in Tim's Marinade for one or more hours covered and refrigerated. Bring to room temperature. Cook over medium fire (about 350°), turning 4 times. Check for doneness with instant-read thermometer (cooking time approximately 50 minutes). Serves 4.

TIM'S SOY MAGIC MARINADE:

Juice of 1 lemon
½ cup soy sauce

2 tablespoons olive oil

Blend well. Makes about ¾ cup.

The Happy Camper's Cookbook (New Mexico)

Lemon Chicken

1¼ cups ketchup
1 can frozen lemonade
¾ cup water
¼ cup Worcestershire
¼ cup prepared yellow mustard

¼ cup corn oil
2 tablespoons instant minced
   onion
1 teaspoon Ac'cent (optional)
2 broilers, quartered

In saucepan, stir together ketchup, lemonade, water, Worcestershire, mustard, corn oil, onion, and flavor enhancer. Heat to boiling; simmer 5 minutes. Place chicken on grill, skin side up, about 8 inches from heat. Cook, basting frequently, turning several times for about 1½ hours.

Beyond Loaves and Fishes (New Mexico)

Chicken Artichoke Casserole

1 (3-pound) chicken, cut into
   serving pieces
1½ teaspoons salt
¼ teaspoon pepper
½ teaspoon paprika
6 tablespoons butter, divided
1 (14-ounce) can artichoke
   hearts, drained

¼ pound fresh mushrooms,
   sliced
2 tablespoons flour
⅔ cup chicken broth
3 tablespoons sherry
¼ teaspoon rosemary

Sprinkle chicken with salt, pepper, and paprika. In skillet, brown chicken in 4 tablespoons of the butter and transfer to a 2-quart casserole. Arrange artichoke hearts between chicken pieces. Melt remaining butter in the skillet and in it, sauté mushrooms until barely tender. Sprinkle flour over mushrooms and stir in broth, sherry, and rosemary. Cook, stirring, until slightly thickened, then pour over chicken and artichoke hearts. Cover and bake in 375° oven for 40 minutes or until tender.

Families Cooking Together (New Mexico)

Microwave Chicken Kiev

Pat Swinney's "micro-quick" recipe for the working girl. Very impressive dish for those unexpected guests.

4 whole chicken breasts
1 cup crushed cheese crackers
1½ tablespoons dry taco
   seasoning mix
3 tablespoons butter
3 tablespoons soft Cheddar
   cheese

2 teaspoons instant minced onion
1 teaspoon monosodium
   glutamate
2 tablespoons chopped green
   chiles
1 teaspoon salt

Skin, bone, and half chicken breasts; pound flat. Set aside. Combine crackers and taco seasoning; set aside. Mix together butter, cheese, onion, MSG, green chiles, and salt. Divide butter mixture into 8 balls. Roll chicken breasts around each butter-cheese ball. Tuck in ends and fasten with a toothpick. Dip each chicken piece in melted butter and roll in cheese-cracker/taco seasoning mix. Lay in pan and cover with wax paper. Microwave on HIGH for 10–12 minutes.

More Calf Fries to Caviar (Texas II)

Barbecued Chicken

4 (4-ounce) skinless boneless chicken breast halves

SAUCE:

¼ cup reduced-sodium ketchup	2 teaspoons firmly packed dark brown sugar
3 tablespoons cider vinegar	1 clove garlic, minced
1 tablespoon ready-made white horseradish	⅛ teaspoon dried thyme
	¼ teaspoon black pepper

Preheat broiler, heat a charcoal grill until coals form white ash, or preheat a gas grill to medium.

In a small saucepan, combine ketchup, vinegar, horseradish, brown sugar, garlic, and thyme. Mix well. Bring to a boil over medium-low heat. Cook, stirring frequently, until thickened, about 5 minutes. Remove from heat; stir in pepper. Brush tops of chicken pieces lightly with sauce. Place chicken, sauce side down, on a foil-lined broiler pan or grill rack. Brush other sides lightly with sauce. Broil or grill 3 inches from heat, basting with remaining sauce and turning until no longer pink in center, 5–7 minutes per side. Let chicken stand for 5 minutes before serving.

What's Cookin' at Casa (New Mexico)

Chicken Fajitas #1 Favorite

This recipe is so good that you can even stir-fry it inside and people will love it! Anything is best grilled outside, but this succeeds either way.

1 cup soy sauce	¼ teaspoon ground ginger
1 cup water	1½ tablespoons liquid smoke
2½ tablespoons honey	2 tablespoons lemon juice
1 tablespoon Worcestershire	6–8 chicken breast halves
½ tablespoon granulated garlic	

Mix ingredients and marinate the chicken for 1 hour. This marinade can be refrigerated and used once or twice more within the week. Serves 6.

Note: To serve, provide guests with warm flour tortillas and bowls of salsa, refried beans, guacamole, grilled onions, bell pepper strips, grated cheese, and chili con queso to make their fajitas just as they want them. Don't forget the Pico de Gallo! Also good with skirt steak, good round steak, or flank steak. Allow ⅓ pound of meat per person.

The Mexican Collection (Texas II)

Cilantro Chicken Cutlets

1 teaspoon seasoned salt
1 teaspoon seasoned pepper
2 teaspoons cilantro
1 teaspoon cumin
6 boned chicken breasts,
   halved, pounded into ¼-inch
   thick pieces
2 cups bread crumbs
Oil

¼ cup flour
3 tablespoons margarine
½ teaspoon salt
¼ teaspoon cumin
1 teaspoon cilantro
2 cups milk
⅓ cup dry white wine
1 cup grated Monterey Jack
   cheese

Mix together seasoned salt, seasoned pepper, cilantro, and cumin. Sprinkle seasonings over chicken cutlets and dip in bread crumbs. Pour oil into a large skillet and brown chicken. Remove to a greased 9x13-inch baking dish. In a saucepan, melt margarine; blend in flour and seasoning. Add milk, and stirring constantly, cook until thickened. Remove from heat and stir in wine. Pour sauce over chicken and bake at 350° for 45 minutes. Remove from oven and sprinkle cheese on top of each piece of chicken; return to oven for 5 minutes. Serves 6.

Southwest Sizzler (Texas II)

Quick Chicken Casserole

3 chicken breasts, cut in halves
½ teaspoon salt
¼ teaspoon pepper
½ teaspoon Ac'cent (optional)
¾ cup Bisquick
¼ cup peanut oil

1 cup instant rice
1 (10-ounce) can cream of chicken soup (low salt)
¾ cup half-and-half (mocha flavor) or canned evaporated milk

Wipe the chicken breasts with paper toweling. Sprinkle with a portion of the salt, pepper, and Ac'cent. Place the Bisquick in a paper sack, then coat each piece of chicken with the mix by shaking up and down vigorously. Heat oil in skillet; brown each piece of chicken on both sides.

Cook rice according to directions on package. Stir cream of chicken soup and half-and-half into cooked rice. Put soup and rice mixture into a buttered casserole, then put the pieces of chicken on the top. Place in a 350° oven for 35 minutes. Serve piping hot. Serves 6

Heavenly Delights (Arizona)

Chicken Catchatuelle

1 bunch green onions, diced
2 large celery stalks, diced
1 small green bell pepper, diced
½ teaspoon garlic powder
3 tablespoons margarine
6 ounces mushrooms, chopped, divided
½ teaspoon basil

½ teaspoon thyme
½ pound ham, chopped or ground
6 chicken breasts, boned, skin on
Salt, pepper, and Lawry's seasoning salt to taste
1 large can stewed tomatoes
1 cup cooking sherry

Sauté onions, celery, and green pepper with garlic powder in margarine. Add 5 ounces mushrooms, basil, and thyme. Add chopped ham. Stuff chicken breasts with mixture (2–3 spoonfuls), roll, and place skin-up in baking dish (place so that pieces don't touch together).

Sprinkle with salt, pepper, and seasoning salt and bake at 425° for ½ hour. In a blender, blend stewed tomatoes, remaining 1 ounce mushrooms, and cooking sherry. Pour over chicken and bake at 350° for 1 hour.

First Baptist Favorites (Arizona)

Flautas

Flautas resemble rolled tacos. They are a delicate blend of chicken, onion, chile pequín, and seasonings, deep-fried and topped with sour cream and guacamole.

3 chicken breasts	**Onion salt**
1 package corn tortillas	**Garlic salt**
Oil for frying	**Guacamole**
¼ cup minced onion	**1 pint sour cream**
¼ cup chile pequín	**Tomato wedges (optional)**

Boil chicken until tender, about one hour. Bone chicken; chop; set aside. Fry corn tortillas in one inch of oil for 5 seconds on each side. Drain on paper towel. Place chicken on one side of tortilla, sprinkle with onion, chile pequín, and salts. Roll jellyroll fashion. Secure with toothpick.

Fry 1–2 minutes until crisp. Drain on paper towels; place in a warm oven until serving time. Serve topped with guacamole and sour cream. Guacamole should be mixed into sour cream for use as topping. Garnish with tomato wedges, if you wish. Makes 12.

Variation: Two pounds cooked beef brisket or 2 pounds cooked pork may be substituted for chicken, if desired.

Comida Sabrosa (New Mexico)

Chicken Enchiladas

3 chicken breasts, cooked and diced (save stock)	**1 soup can of water**
2 cans cream of chicken soup	**2 cups grated Cheddar cheese**
½ pint sour cream	**1 cup chopped onion**
2 small cans green chiles	**12 tortillas**

Boil chicken in seasoned water. Make sauce of soup, sour cream, chiles, and water. Add diced chicken. Combine cheese and onion. Dip tortillas in chicken stock. Stuff with sauce and 1 tablespoon of cheese and onion. Roll up in casserole and cover with remaining sauce. Bake 325° for 30 minutes.

Gingerbread . . . and all the trimmings (Texas II)

Sour Cream Chicken Enchiladas

1 chicken, stewed and cut into bite-size pieces	1 teaspoon cumin
1 large bunch green onions and tops, chopped	½ teaspoon salt
	½ teaspoon oregano
	½ teaspoon basil
½ stick margarine, or ¼ cup butter	2 cups grated Monterey Jack cheese
1 garlic clove, minced	2 cups grated Longhorn Cheddar cheese
1 (16-ounce) can tomato sauce	
1 (4-ounce) can chopped green chiles, drained	1 pint sour cream
	12 tortillas
1 teaspoon sugar	

Set aside stewed, boned, and cut-up chicken. Sauté together onions, margarine, and minced garlic. Add tomato sauce, chiles, sugar, cumin, salt, oregano, and basil. Simmer approximately 15 minutes. In separate bowl, mix together Monterey Jack and Cheddar cheese. Mix the cubed chicken with enough sour cream to just moisten. Save remainder of sour cream.

Dip each tortilla into hot tomato sauce to soften tortilla. Place a portion of the chicken mixture on the tortilla and add a portion of the grated cheeses. Roll up and place seam side down in a greased baking dish. This will do 12 tortillas. Mix remaining tomato sauce with the remaining sour cream and smooth over top of casserole, allowing it to seep between tortillas. Sprinkle cheeses over top. Cover and bake at 350° for 30–45 minutes, or until hot. Preparation time: 1 hour with fresh chicken, ½ hour with canned chicken. Serves 6 and is very good warmed over.

Entertaining at Aldredge House (Texas)

Texas has far more farms than any other state—247,000—on an awesome 142 million acres of private farms, ranches, and forests land. Agriculture was the leading industry for more than 100 years, but since the forties, the oil and gas industry has generated more income. Texas still leads the nation in cotton production.

Green Chile Cream Chicken Enchiladas

CREAM CHEESE FILLING:

1–2 large onions, sliced thin or chopped
2 tablespoons butter
2 cups diced cooked chicken
½ cup roasted sweet pepper or red bell pepper or pimentos
2 (3-ounce) packages cream cheese, diced
12 corn tortillas (blue preferred)

Sauté onion in large skillet in butter until limp and beginning to brown. Remove from heat and add chicken, red pepper, and cream cheese; mix well. Fry tortillas in small amount of oil in frying pan or microwave. Spoon ⅓ cup filling in center of tortilla and roll up. Place seam side down in a shortening-sprayed 9x13-inch baking dish. Fill all tortillas in this way.

GREEN CHILE SAUCE:

2 cloves garlic, minced
½ cup minced onion
¼ cup oil
1 tablespoon flour
1 cup chicken broth or water
1 cup diced green chiles
Salt and pepper to taste
½ cup chopped tomato (optional)
2 cups shredded Jack cheese

Sauté garlic and onion in oil. Blend in flour and add broth and green chiles. Season to taste. Add chopped tomato, if desired. Bring to a boil and simmer 15–20 minutes. Pour Green Chile Sauce over filled tortillas. Sprinkle with cheese. Bake covered for 10 minutes at 375°. Uncover and bake another 10 minutes.

Bon Appétit de Las Sandias (New Mexico)

Fiesta Tortilla Stack

1 (9-ounce) can bean dip
½ cup plus 2 tablespoons sour cream, divided
1 tablespoon plus ½ teaspoon Mexican seasoning mix, divided
2 cups chopped, cooked chicken
1 medium red bell pepper, chopped
½ cup thinly sliced green onions with tops
¾ cup sliced olives, divided
¼ cup snipped cilantro, divided
5 (10-inch) flour tortillas
8 ounces mild Cheddar cheese, shredded
2 medium tomatoes, seeded and chopped
Salsa (optional)

Heat oven to 375°. In a 1-quart glass bowl, combine dip, 2 tablespoons sour cream, and 1 tablespoon seasoning mix. Mix well. Place chicken and bell pepper in bowl. Add green onions, ½ cup olive slices, and 2 tablespoons cilantro. Mix gently. Place one tortilla in a 13-inch round baking dish. Top tortilla with two scoops of bean mixture, spread chopped chicken evenly over mixture and top with grated cheese. Repeat layers three more times. Top with remaining tortilla and spray with vegetable oil. Bake 25–30 minutes or until top of tortilla is golden brown. Place remaining mixture on top of warm tortilla. Add remaining olives, tomatoes, and remaining cilantro for garnish.

Kids in the Kitchen (Arizona)

WIKIPEDIA.ORG

Phoenix, Arizona, is named for the mythical Egyptian bird that rose from the ashes of its open funeral pyre, reborn to a new life. Modern Phoenix was built over the ruins of an advanced prehistoric civilization that we call the Hohokam. The Hohokam flourished here in the inhospitable desert for centuries, then mysteriously vanished.

Chinese Chicken

Quick, crunchy, and wonderful

SAUCE:

¼ cup honey	2 tablespoons sesame seed,
½ cup soy sauce	toasted
¼ cup red wine vinegar	⅛ teaspoon red pepper
1 clove garlic, minced	

Combine all ingredients.

4 cups cooked, shredded chicken	2 tablespoons oil
1 (3¾-ounce) package bean	2–3 bunches scallions
threads, or 1½ cups bean	½–1 head iceberg lettuce,
sprouts	shredded

Marinate chicken in Sauce 30 minutes. Using wok or large saucepan, sauté bean threads in oil over high heat 1 minute; drain. Mix chicken, marinade, scallions, and lettuce with bean threads. Toss briefly over low heat to blend thoroughly. Serve immediately so that vegetables remain crisp. Serves 4.

The Dallas Symphony Cookbook (Texas)

Weekender Party Pleaser

2 cups diced cooked chicken	2 cloves garlic, chopped
½ cup shredded carrots	¼ teaspoon salt
½ cup chopped fresh broccoli	Pepper to taste
½ cup chopped sweet red bell	2 (8-ounce) tubes refrigerated
pepper	crescent rolls
1 cup shredded sharp cheese	1 egg white, beaten
½ cup mayonnaise	2 tablespoons slivered almonds

In a bowl, mix chicken, carrots, broccoli, red pepper, cheese, mayonnaise, garlic, salt, and pepper; mix well. Unroll crescent roll dough and place on cookie sheet side by side, pressing out perforations and making a 15x12-inch rectangle (dough will hang over pan). Spread filling down center of dough. On each side, cut wide strips. Start at one end and alternate strips, twisting the ends across the filling. Seal ends. Brush with egg white and top with almonds. Bake at 375° for 30–35 minutes. Makes 12 servings.

Kingman Welcome Wagon Club Cookbook (Arizona)

Ruidoso Winner

1 (8-ounce) package green
  spinach noodles
¼ cup butter
¼ cup flour
1 cup milk
1 cup chicken stock
1 pint sour cream
⅓–½ cup lemon juice
1 (6-ounce) can mushroom
  pieces and juice
2 teaspoons seasoned salt

1 teaspoon MSG (optional)
½ teaspoon nutmeg
2 teaspoons pepper
½ teaspoon cayenne pepper
  (optional)
1 teaspoon paprika
1 tablespoon parsley flakes
4 cups cooked cubed chicken
½ cup toasted bread crumbs
Parmesan cheese

Cook noodles; drain. Melt butter in a large saucepan. Stir in flour.
Add milk and chicken stock. Cook over low heat, stirring constantly until sauce thickens. To the cream sauce, add sour cream, lemon
juice, mushrooms, seasoned salt, MSG, nutmeg, paprika, pepper,
and parsley flakes. Mix well.

Butter a 3-quart casserole. Place drained noodles in casserole.
Add layer of chicken. Pour some sauce over chicken. Sprinkle with
bread crumbs and Parmesan cheese. Repeat layers, ending with
cheese on top. Heat in 350° oven until bubbly, about 25 minutes.
Can be made the night before and refrigerated. Bake at 325° for
one hour. Serves 8–10.

Savoring the Southwest (New Mexico)

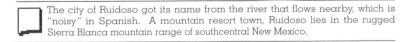
The city of Ruidoso got its name from the river that flows nearby, which is
"noisy" in Spanish. A mountain resort town, Ruidoso lies in the rugged
Sierra Blanca mountain range of southcentral New Mexico.

Cheese Tortilla Torta

2 cups cooked turkey or
  chicken
1 (11-ounce) can Mexican-style
  corn, drained
2 cups or 2 (4-ounce) cans
  diced or chopped green
  chiles, undrained
½ cup chopped red onion
  (optional)
1 pound container sour cream
  mixed with 1 tablespoon flour

2 (10-ounce) cans enchilada
  sauce or same amount of
  homemade chile sauce
12 corn tortillas, halved
10 ounces shredded sharp
  Cheddar cheese, or your
  choice
¼ cup sliced, pitted black
  olives, if desired

Preheat oven to 350°. Lightly grease a 9x13-inch pan. In medium bowl, combine turkey or chicken, corn, chiles, red onion, and half of the sour cream mixture. Pour enchilada sauce into another medium bowl. Dip 8 tortilla halves, one at a time, in sauce; arrange on bottom of prepared dish. Add half the meat mixture, spreading evenly with spatula to cover. Sprinkle one cup of the cheese over meat layer. Add another layer of 8 dipped tortilla halves, the remaining meat mixture (spread evenly), and one cup of the cheese. Top with remaining 8 tortilla halves, dipped in sauce. Pour any remaining sauce over dish. Spoon remaining sour cream mixture into plastic food storage bag and snip off one corner. With this, make a lattice design over top of the dish. Decorate here and there with green chiles and olives. Sprinkle with cheese and bake 30 minutes or until bubbly. Let stand 15 minutes before serving.

The Eagle's Kitchen (New Mexico)

Fried Wild Turkey

Breast of turkey (domestic turkey
**   may be substituted)**
Salt and pepper to taste

2½ cups or more buttermilk
2 cups vegetable oil
Flour

Bone the breast of turkey. Slice the breast in ¼-inch thick slices or thicker, if desired. Salt and pepper to taste. Soak turkey slices in buttermilk for 2–3 minutes. While turkey is soaking, heat vegetable oil in frying pan. Roll turkey slices in flour. Drop in heated oil (327°) and fry until golden brown. (Do not overcook.) Drain on a paper towel. Best served with cream gravy.

Recipe by Mrs. Madeline Russell
Texas Celebrity Cookbook (Texas)

Wild Turkey in a T-Shirt

1 wild turkey, skinned
Salt and pepper to taste
1 onion, chopped
2 ribs celery, chopped

1 old clean T-shirt
1 stick margarine or butter, or
**   bacon drippings**

Imagine our distress when we found our Thanksgiving wild turkey, brought home from the locker plant still wrapped, had been skinned rather than picked. The only thing we had to wrap the bare bird in was a clean old T-shirt.

The bird was salted, peppered and stuffed with the chopped onion and celery. The T-shirt was dampened and dipped in melted butter. We clothed the turkey in the T-shirt and cooked it in a 325° oven for 2½ hours. It was the best wild turkey ever.

The New Texas Wild Game Cook Book (Texas II)

East Texas Turkey Dressing

This recipe (Susan Cooper's) can be traced to my great-grandmother. It is likely that it has been served on every Thanksgiving since 1883 by some descendant. My ancestors came from Shelby County near Timpson, and many still remember the thrill of occasionally having fresh oysters in the tiniest town in east Texas.

1 (12-serving size) cornbread (made according to recipe of choice)
6 slices stale bread ends, crumbled
1 cup chopped onion
1 tablespoon sage

1 teaspoon salt
2 eggs, not beaten
½ teaspoon pepper
2 cups chicken or turkey broth
4 teaspoons bacon drippings, melted
1 cup drained oysters (optional)

Prepare cornbread to serve 12. Set aside. Combine bread, cornbread, onion, sage, salt, pepper, eggs, stock, and bacon drippings. Add oysters, if desired. Stir ingredients lightly and stuff into fowl (or bake separately at 350° for 30 minutes). Makes about 3 quarts.

Through Our Kitchen Door (Texas)

LIBRARY OF CONGRESS

Native born Texan Howard Hughes was an American aviator, engineer, industrialist, film producer and director, philanthropist, and one of the wealthiest people in the world. Hughes did not get his fortune from his movies or aviator skills, but rather from the inheritance from his father's invention of the Hughes Drill Bit, which revolutionized the oil industry.

Stuffed Peppers à la Phoenix

¾ pound ground turkey breast
¼ cup chopped scallions
1 tablespoon chopped cilantro
Freshly ground black pepper to
   taste
1 cup shredded part-skim
   mozzarella cheese
4 Anaheim or Poblano peppers,
   seeded and halved
1 tablespoon chopped parsley

Cook turkey, scallions, cilantro, and pepper over medium heat until the turkey is no longer pink. Stir in half of the cheese. Spoon mix into the pepper halves. Arrange the peppers in a casserole dish lightly coated with vegetable spray. Bake at 350° for 15 minutes. Sprinkle remaining cheese and parsley over the peppers and bake until cheese is melted, about 10 minutes. Serves 4.

Variation: Two medium bell peppers may be substituted for the Anaheim or Poblano peppers.

Cal 163; %Fat 28; Fat 5g; Sat Fat 2.3g; Chol 58mg; Sod 125mg; Carbo 4g; Prot 24g; Fiber 1g. Exchanges: Vegetable 1, Low-fat protein 3.

Arizona Heart Institute Foundation Cookbook (Arizona)

Smothered Quail

6 quail, dressed
6 tablespoons butter
3 tablespoons flour
2 cups chicken broth
½ cup sherry
Salt and pepper to taste
1 (3-ounce) can mushrooms,
   chopped
1 (6-ounce) box Uncle Ben's Long
   Grain Wild Rice

Brown quail in butter. Remove to baking dish. Add flour to butter. Stir well. Slowly add broth, sherry, and seasonings. Blend thoroughly. Add mushrooms. Pour over quail. Cover and bake at 350° for 1 hour. Serve over rice prepared according to package directions. Serves 6.

Hullabaloo in the Kitchen (Texas)

Proud Bird with a Golden Taste

4–6 quail
1 cup flour
3 tablespoons salt and pepper
¼ cup butter or margarine
¼ cup chopped onion

½ cup fresh mushrooms
½ cup white wine
½ cup whipping cream
Cooked rice
1 tablespoon snipped fresh parsley

Dredge cleaned birds in flour mixed with seasoning. Sauté in butter until slightly browned. Remove birds. Sauté onion and mushrooms in butter. Add birds. Add wine. Cook 30 minutes. Add cream and blend well. Serve over white rice. Sprinkle with parsley. Makes 4 servings.

The Wild Wild West (Texas II)

Jalapeño Dove Breasts

Jacque Wynne and Steve Kanaly won both American Regional Cuisine and Gala awards with this recipe.

10 dove breasts
30 jalapeño peppers, seeded

1 can water chestnuts
30 bacon slices

Carefully remove meat from each side of dove breast with a sharp knife and slice each half lengthwise into 2–3 pieces.

Cut jalapeño pepper lengthwise into strips about the same size as the dove breast. Be sure to remove the seeds. Cut canned water chestnuts into small bite-sized chunks, cut bacon slices into halves. Wrap 1 dove breast slice, 1 jalapeño slice, 1 water chestnut in half slice of bacon and skewer with toothpick. Cook in broiler or on barbecue coals until bacon is brown. Serves about 60.

March of Dimes Gourmet Gala Cookbook (Texas)

SEAFOOD

WIKIMEDIA COMMONS

The Glen Canyon Dam is on the Colorado River at Page, Arizona. It provides water storage for the arid southwestern United States, generates electricity for the region's growing population, and provides water recreation opportunities. Damming the river flooded Glen Canyon and created a large reservoir called Lake Powell.

Crabmeat Sharman

Delicious! This dish makes a fabulous main dish or hot dip.

2 (8-ounce) packages cream
  cheese, softened
2 tablespoons mayonnaise
4 tablespoons grated onion
1 tablespoon cream-style
  horseradish

2 tablespoons milk
13 ounces crabmeat (fresh)
Lea & Perrins Worcestershire
Juice of 1 lemon

Mix all ingredients together until smooth. Add a dash of Lea & Perrins Worcestershire and juice of lemon. Bake in 10-ounce buttered pie plate for 30 minutes at 350°. Cover with a sprinkle of paprika. Serve with sesame or rye Old London Melba rounds and toast. This and a good salad are quite a meal! Serves 6 as a main dish or 20 as a dip.

Cuckoo Too (Texas)

Crabmeat à la Lulu

What else can I say!

¼ cup butter (½ stick)
1 cup thinly sliced fresh
  mushrooms
1 cup milk
1 egg yolk
2 tablespoons lemon juice
1½ tablespoons flour
1 tablespoon finely chopped
  green onion

1 teaspoon parsley flakes
¼ teaspoon salt
⅛ teaspoon cayenne pepper
⅛ teaspoon Tabasco
6 ounces cooked crabmeat, if
  frozen, thaw
½ cup grated Swiss cheese

1. Preheat oven at 350°.
2. In a small skillet, melt the butter and cook the mushrooms for 10 minutes. Remove from heat.
3. In a blender, combine the milk, egg yolk, lemon juice, flour, onion, parsley flakes, salt, cayenne, and Tabasco, and blend briefly.
4. Pour blender mixture into a bowl; add mushrooms, butter, crabmeat, and cheese. Mix well.
5. Pour into baking dish and bake at 350° for 30 minutes.
6. Serve over cooked rice or noodles. Serves 3.

Leaving Home (Texas)

Texas Star Crabmeat Casserole

1 pound lump crabmeat
¼ cup lemon juice (juice of 3
  lemons)
½ teaspoon salt
½ cup butter or margarine
2½ tablespoons all-purpose
  flour
1½ cups milk
½ teaspoon garlic salt

½ teaspoon celery salt
1 teaspoon parsley flakes
1 cup grated Cheddar cheese
2 tablespoons white wine
  (optional)
6 cups cooked wild rice or
  Uncle Ben's Wild Rice Mixture
1 (6-ounce) can sliced mushrooms,
  drained

Combine crabmeat, lemon juice, and salt in a medium bowl and refrigerate while preparing sauce.

Melt butter or margarine in a medium saucepan. Add flour; stir and cook for about 1 minute. Add milk slowly, stirring constantly, and cook until sauce thickens. Add seasonings, cheese, and wine, if desired. Stir until cheese is melted and sauce is smooth. Drain crabmeat, add to sauce, and heat until bubbly.

Layer cooked wild rice in bottom of a lightly oiled 2-quart casserole dish. Pour crabmeat and sauce over rice. Top with mushroom slices and bake at 350° for about 30 minutes or until lightly browned. Serve with a crisp green salad and crunchy rolls. Yields 6 servings.

More Tastes & Tales (Texas II)

Perhaps one of the most recognized nicknames of any state, the Lone Star State signifies Texas as an independent republic and as a reminder of the state's struggle for independence from Mexico. The "Lone Star" is on the Texas state flag and on the Texas state seal.

El Tovar Dining Room's
Black Bean and Crabmeat Cakes
with Avocado Salsa

1 pound black beans
4 cups water
1 medium onion, chopped
2 tablespoons minced garlic
2 cups chicken stock
1 bunch fresh cilantro

1 cup lump crabmeat
2 tablespoons Tabasco
1 tablespoon salt
Flour
Cooking oil or butter

Soak beans overnight in water. Drain beans and discard soaking water. Cook beans, onion, and garlic in chicken stock over low heat until tender, about 1½ hours. Drain and cool. Run through a grinder on large die with cilantro. Add crabmeat and seasonings. Form into 16 equal patties. Dust with flour. Sauté a few minutes on each side until heated throughout. Top with Avocado Salsa. Makes 16 cakes or 8 servings.

AVOCADO SALSA:

2 avocados, diced
½ medium red onion, diced
1 medium red pepper, diced
1 medium yellow pepper, diced
½ bunch green onions, chopped

⅓ bunch fresh cilantro, chopped
1 tablespoon fresh lemon juice
¼ cup olive oil
2 tablespoons rice wine vinegar

Mix all ingredients together. Allow to sit for 1 hour before serving.

Arizona's Historic Restaurants and their Recipes (Arizona)

EL TOVAR HOTEL

El Tovar Hotel, located on the rim of the Grand Canyon, opened its doors in 1905. In the past, the hotel has hosted such luminaries as Theodore Roosevelt, Albert Einstein, western author Zane Grey, and many others. Today, El Tovar is a Registered National Historic Landmark and still open to the public.

Crabmeat Quesadillas

1 cup fresh crabmeat
½ cup sour cream
1 teaspoon lemon juice
3 green onions, chopped
1 (4-ounce) can chopped
  green chiles
1 heaping tablespoon finely
  chopped cilantro
1 teaspoon chili powder

¼ teaspoon red pepper
1 jalapeño pepper, chopped
  (optional)
12 tortillas
1 cup grated Cheddar cheese
1 cup grated Monterey Jack
  cheese
1 egg white
1 tablespoon vegetable oil

In a bowl, combine the crabmeat, sour cream, lemon juice, green onions, green chiles, cilantro, chili powder, red pepper, and jalapeño, if desired. Place 2 tablespoons of the mixture on a tortilla (small ones work better, easier to turn), spreading to ¾ inch of the edge. Top with a tablespoon of each of the cheeses. Brush the rim of the tortilla with egg white. Place a second tortilla on top and press to seal. Repeat. Heat vegetable oil in large skillet. Brown the tortillas on both sides to heat and melt the cheese. Cut into wedges. Serve with salsa, sour cream, and/or guacamole.

Bon Appétit de Las Sandias (New Mexico)

Seafood Casserole for a Crowd

3 pounds shrimp, cooked and
  chopped
3 pounds crabmeat (imitation
  or genuine crab)
2 cups finely chopped celery
1 large bell pepper, chopped
1 large onion, chopped

1 tablespoon Worcestershire
2 cups (1 pint) mayonnaise
Dash of hot pepper sauce
2 cups bread crumbs
½ cup (1 stick) margarine or
  butter, melted

Combine shrimp, crab, celery, bell pepper, onion, and Worcestershire; mix well. Spoon mixture into greased extra large (18x14x3-inch) casserole dish.

Mix mayonnaise with dash of hot pepper sauce; mix bread crumbs with melted butter; combine mayonnaise and bread mixture. Spoon over shrimp mixture. Bake at 350° for 30 minutes. Serves 30.

Coastal Cuisine (Texas II)

Shrimp Quesadillas

4 (16- to 20-count) shrimp, peeled
  and deveined
4 tablespoons butter, divided
1 green chile, roasted, peeled
  seeded and diced
1 tablespoon cilantro
1 teaspoon Southwestern Spice

1 (10-inch) flour tortilla
3 ounces Jack and Cheddar
  cheese, shredded and mixed
  together
2 ounces salsa
Parsley

Cook shrimp in 2 tablespoons butter with green chile, cilantro, and Southwestern Spice. When cooked, dice shrimp. Heat remaining 2 tablespoons of butter in large frying pan. Add flour tortilla. Sprinkle cheese and shrimp over half of tortilla. Fold over and turn. Cook until both sides are golden brown. Cut into 4 pieces. Serve with salsa and garnish with parsley.

SOUTHWESTERN SPICE:
¼ cup chili powder
4 teaspoons ground cumin

½ tablespoon ground oregano
1 teaspoon ground basil

Combine in small bowl and stir well.

Sedona Cook Book (Arizona)

Hot Seafood Salad

2 cups cut-up, cooked shrimp
  (1-pound frozen package)
2 cups cubed brick cheese
  (Monterey Jack)
1 cup chopped celery
¼ cup toasted, slivered almonds
¼ cup chopped green bell
  pepper

1 cup sour cream
2 tablespoons minced onion
2 tablespoons fresh lemon juice
1 teaspoon salt
2 tablespoons margarine, melted
½ cup cornflake crumbs or bread
  crumbs

Combine shrimp, cheese, celery, almonds, and green pepper. Set aside. Blend sour cream, onion, lemon juice, and salt. Blend 2 mixtures well. Spoon about 1 cup onto individual baking shells or ramekins. Combine margarine and crumbs. Sprinkle over top. Bake at 300° for 10–15 minutes, until just heated. Garnish with lemon wedges.

The Garden Patch (Arizona)

Camarones Veracruz
(Veracruz-style Shrimp)

1 tablespoon butter or margarine
1 tablespoon vegetable oil
2 medium onions, thinly sliced
  and cut in half-rings
1 large garlic clove, thinly sliced
2 large green bell peppers,
  seeded and deveined, thinly
  sliced into rings

2 serrano chiles, seeded and
  deveined, cut in thin strips
2 large (about 1 pound) fresh
  tomatoes
Salt and freshly ground pepper
1 pound raw medium shrimp,
  peeled and deveined
1 cup green olives

Use an extra large (12-inch) skillet to melt butter or margarine with oil, and sauté onion rings and garlic until soft. Add bell pepper rings and chile strips; cook only until they begin to soften.

Meanwhile, place washed tomatoes in a shallow pan, set on rack 5–6 inches from heat, and broil 5 minutes, then turn over and broil another 2–3 minutes. Remove to cool, then core, peel, and coarsely chop, saving all juices. Add tomatoes and juices to skillet, breaking up further as you stir them into other ingredients. Salt and pepper to taste.

Cover and simmer 15 minutes. Stir shrimp and olives into sauce to completely cover; simmer an additional 5 minutes. Can be served with sauce either over rice or offer rice on the side. Serves 6.

Gourmet Gringo (Arizona)

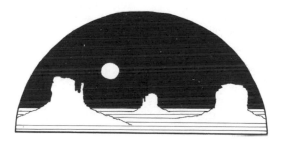

Shrimp 'n Pasta

5 pounds shrimp, unpeeled
¾ cup butter
½ cup vegetable oil
¼ cup olive oil
1 cup chopped green onions
1 cup chopped white onion
1½ tablespoons minced garlic
½ cup chopped parsley
2 teaspoons Konriko Creole
   Seasoning

2 teaspoons salt
1 teaspoon white pepper
¾ teaspoon cayenne
¾ teaspoon thyme
1½ teaspoons black pepper
¾ teaspoon oregano
¾ cup white wine
1 cup seafood stock
1 (12-ounce) package fettuccine,
   cooked and drained

Peel shrimp and butterfly. Place in boiling salted water for 30 seconds; drain. Combine butter and oils in large skillet on medium heat. Add onions, garlic, and parsley; cook, stirring often, until onion is soft. Add seasonings, wine, stock, and shrimp. Cook on low heat for 5 minutes or until shrimp is done. Toss with fettuccine. Serves 8–10.

Best of Friends Two (Texas II)

Shrimp Creole

⅓ cup shortening
¼ cup flour
1 cup hot water
1 (8-ounce) can tomato sauce
1 pound medium shrimp, cleaned
   and deveined
½ cup chopped green onions
   and tops
4 cloves garlic, pressed
½ cup chopped fresh parsley

¼ cup chopped green bell pepper
1½ teaspoons salt
2 whole bay leaves
½ teaspoon crushed thyme
1 lemon slice
Cayenne pepper
2–3 cups cooked rice (prepared
   according to package
   directions)

1. In a large skillet, melt shortening. Blend in flour, stirring constantly until mixture is brown (5–10 minutes). Add water and cook until thick, stirring constantly.
2. Add tomato sauce and mix thoroughly.
3. Add remaining ingredients, using cayenne pepper to personal taste. Serve over rice. Yields 4 servings.

Preparation time: 30 minutes.

Rare Collection (Texas)

My Barbequed Shrimp

Bring on the cold beer

1 pound (18- to 21-count) raw
  shrimp in shells
½ cup oil
¼ cup butter, no substitute,
  please
2 tablespoons fresh lemon juice
2 tablespoons dry white wine
1 tablespoon Worcestershire

1 tablespoon parsley flakes
1 teaspoon cracked black pepper
1 teaspoon pressed fresh garlic
½ teaspoon salt
½ teaspoon Knorr Swiss Aromat
  Seasoning for Meat
½ teaspoon Lawry's lemon pepper
2 shakes Tabasco

1. Rinse and drain shrimp and place in the bottom of a baking dish.
2. In a small bowl, combine and mix together all the remaining ingredients.
3. Pour sauce over shrimp.
4. Bake in preheated 400° oven for about 20 minutes, stirring once or twice. When cooked, the shells will turn a red color.
5. Serve with crusty French bread, for dipping in sauce. Serves 4 people 5 shrimp each.

Leaving Home (Texas)

Ceviche II

1 pound fresh, sweet white fish
  (snapper, redfish, etc.)
Juice of 3 limes, or enough to
  cover fish
1 teaspoon salt
1 tablespoon chopped fresh
  cilantro

3 serrano peppers (packed in
  vinegar), cut up
Juice of 1 orange
2 tablespoons olive oil
1 large onion, finely chopped
2 fresh tomatoes, peeled and
  chopped

Cut fish into thin bite-sized pieces. Combine lime juice, salt, cilantro, and peppers. Pour over fish. Be sure there is enough juice to cover fish. Marinate in refrigerator 4 hours. Add orange juice, oil, onion, and tomatoes. Serve in cups with juice and saltine crackers. Serves 6.

San Antonio Conservation Society Cookbook (Texas)

Easy Tasty Bass

4 tablespoons butter
1 clove garlic, crushed
1 green onion, chopped fine
3 sprigs parsley, chopped

1 teaspoon tarragon
1 large or 2 small bass
Salt and pepper to taste
2 tablespoons lemon juice

In a skillet, melt the butter and add the garlic, onion, parsley, and tarragon. Simmer for 2 minutes. Season fish with salt and pepper and cook gently in the herb-butter mixture until fish flakes. Remove bass to a serving dish. Add lemon juice to the sauce in the skillet, heat 1 minute, then pour over the fish.

Arizona Small Game and Fish Recipes (Arizona)

Fillet of Sole à L'Orange

This wonderfully delicate fish dish makes a great holiday offering either on a buffet or for a special luncheon. You can substitute pollack or any other tender white fish fillets, if you wish.

1½–2 pounds fillet of sole or
   other white fish
1½ cups chicken broth, divided
3 medium-size green onions,
   chopped
1 tablespoon chopped fresh
   parsley

1 teaspoon cornstarch
½ cup fresh orange juice
1 tablespoon orange-flavored
   liqueur
1 teaspoon orange peel
Orange slices
Cilantro sprigs

Arrange the fillets in a microwave-safe cooking dish. Pour ½ cup chicken broth over fish, sprinkle onions and parsley on top, cover with plastic wrap, and cook in the microwave on HIGH for 6–8 minutes or until fish tests done when tested with a fork. While the fish is cooking, dissolve cornstarch in orange juice in a saucepan. Add remaining 1 cup chicken broth. Stir in orange liqueur and orange peel and cook over medium heat until sauce has thickened.

Remove fish from microwave, drain off liquid, and arrange on warm plates or serving platter. Spoon orange sauce over fish, arrange orange slices and cilantro around fish, and serve. Serves 4.

Christmas in Arizona Cook Book (Arizona)

Red Snapper Vera Cruz

1 pound red snapper fillets
1½ cups milk
2 teaspoons crushed oregano
   leaves
¼ teaspoon pepper
1 teaspoon each vegetable oil
   and butter
1 cup thinly sliced onion
2 cloves garlic, finely chopped
4 cups chopped tomatoes

2½ cups green bell pepper, cut in
   1-inch matchsticks
1 cup medium pitted ripe olives
¼ cup plus 2 tablespoons dry red
   wine
¼ cup lemon juice
1 teaspoon ground cumin
¾ teaspoon salt
Hot pepper sauce to taste
Lemon wedges and sour cream

Place fillets in a 9x13x2-inch pan. Pour milk over and sprinkle with oregano and pepper. Cover and refrigerate 1 hour. Turn fillets after ½ hour.

Heat oven to 350°. In large skillet, heat oil and butter over medium-high heat. Sauté onion and garlic until onion is tender. Add remaining ingredients except fillets; simmer about 15 minutes, or until mixture is thickened. Set sauce aside.

Remove fish from milk and discard milk. Divide fish among 4 large squares of aluminum foil. Spoon sauce evenly among packets; fold over and seal. Place in a 15½x10½x1-inch jellyroll pan. Bake for 30 minutes, or until fish is opaque. Serve with lemon wedges and dairy sour cream. Serves 4.

Recipes from Arizona with Love (Arizona)

WIKIMEDIA COMMONS

Lake Mead National Recreation Area exhibits a startling contrast of desert and water, mountains and canyons, primitive backcountry and modern technology. Lake Mead and Lake Mohave (man-made reservoirs on the Colorado River created by the construction of Hoover Dam and Davis Dam, respectively) and their shorelines form the recreation area, located on the Arizona/Nevada border.

Red Snapper Fiesta

1 pound (about 4 fillets) red
  snapper
Salt and pepper to taste
¾ cup chopped onion
¾ cup chopped tomato
¼ cup chopped green bell
  pepper

1 (4-ounce) can mushroom pieces,
  drained
1–2 tablespoons butter or
  margarine
1 cup shredded Cheddar cheese

Check fillets for bones, and remove any you find. Place snapper in a 10x10-inch microwave-safe baking dish that has been coated with nonstick cooking spray. Sprinkle with salt and pepper. Sprinkle onion, tomato, green pepper, and mushrooms on top of fillets. Dot with butter.

Cook, uncovered, in microwave oven at full power for 3 minutes. Turn dish halfway and cook another 3 minutes. Turn dish halfway and cook another 3 minutes or until fish flakes when tested with fork. Sprinkle cheese over fish. Cook another 2 minutes or until cheese has melted. Makes 4 servings.

Savory Southwest (Arizona)

Grilled Texas Tequila Tuna

Prepare ahead. Heat up outdoor grill!

¼ cup tequila
¼ cup red wine vinegar
2 tablespoons lime juice
1 tablespoon ground red
  chiles

2 cloves finely chopped garlic
1 red bell pepper, finely
  chopped
2 pounds fresh tuna (4 steaks,
  approximately ¾ inch thick)

In a bowl, mix all ingredients together except tuna. Place tuna in shallow dish. Pour marinade over. Refrigerate for 1 hour. Remove tuna from marinade and reserve liquid. Place tuna on grill over medium hot coals, turning once. Cook until done, 6–7 minutes per side. Heat marinade to boiling in saucepan. Cook until bell pepper is tender. Serve over tuna. Serves 4.

Note: Alternative fish: swordfish and halibut.

Texas Sampler (Texas II)

Orange Roughy with Tomatoes

2 large onions, sliced
1 medium bell pepper, sliced
1 clove garlic, minced
1 (1-pound) can no-salt-added
   stewed tomatoes, crushed
1 teaspoon oregano

1 pound orange roughy, cut into 4
   serving-size pieces
1 lemon, sliced
Freshly ground black pepper to
   taste

Sauté onions and bell pepper until tender. Stir in garlic, tomatoes and oregano, cooking for 1 minute. Place fish in a single layer in a nonstick baking dish. Top with lemon slices and pepper; add vegetable mixture. Bake, uncovered, at 350° for 45 minutes. Fish is done when it is opaque and flakes easily with fork. Serves 4.

Cal 290; %Fat 31; Fat 10g; Sat Fat 1.9g; Chol 45mg; Sod 143mg; Carbo 22g; Prot 28g; Fiber 4g.
Exchanges: Starch ½, Vegetable 3, Lowfat protein 4

Arizona Heart Institute Foundation Cookbook (Arizona)

Seasoned Catfish

1 teaspoon onion powder
1 teaspoon garlic salt
1 teaspoon ground red pepper
1 teaspoon dried basil
½ teaspoon thyme

¼ teaspoon sage
4 catfish fillets
¼ cup margarine or butter,
   melted
Lemon slices

In a shallow dish, combine all seasonings. Brush both sides of fish with some of the melted margarine or butter. Coat both sides of fish with the seasoning mixture.

Grill fish or use a nonstick frying pan with 2 teaspoons margarine or butter and quick-fry them.

Arizona Small Game and Fish Recipes (Arizona)

Pan-Fried San Juan Trout

Sportsmen from around the world travel to northern New Mexico's San Juan River to fly-fish for trophy trout. This recipe will transform any fresh trout into award-winning dinner fare.

½ cup all-purpose flour, sifted	2 tablespoons vegetable oil
1 teaspoon Chimayó chili powder, or to taste	3–4 tablespoons unsalted butter, softened
1 teaspoon salt	¼ cup chopped fresh parsley
1 pinch freshly ground black pepper	1 tablespoon chopped cilantro leaves
8 small trout fillets, 3–4 ounces each, rinsed and dried	Juice of 2 lemons

Mix the sifted flour with the chili powder, salt, and pepper and spread out on a flat plate. Dredge the trout fillets in the flour, and lay out on a flat dish or baking rack.

Heat the vegetable oil to hot, but not smoking, in a heavy nonstick skillet. Pan-fry the fillets in the hot oil for about one minute on each side, then add the softened butter and cook until the fillets are golden, another minute on each side. With a slotted spatula, remove the fillets to 4 warmed plates. Toss the parsley, cilantro, and lemon juice into the skillet and whisk together 1 or 2 minutes until hot. Pour the sauce over the trout fillets, garnish with parsley and lemon wedges, and serve. Serves 4.

Red Chile Bible (New Mexico)

Smokey Bear Historical Park in Capitan, New Mexico, is the birthplace and burial site of the world's most well-known bear. In May of 1950, man-made fires destroyed 17,000 acres of forest and grasslands. A fire crew rescued a badly singed bear cub clinging tenaciously to the side of a burnt pine tree. After being treated at a veterinary hospital in Santa Fe, "Smokey Bear" was kept by Game Warden Ray Bell in his home, where Smokey was said to be somewhat of a ham and a "mite domineering." Smokey was later taken to the National Zoo in Washington DC, and became the National Fire Safety symbol, Smokey the Bear. Remember, "Only YOU can prevent forest fires."

Lime Marinated Grilled Salmon

LIME MARINADE:

⅓ cup freshly squeezed lime
  juice
2 cups coarsely chopped onions
1½ teaspoons coarsely chopped
  garlic

2 large jalapeños, minced
1 bunch cilantro, coarsely
  chopped
1 tablespoon honey
1 teaspoon salt

Combine marinade ingredients in the work bowl of a food processor and pulse for 30 seconds. Taste and adjust seasoning.

2 pounds salmon fillets,
  cut in 4- to 5-ounce portions

Salt and pepper to taste

Pour half the marinade over the bottom of a glass or stainless steel baking dish. Place the fillets on the marinade and pour the remaining marinade to cover the fillets. Marinate for at least one hour at room temperature or refrigerate overnight.

Wipe the marinade from the salmon, sprinkle the fish with salt and pepper to taste, and grill the salmon to desired doneness. Yields 6–8 servings.

The Santa Fe School of Cooking Cookbook (New Mexico)

KEITH ODOM

King Arthur's Oysters

There is never enough.

2 tablespoons butter, melted
¼ cup lemon juice
½ cup dry sherry
1 cup A-1 steak sauce

2 tablespoons flour
3 tablespoons water
2 dozen oysters
Salt and pepper to taste

1. In medium-size saucepan, combine butter, lemon juice, sherry, and steak sauce. Cook over low heat.
2. Blend flour and water together. Slowly stir into sauce being careful not to let boil.
3. Add oysters to sauce and heat for 1 minute. Adjust seasonings to taste with salt and pepper.
4. Transfer to chafing dish to keep warm. If oysters are to be eaten immediately, they can be placed in a shallow baking dish or serving dish. Yields 6 servings (4 each).

Preparation time: 30 minutes.

Rare Collection (Texas)

Beer Batter

Good with vegetables (mushrooms, onions, bell peppers, all types squash, etc.). Also good with shrimp, fish, crab, and crayfish tails.

1 can beer
1 cup all-purpose flour
1 egg, beaten
1 tablespoon Worcestershire

1 tablespoon mustard
2 cups crushed potato chips

Pour beer in flour until thin mixture forms. Add egg, Worcestershire, and mustard. Dip vegetable or fish in batter; then roll through crushed potato chips. Drop into deep fryer at 300°. Cook 3–4 minutes until light brown.

"I'm Glad I Ate When I Did, 'Cause I'm Not Hungry Now" (Texas)

CAKES

The Lyndon B. Johnson Space Center is NASA's center for human spaceflight activities. The center consists of a complex of 100 buildings on 1,620 acres in southeast Houston. Space Center Houston, the official visitors center for NASA's Johnson Space Center, features a multitude of permanent exhibits, attractions, and theaters, taking visitors on a journey through human adventures in space.

WWW.TRAVELTEX.COM

Party Cake Elegante

1 (2-layer) package yellow cake
  mix
1½ cups plain yogurt
1 (6-ounce) can frozen lemonade
  concentrate, thawed

1 (14-ounce) can sweetened
  condensed milk
4 kiwi fruit, peeled, sliced
1 pint fresh strawberries or
  raspberries, sliced

Prepare and bake cake mix using package directions for 2 (9-inch) cake pans. Remove layers to wire rack to cool. Split layers horizontally into halves. Combine yogurt, lemonade concentrate, and condensed milk in bowl; mix well. Spread mixture over cake layers. Stack cake layers with fruit between, alternating kiwi fruit and strawberries. Spread remaining lemonade mixture over top of cake; mixture will run down sides of cake. Decorate top of cake with concentric rings of remaining fruit. Chill until serving time. Yields 10–12 servings.

Heard in the Kitchen (Arizona)

Strawberry Chocolate Mousse Cake

1 cup chocolate cookie crumbs
3 tablespoons butter, melted
2 pints strawberries, stemmed
  and halved
12 ounces semisweet chocolate
  chips

2 tablespoons light corn syrup
½ cup orange liqueur
2½ cups whipping cream, divided
1 tablespoon powdered sugar

In a 9-inch springform pan, mix the cookie crumbs and butter thoroughly. Press evenly into the bottom of the pan. Stand strawberry halves around pan, touching, side by side, pointed ends up, with cut sides against the side of pan. Set aside. Place chocolate chips, corn syrup, and orange liqueur in bowl. Microwave for 1 minute or until the mixture is smooth when stirred. Beat 1½ cups of cream until it forms stiff peaks. Fold the cooled chocolate mixture into the cream. Pour into strawberry-lined bowl. Refrigerate. When ready to serve, unmold the dessert and whip the remaining cream with 1 tablespoon powdered sugar. Arrange cream on top of dessert and top with the remaining strawberries. Serves 12.

Favorites for All Seasons (Arizona)

Strawberry Meringue Cake

1 package yellow cake mix
1⅓ cups orange juice
4 egg yolks
1½ teaspoons grated orange
  peel
4 egg whites

¼ teaspoon cream of tartar
1 cup sugar
1 quart fresh strawberries,
  divided
2 tablespoons sugar
2 cups heavy whipping cream

Combine cake mix, orange juice, egg yolks, and orange peel, beat 4 minutes at medium speed of electric mixer. Pour into 2 greased and floured 9-inch round pans. Beat egg whites with cream of tartar to soft peaks; gradually add the one cup sugar, beating to stiff peaks. Spread meringue over batter evenly. Bake at 350° for 35 minutes. Cool. Remove from pans, meringue side up.

Mash ½ cup strawberries with 2 tablespoons sugar; add cream; whip till stiff. Add more sugar to whipped cream as desired. To assemble cake, spread ½ of cream mixture over bottom meringue. Reserve 2 cups whole berries; slice remainder and place over cream mixture. Add top layer; garnish with remaining cream mixture and reserved berries.

Recipes from the Cotton Patch (New Mexico)

Cake That Never Lasts

3 cups all-purpose flour
1 teaspoon cinnamon
1 teaspoon baking soda
1 teaspoon salt
2 cups sugar
1¼ cups cooking oil

1 (8-ounce) can crushed
  pineapple with juice
½ teaspoons vanilla
3 eggs
2 cups diced ripe bananas
1 cup chopped pecans

Sift together into a large mixing bowl the flour, cinnamon, baking soda, salt, and sugar, then add the cooking oil, pineapple, vanilla, eggs, bananas, and pecans. Mix all together but do not beat. Pour into 9-inch greased Bundt or tube pan. Bake at 350° for 1 hour and 20 minutes. Cool before removing from the pan.

Chuckwagon Recipes (Texas II)

Banana Cake with Sour Cream

2½ cups all-purpose flour
2 teaspoons baking powder
1 teaspoon baking soda
¼ teaspoon salt
½ cup margarine
1½ cups sugar

3 whole eggs, beaten
1 teaspoon vanilla
1 cup sour cream
1 cup mashed ripe bananas
½ cup chopped pecans or walnuts

Sift flour, baking powder, baking soda, and salt. Cream margarine, sugar, and eggs; add vanilla. Add sour cream, bananas, and nuts, alternating with dry ingredients. Bake in 2 well-greased and floured 9-inch baking pans. Bake at 350° for 30–45 minutes, or until cake tests done. Frost with Butter Cream Frosting.

BUTTER CREAM FROSTING:

1½ sticks margarine,
    divided
3 tablespoons flour

¾ cup milk
¾ cup granulated sugar
⅓ teaspoon vanilla

In saucepan, melt ½ stick margarine. Slowly add flour and milk over low heat. Cook to a pudding consistency and chill thoroughly in refrigerator. In a bowl, cream remaining 1 stick margarine and gradually add sugar. Beat until sugar seems to dissolve. Add pudding mixture gradually, beating until fluffy. Add vanilla and continue to beat until light, about 1 minute.

The Second Typically Texas Cookbook (Texas II)

WWW.TEXASROSEFESTIVAL.COM

Tyler, Texas, has been nicknamed the "Rose Capital of America" because of its large role in the rose-growing industry; about 20% of commercial rose bushes produced in the United States are grown in the area. The Tyler Municipal Rose Garden is the largest rose garden in the nation.

Esther's Blueberry Sour Cream Cake

½ cup butter or margarine
1 cup sugar
3 eggs
1 cup sour cream
1 teaspoon vanilla
2 cups all-purpose flour, sifted

1 teaspoon baking soda
1 teaspoon salt
2 cups blueberries
⅓ cup packed brown sugar
½ cup chopped nuts
½ teaspoon cinnamon

Cream butter and sugar together until fluffy. Add eggs, one at a time, beating well after each addition. Blend in sour cream and vanilla. Sift together flour, baking soda, and salt; add to creamed mixture, beating until smooth. Fold in blueberries. Spread one-third of batter into greased and floured Bundt pan. In a small bowl, combine brown sugar, nuts, and cinnamon; spread half evenly over top of batter in the pan. Spread another third of batter evenly over nut mixture, then top with remaining nut mixture, then remaining batter. Bake at 350° for 1 hour or until done. Cool cake in pan on wire rack. Sprinkle with powdered sugar before serving. Makes 12–16 servings.

The Blueberry Lover's Cookbook (Texas II)

Bride's Delight

1 cup butter
1½ cups sugar
1 egg plus 1 egg yolk
    (save white)
2 teaspoons almond extract

2½ cups all-purpose flour, sifted
½ teaspoon salt
1 egg white
2 teaspoons water
½ cup almonds, sliced

Cream butter, sugar, egg, egg yolk, and almond extract until fluffy. Add flour and salt. Press into 2 (8- or 9-inch) round cake pans. Mix egg white with 2 teaspoons water and brush over cakes. Sprinkle with sliced almonds and lightly with sugar. Bake at 325° for 25–35 minutes (it should not brown). Serve cut in wedges either alone or with strawberries and whipped cream. Makes 12–16 servings.

Pass it On... (Texas II)

Super Buttermilk Cake

This cake is very light and of a sponge-cake consistency! It can be used as is, without the glaze, with a topping of fruit and whipped cream, or a dessert sauce. It is also delicious with just the glaze.

CAKE:

2 cups all-purpose flour
½ teaspoon baking soda
½ teaspoon baking powder
Pinch of salt
2 sticks margarine

2 cups sugar
1 teaspoon pure vanilla
4 large eggs
1 cup buttermilk

Sift dry ingredients together. Cream margarine with 2 cups sugar, vanilla, and eggs, one at a time. Beat until fluffy. Add sifted flour mixture alternately with buttermilk, beginning and ending with flour. Pour into a greased and floured 13x9x2-inch baking dish. Bake in a preheated 350° oven for 40–45 minutes or until it tests done in center. Pour warm glaze over cooled cake in pan. This cake must be served from the pan.

GLAZE:

1 cup heavy cream   2½ tablespoons sugar

Heat the sugar and cream in a saucepan, stirring, until hot. Do not boil. Yields 1 (13x9x2-inch) cake.

Note: Evaporated milk (not condensed milk) may be substituted for whipping cream if you want to cut calories.

Raleigh House Cookbook II (Texas II)

WIKIPEDIA.ORG

22-Minute Cake

CAKE:

2 cups all-purpose flour
2 cups sugar
1 stick margarine, softened
1 cup water
½ cup shortening
3½ tablespoons cocoa

½ cup buttermilk
2 eggs
1 teaspoon baking soda
1 teaspoon vanilla
1 heaping teaspoon instant
  coffee

Do not use mixer. Combine flour and sugar in large bowl. In a saucepan, combine and bring to a boil the margarine, water, shortening, and cocoa; pour over flour and sugar mixture. Combine buttermilk, eggs, baking soda, vanilla, and coffee and add to the mixture; mix all together. Pour into a greased 12x7-inch pan and bake 20 minutes at 400°.

ICING:

1 stick margarine
3½ tablespoons cocoa
⅓ cup milk
1 pound powdered sugar

1 cup chopped pecans
1 heaping tablespoon instant
  coffee

When cake has baked for 18 minutes, combine in saucepan the margarine, cocoa, and milk. Bring to a boil. Add the powdered sugar, nuts, and coffee. Pour over cake when removed from oven.

Recipes for Rain or Shine (New Mexico)

Gallup, New Mexico, is the only large settlement in the Southwest that still hosts, in any significant number, the unique mercantile tradition of trading post. Located between the Navajo and Zuni reservations, the town has 110 trading posts, shops, and galleries, making it the undisputed southwestern center for original, authentic Native American arts and crafts. In August of each year the Inter-Tribal Ceremony attracts upwards of 50,000 visitors, making it one of the largest annual events in the Southwest. Permanent grandstands built against towering red rock formations create an unforgettable amphitheater for the event.

Decadent Chocolate Cake

¾ cup butter, softened
2 cups sugar
2 eggs, separated
1 teaspoon vanilla
1 cup sour cream
1 teaspoon baking soda
1 package powdered whipped
  topping mix

2 cups all-purpose flour
¾ cup cocoa
1 teaspoon baking powder
1 (3-ounce) package chocolate
  fudge pudding mix
1¼ cups half-and-half

Cream butter and sugar; add egg yolks and vanilla. Beat one minute on HIGH speed; set aside. Beat egg whites until soft peaks form; fold into sour cream; add baking soda and whipped topping mix. Add sour cream mixture to butter mixture. Mix flour, cocoa, baking powder, and pudding mix. Add alternately with half-and-half and butter mixture. Beat 2 minutes on HIGH. Pour into 2 greased and lightly floured 8-inch pans. Bake at 350° for 35–40 minutes.

CREAMY CHOCOLATE FROSTING:

6 tablespoons butter,
  softened
¾ cup cocoa

3 cups powdered sugar
⅓ cup half-and-half
1 teaspoon vanilla

Cream butter; add cocoa and sugar alternately with cream and vanilla. With electric mixer, beat until smooth. When cake is done, cool in pans for 10 minutes. Remove to wire rack to complete cooling. Frost.

Beyond Loaves and Fishes (New Mexico)

Heavenly Chocolate Cake

2 squares unsweetened
  chocolate
¼ cup boiling water
¼ cup tequila
2 eggs, well beaten
1½ cups sugar
½ cup butter, room temperature

Pinch of salt
1 teaspoon vanilla
¾ cup buttermilk
1 teaspoon baking soda
1½ cups all-purpose flour

Preheat oven to 375°. Put chocolate, water, and tequila in a saucepan and cook over low heat until chocolate is melted. Let cool, then stir the eggs into the chocolate mixture. Cream sugar and butter together and stir into the chocolate and egg mixture. Add salt, vanilla, buttermilk, baking soda, and flour and stir until blended, but do not overbeat. Pour into 2 lightly greased and floured 8-inch-round cake pans. Bake in a 375° oven for 45 minutes or until a toothpick comes out clean when inserted in the center. Let the cake cool in the pans on a wire rack. Remove from the pans and frost with Tequila Frosting.

TEQUILA FROSTING:

½ cup butter or margarine,
  room temperature
½ teaspoon salt
2½ cups powdered sugar

½ teaspoon vanilla
1 tablespoon Grand Marnier
3–4 tablespoons tequila

Cream butter, salt, and sugar together. Add vanilla and Grand Marnier. Then slowly add tequila until the frosting is a spreadable consistency. Spread smoothly over cake.

The Tequila Cook Book (New Mexico)

Heath Torte

6 egg whites
1 teaspoon vinegar
⅛ teaspoon salt

1 teaspoon vanilla
2 cups sugar

Beat egg whites with vinegar, salt, and vanilla until very stiff. Add sugar and beat until very stiff. Pour into 2 (9-inch) cake pans, buttered on sides and greased brown paper on bottom. Bake in 300° oven for 1 hour. Cool.

FILLING:
1 pint heavy cream, whipped
2 tablespoons powdered sugar
1 tablespoon vanilla

10–15 Heath bars, finely ground
Chopped nuts

Whip cream and add sugar and vanilla. Fold in ground Heath bars. Place half of Filling between layers and other half on top. Cover top with chopped nuts. Cover with plastic wrap. Refrigerate overnight. Yields 15 servings. Preparation time: 1 hour.

Rare Collection (Texas)

Eclair Cake

1 cup water
1 stick margarine
1 cup all-purpose flour
4 eggs
1 large package vanilla instant
   pudding

1 (8-ounce) package cream
   cheese, softened
1 (8-ounce) tub Cool Whip
Hershey's syrup

Heat water and margarine. Add flour; stir. Add eggs, one at a time; beat well. Spread in a greased 9x13-inch pan. Bake at 400° for 30 minutes. Don't mind how it looks; cool. Fix instant pudding according to directions on box, then add cream cheese and beat thoroughly. Pour on cake. Top with Cool Whip. Drizzle with Hershey's syrup. Cut in 16–20 servings.

Saint Joseph's Really Grande Cookbook (New Mexico)

Harvey House Chocolate Puffs

1 cup all-purpose flour
1 cup water
1½ cups butter
1 ounce chocolate, melted

3 eggs
1 teaspoon strawberry preserves
   or sugared fresh berries
Whipped cream, sweetened

Boil together flour, water, and butter. Remove from fire and beat in melted chocolate and eggs, one at a time. Bake in a gun pan (muffin tins), lightly greased, filled half full. Bake in hot oven (400°) until done in peaks, 20–25 minutes.

Allow to cool, then cut off top of each cake and put in a teaspoon of strawberry preserves or fresh berries. Heap with sweetened whipped cream. (I have no record of what happened to the tops, but I am positive they were not thrown out.) Makes 10 puffs.

Arizona Highways Heritage Cookbook (Arizona)

Mexican Cake

1 (20-ounce) can crushed
   pineapple, undrained
1 cup all-purpose flour
1 teaspoon baking soda

2 eggs
2 cups sugar
Pinch of salt
1 cup chopped pecans

Put all ingredients into mixing bowl. Mix with spoon. Pour into greased 9x13-inch pan and bake at 350° for 35–45 minutes.

FROSTING:

4 (3-ounce) packages cream
   cheese, softened

1 stick margarine, melted
1 teaspoon vanilla

Combine ingredients. Frost cake while still hot. Cover with foil.

Our Best Home Cooking (New Mexico)

Sam Houston's Golden Spice Cake

7 egg yolks	1 teaspoon ground cloves
1 whole egg	2 teaspoons ground cinnamon
2 cups brown sugar	2 teaspoons ginger
1 cup sweet butter	1 nutmeg, ground
1 cup molasses	A speck of cayenne pepper
1 teaspoon baking soda	1 teacup sour milk
5 cups all-purpose flour	2 cups raisins (optional)

Beat eggs, sugar, and butter to a light batter before adding the molasses. Then add the molasses, baking soda, flour, spices, and milk. Heat it well together and bake in a moderate oven (350°, in 2 loaf pans about 35–45 minutes). If you use fruit, take 2 cupfuls of raisins, flour them well, and put them into the batter last.

Jane Long's Brazoria Inn (Texas II)

WIKIMEDIA COMMONS

Houston, Texas, is the fourth largest city in the United States (after New York, Los Angeles, and Chicago), the largest city within the state of Texas, and "the Energy Capital of the world" (five of the six major energy companies maintain a large base of operations in Houston). Houston was founded in 1836 and named after then-President of the Republic of Texas—former General Sam Houston. In the mid-twentieth century, Houston became the home of the Texas Medical Center—the world's largest concentration of healthcare and research institutions—and NASA's Johnson Space Center, where the Mission Control Center is located. Only New York City is home to more Fortune 500 headquarters in the city limits than Houston.

Wini's Carrot Cake

2 cups sugar
4 eggs
1½ cups oil
3 cups all-purpose flour
2 teaspoons baking soda
3 cups grated carrots
1 cup broken pecans

1 teaspoon lemon flavoring
1 teaspoon coconut flavoring
Curacao or Triple Sec Liqueur or
  2 cups sugar, 1½ cups fresh
  orange juice, and 2 tablespoons
  grated orange rind

Blend sugar, eggs, and oil. Add flour and baking soda. Mix thoroughly. Fold in carrots, pecans, and lemon and coconut flavorings. Pour into greased and floured Bundt pan. Bake for 1½ hours at 300°. As soon as cake is removed from oven, pour Curacao or Triple Sec, any amount desired, over warm cake. Or, mix together 2 cups sugar, orange juice and orange rind, and brush over all sides of warm cake. Let cool completely in pan. Yields 16 servings.

Keepers (Texas)

A Pioneer Birthday Cake

This recipe was used to make a birthday cake for a little Texas girl long ago when there was no flour to be had. Corn was ground on a hand mill. The meal was carefully emptied from one sack to another, and the fine meal dust clinging to the sack was carefully shaken out on a paper. The sack was again emptied and shaken, and this process was repeated laboriously, time after time, until two cups of meal dust was obtained. The rest of the ingredients were as follows: One half cup of wild honey, one teaspoon of homemade soda, one wild turkey egg, one scant cup of sour milk, and a very small amount of butter, to all of which was added the two cups of meal dust.

    The batter was poured into a skillet with a lid and placed over the open fire in the yard; the skillet lid was heaped with coals.

Seconds of A Pinch of This and A Handful of That (Texas II)

A Good Cake

One cup sweet milk, one cup butter, three cups sugar, five cups of flour, two teaspoons baking powder.

The First Texas Cook Book (Texas II)

Texas Buttermilk Pound Cake

1 cup shortening
3 cups sugar
6 egg yolks
3 cups all-purpose flour
¼ teaspoon baking soda

½ teaspoon salt
1 cup buttermilk
2 teaspoons lemon flavoring
6 egg whites

Preheat oven to 325°. Cream shortening and sugar together. Add egg yolks, one at a time, mixing after each addition. Sift together the flour, baking soda, and salt, and add alternately with buttermilk. Add lemon flavoring and fold in stiffly beaten egg whites. Pour this mixture in an ungreased tube or Bundt pan and bake at 325° for 1 hour and 20 minutes.

SWEET MILK VARIATION:

Substitute 1 cup sweet milk for buttermilk, and substitute 2 teaspoons vanilla for lemon flavoring. Bake in greased and floured Bundt pan at 350° for 1 hour and 15 minutes. Pour Buttermilk Glaze over cake.

BUTTERMILK GLAZE:

½ cup sugar
¼ cup buttermilk

½ stick butter or margarine

Combine in a saucepan and cook 6 minutes. Pour over cake.

Cookin' Wise (Texas)

Lemon Apricot Pound Cake

CAKE:

1 (3-ounce) package instant
  lemon pudding mix
1 cup apricot nectar
1 box lemon supreme cake mix

4 eggs
¾ cup oil
1 tablespoon lemon extract

Place pudding into bowl with apricot nectar and let sit while mixing the rest of ingredients. Combine the cake mix, eggs (beating well after each addition of egg), oil, and lemon extract, then add the pudding mixture. Beat well with mixer and pour batter into greased and floured tube or Bundt pan. Cook at 350° for 40–50 minutes. Remove from oven and take out of pan immediately. Prick top with a toothpick and spoon Glaze over the cake.

GLAZE:

¼ cup fresh lemon juice
¼ cup apricot nectar

1½ cups powdered sugar

Mix lemon juice, apricot nectar, and powdered sugar until smooth. Yields 24 servings. Freezes well.

Variation: Delicious with glaze alone, but for a special treat add this icing over glaze: a box of Fluffy Lemon Frosting and 1 cup whipping cream. Mix until stiff and ice.

La Piñata (Texas)

March Second Cheesecake

A dandy dessert for Texas Independence Day.

1 (8-ounce) package cream
  cheese, softened
⅓ cup sugar
1 cup sour cream
2 teaspoons vanilla

1 (8-ounce) container
  nondairy whipped topping
1 prepared graham cracker
  crust
Fresh strawberries for garnish

Cream cheese until smooth; gradually beat in sugar. Blend in sour cream and vanilla. Fold in whipped topping, blending well. Spoon into crust and chill until set . . . at least 4 hours. Garnish with fresh strawberries, if desired.

Cook 'em Horns: The Quickbook (Texas II)

Cafe Mexicana Cheesecake

CRUST:

¼ cup chocolate wafer crumbs
¼ cup butter, melted

1 tablespoon sugar
¼ teaspoon cinnamon

Combine crumbs, butter, sugar, and cinnamon in small bowl. Press evenly over bottom of a buttered 9-inch springform pan. Refrigerate.

FILLING:

4 (8-ounce) packages cream
    cheese, softened
1½ cups sugar
4 large eggs
1 cup sour cream
¼ cup coffee-flavored liqueur
1 teaspoon vanilla

1 cup whipping cream
1 cup semisweet chocolate chips,
    melted
½ teaspoon cinnamon
Sweetened whipped cream
Candy coffee beans

Beat cream cheese until smooth. Gradually beat in 1½ cups sugar; add eggs, one at a time, beating well. Stir in sour cream, liqueur, vanilla, whipping cream, melted chocolate, and cinnamon. Blend well. Pour into crust-lined pan. Bake at 325° for 1 hour and 15 minutes. Do not open oven door. Turn oven off and leave cheesecake in another hour. Remove and cool slightly, then refrigerate. To serve, remove cake from pan. Garnish with sweetened whipped-cream rosettes, sprinkled lightly with cinnamon and topped with candy coffee beans. Makes 8–12 servings.

Savory Southwest (Arizona)

Lemon Cheesecake
with Berry Topping

¾ cup fat-free granola
16 ounces fat-free cottage
    cheese
8 ounces fat-free cream cheese,
    softened
¼ cup plus ½ tablespoon flour
1¼ cups sugar

4 egg whites, beaten
1 tablespoon lemon juice
1 tablespoon grated lemon rind
¼ cup blueberries
¼ cup strawberries
¼ cup raspberries

Preheat oven to 325°. Place granola in food processor or blender, and blend until slightly ground. Lightly spray 8-inch springform pan with cooking spray and place ground granola in pan.

Combine cottage cheese and cream cheese in food processor or blender, and process until smooth. Add flour, sugar, egg whites, lemon juice, and lemon rind to cheese mixture. Pour into prepared pan and bake in preheated oven for 50 minutes. Turn oven off and let the cheesecake remain in oven for another hour, with the door slightly open. Remove pan from oven and allow cheesecake to cool completely before removing sides of pan. Top cheesecake with mixed berries and serve. Serves 12.

Nutritional Analysis Per Serving: Cal 151; Prot 9g; Carbo 29g; Chol 5mg; Sod 228mg; Dietary Fiber < 1 gram; Exchanges: 2 starch; ½ meat.

Recipes for Fat Free Living Cookbook (Arizona)

The Gadsden Purchase is a 29,670-square-mile region of what is today southern Arizona and southwestern New Mexico. It was purchased by the United States in a treaty signed by President Franklin Pierce in 1853, and then ratified by the U.S. Senate on April 25, 1854. It is named for James Gadsden, the American ambassador sent to Mexico at the time. The purchase included lands south of the Gila River and west of the Rio Grande. The Gadsden Purchase was intended to allow for the construction of a transcontinental railroad along a very southern route, and it was part of negotiations needed to finalize border issues that remained unresolved from the Treaty of Guadalupe-Hidalgo, which ended the Mexican-American War of 1846–48.

Pumpkin Cheesecake

The use of pumpkins and squash is centuries old in New Mexico, and this recipe gives a new twist to an old favorite.

CRUST:

¾ cup graham cracker crumbs   2 tablespoons melted butter
2 tablespoons sugar

Preheat the oven to 350°. Combine the cracker crumbs, sugar, and butter thoroughly. Press the mixture into the bottom of a 9-inch springform pan. Chill in the refrigerator for 15 minutes.

CHEESECAKE:

1½ pounds cream cheese, at   2 teaspoons ground cannèlla, or
   room temperature   1 teaspoon ground cinnamon
1½ cups sugar   1 tablespoon Mexican vanilla
4 large eggs   Whipped cream for garnish
¾ cup canned solid-pack
   pumpkin

In a mixer with a paddle attachment, whip the cream cheese and sugar until light and fluffy. Add the eggs and the pumpkin, and continue beating until the mixture is smooth. Add the cannèlla and vanilla and incorporate thoroughly. Pour the cream cheese mixture into the prepared Crust and bake for approximately one hour, or until the cheesecake is set all the way through. Turn off the oven and let the cake sit for 15 minutes. Remove the cake from the oven and chill. Top with whipped cream. Yields 10–12 servings.

The Santa Fe School of Cooking Cookbook (New Mexico)

COOKIES and CANDIES

Over 25,000 tons of rock were removed to build the Chapel of the Holy Cross into the mesas of Sedona, Arizona. Inspired and commissioned by sculptor Marguerite Brunswig Staude, student of Frank Lloyd Wright, the Catholic chapel was built in 18 months at a cost of $300,000. It was completed in 1956.

GWEN McKEE

Churros
(Mexican Crullers)

1 cup water
1 cup all-purpose flour
¼ teaspoon salt
1 egg, lightly beaten

1 teaspoon sherry wine
1 cup cooking oil
Powdered sugar

Bring water to boiling point in a saucepan. Remove saucepan from fire and gradually add sifted flour with salt. Beat vigorously until fluffy and smooth. Add egg with wine and continue beating until batter is smooth and shiny. Heat oil in a deep pan until medium hot. Pour batter in a pastry tube and drop small amounts of batter, about 4–5 inches long, in the hot oil. Fry both sides until golden brown and remove Churros to absorbent paper to drain. Roll each one in powdered sugar while still hot. Serve with hot cocoa. Yields 12.

Vistoso Vittles II (Arizona)

Butter Cookies
(Vajas Pogacsa)

5 cups all-purpose flour
2 teaspoons baking powder
1 cup sugar or 9 packets artificial
  sweetener

Pinch of salt
1 pound butter or margarine
3 eggs
1 tablespoon sour cream

Preheat oven to 350°. In a mixing bowl, mix together flour, baking powder, sugar, and salt. Cut in softened butter or margarine and mix together. Make a hole in the center and add eggs and sour cream. Mix together into a soft dough. Cut dough in 2 pieces. Roll out each dough piece on a floured board to about ¼-inch thickness. Cut with a small round cookie cutter. Place cookies on a greased cookie sheet and bake in a 350° oven for 20–22 minutes until light beige. Yields 12 dozen cookies.

Kosher Kettle (Arizona)

Frosty Apple Bites

COOKIES:

2 cups sifted all-purpose flour
½ teaspoon baking soda
½ teaspoon salt
¼ teaspoon nutmeg
½ cup margarine or butter
1 cup firmly packed brown sugar
1 egg, unbeaten

1 teaspoon vanilla
⅔ cup evaporated milk
1 cup chopped walnuts
1 cup pared and chopped apples
½ cup semisweet chocolate
  chips

Sift together all the dry ingredients. Then cream margarine and brown sugar and then add the unbeaten egg and vanilla. Beat well. Add the dry ingredients alternately with evaporated milk, beginning and ending with dry ingredients. Stir in walnuts, apples, and chocolate chips. Drop by teaspoonfuls onto lightly greased cookie sheets. Bake at 375° for 12–15 minutes. Frost while warm with Cinnamon Glaze.

CINNAMON GLAZE:

2 cups powdered sugar, sifted
3 tablespoons butter, melted

1 teaspoon cinnamon
2–3 tablespoons evaporated milk

Combine sugar, butter, and cinnamon. Add evaporated milk until of spreading consistency. Yields 4 dozen cookies.

Cowtown Cuisine (Texas)

Mrs. Lyndon Johnson's Sand Tarts

These are the real McCoy. Light and tasty—you'll see why LBJ loved them.

½ pound butter, softened
4 tablespoons powdered sugar
2 tablespoons water

3 cups all-purpose flour
1 cup pecans, chopped
2 teaspoons vanilla

Blend butter and sugar; add other ingredients. Roll with the hand to finger size and turn into half moons. Bake about 25 minutes in 350° oven. Roll in powdered sugar.

Ma's in the Kitchen (Texas II)

Oatmeal Carmelitas

1 (14-ounce) package caramels
½ cup heavy cream
1½ cups all-purpose flour
1½ cups rolled oats
1½ cups packed light brown
  sugar
1 egg (optional)
½ teaspoon baking soda
½ teaspoon salt
¾ cup unsalted butter, cut into
  pieces
12 ounces semisweet chocolate
  chips
1 cup chopped pecans or walnuts

Heat the caramels and cream in a saucepan over medium heat. Cook until the caramels are melted, stirring constantly; set aside. Process the flour, oats, brown sugar, egg, baking soda, and salt in a food processor until well mixed. Add the butter. Pulse on and off until the mixture begins to clump. Press ½ of the mixture into a greased 9x13-inch baking pan. Bake at 350° for 8–10 minutes. Scatter the chocolate chips and nuts over the crust. Drizzle with the caramel mixture. Sprinkle the remaining crumb mixture over the top. Bake for 20 minutes or until golden brown around the edges. Loosen the edges from the sides of the pan. Cool completely. Cut into squares. Chill until firm. Store in the refrigerator. Serves 20.

Reflections Under the Sun (Arizona)

Orange-Oatmeal Cookies

2 cups all-purpose flour
1 teaspoon baking soda
¼ teaspoon salt
½ teaspoon cinnamon
⅛ teaspoon allspice
1 cup shortening
½ cup packed light brown
  sugar
½ cup sugar
2 eggs
2 cups quick-cooking rolled oats
⅓ cup orange juice
1 cup raisins
½ cup chopped pecans
2 teaspoons grated orange rind

Sift flour, baking soda, salt, cinnamon, and allspice together. Cream shortening and sugars in mixer bowl until smooth. Add eggs, beating until light and fluffy. Stir in oats. Add sifted dry ingredients alternately with orange juice, beating well after each addition. Stir in raisins, pecans, and orange rind. Drop by teaspoonfuls onto greased cookie sheets. Bake at 350° for 10–15 minutes or until golden brown. Yields 48 servings.

Approx. Per Serving: Cal 111; Prot 2g; Carbo 14g; Fiber 19; T Fat 6g; 44% Calories from Fat; Chol 9mg; Sod 55mg.

Gatherings (Texas II)

Butter Mint Delights

Now we've come to my favorite cookie—they are soo-oo-ooo good! They used to spread in a very uncontrolled manner, but I have really worked at getting them to behave. This is the reason for the chilling and freezing. I like to use a pretty cookie stamp on the tops before they go to the freezer, as without it, they look rather plain. And if your candy tooth has as much weakness as mine does, you will have a difficult time to keep that full cup of mints when it's time to add them!

1 cup ground butter mints	**2 cups all-purpose flour**
1 cup softened butter	**1 tablespoon granulated sugar**

Preheat oven to 300°. Line a 9-inch square baking pan with wax paper.

Grind the butter mints to a medium fine texture in an electric blender. Knead the butter into the flour until thoroughly blended. Add the ground mints and continue kneading until dough is of a soft but solid consistency. Put dough evenly into the prepared baking pan and refrigerate for 1 hour. Remove from refrigerator and sprinkle surface of pastry with the granulated sugar. Cut the pastry into small 1-inch squares. Lift the wax paper with the cookies intact from the baking pan and place cookies about 1 inch apart on an ungreased baking sheet. Place in freezer for 30 minutes. Bake frozen cookies for 16–18 minutes. Butter Mint Delights should not brown at all. Remove from oven and cool on wire rack.

I used to crush these delicious mints between two sheets of wax paper with a rolling pin but it wasn't enough protection for the mints—from me! This is not only my favorite cookie—the butter mints are my favorite candy, too. I wonder if that could have anything to do with my being willing to make them at any time!

Sweets . . . From Marina with Love . . . (Texas)

White Chocolate and Almond Cookies

¾ cup brown sugar, firmly
  packed
½ cup sugar
½ cup butter, softened
½ cup shortening
1½ teaspoons vanilla

1 egg
1¾ cups all-purpose flour
1 teaspoon baking soda
½ teaspoon salt
8 ounces white chocolate, chopped
¼ cup sliced almonds

In large bowl, combine brown sugar, sugar, butter, shortening, vanilla, and egg. Blend well. Stir in flour, baking soda, and salt. Blend well. Stir in white chocolate and almonds. Mix well. Drop by rounded teaspoonfuls, 2 inches apart, onto an ungreased baking sheet. Bake at 375° until light golden brown, 8–10 minutes. Remove immediately. Makes 4 dozen.

Purple Sage and Other Pleasures (Arizona)

How big is the Grand Canyon? Counted in river miles, it is 277 miles long. The width is as much as 18 miles and the deepest point is 6,000 vertical feet from rim to river. A trip to the bottom of the Canyon and back (on foot or by mule) is a two-day journey. Rim-to-rim hikers generally take three days one-way to get from the North Rim to the South Rim. A trip through Grand Canyon by raft can take two weeks or longer.

Peanut Butter Chocolate Balls

1 stick margarine, softened
1 box powdered sugar, sifted
2 cups crunchy peanut butter
3 cups Rice Krispies

1 (6-ounce) package chocolate
  chips
½ square paraffin

Cream margarine and powdered sugar. Add peanut butter and Rice Krispies, mixing well. Form into small balls. Melt chocolate chips and paraffin. Roll balls in chocolate and place on wax paper to cool.

Entertaining in Texas (Texas)

Jean's Chocolate Cookies

Wonderful!

2 tablespoons margarine
1 (12-ounce) package
  semisweet chocolate chips
1 can sweetened condensed
  milk

1 cup all-purpose flour
1 teaspoon vanilla
1 cup chopped pecans

Melt margarine and chocolate chips in a double boiler. Add milk and mix well. Remove from heat. Add flour and vanilla. Add nuts. Roll walnut-size balls of dough and put on cookie sheet. Bake at 350° for 10 minutes.

Central Texas Style (Texas II)

Nell's Apricot Bars

1½ sticks margarine, softened
1 Duncan Hines (only) Yellow
  Butter Recipe Cake Mix
1 cup flour mixed with cake mix

1 cup chopped pecans
1 cup flaked coconut
1 (10- to 12-ounce) jar apricot
  preserves

Cut butter into cake mix and flour. Add nuts and coconut. Mix well. Pat ⅓ mixture into an ungreased 9x13-inch pan. Spread apricot preserves over mixture. Crumble remaining mixture over preserves. Bake 1 hour at 325°.

Gingerbread . . . and all the trimmings (Texas II)

Nita's Hidden Treasures

The following recipe was known just as Lemon Bars until it was discovered that our daughter Nita was secretly wrapping them in wax paper and hiding them in her bureau to eat unshared when she was alone! Anyone who has lived in a large family knows how quickly Nita's Hidden Treasure secret was exposed! However the name has become permanent—and here is Nita's favorite cookie. Do be sure to make enough to share!

⅔ cup butter
1 cup dark brown sugar, firmly
  packed
1 cup regular oats
1½ cups sifted all-purpose flour
1 teaspoon baking powder

½ teaspoon salt
1 (14-ounce) can sweetened
  condensed milk
½ cup lemon juice (2 lemons)
1 teaspoon lemon rind

Preheat oven to 350°. Generously butter a 9x13-inch baking pan.

Thoroughly cream the butter and sugar together until light. Stir in the oats, blending well. Sift together the flour, baking powder, and salt and mix in until texture is evenly crumbly. Reserve half the crumb mixture and spread the remaining half evenly over the bottom of the prepared baking pan, pressing lightly into place. Mix together the milk, lemon juice, and rind until very smooth and creamy. Spread carefully and evenly over the crumb layer and cover the cream layer with the remaining reserved crumbs. Bake for 25–30 minutes until lightly golden in color. Remove from oven and cool on wire rack. When completely cool, cut into 48 squares.

Sweets . . . From Marina with Love. . . . (Texas)

Lemon Squares

CRUST:

2 cups all-purpose flour
½ cup powdered sugar

1 cup margarine, softened

Mix well and spread in a 9x13-inch pan.

FILLING:

4 eggs, beaten (do not
  overbeat)
3 tablespoons flour
1 teaspoon baking powder

Grated rind and juice of 2 lemons
2 cups sugar
Powdered sugar

Mix all ingredients except powdered sugar together and pour over Crust. Bake 20 minutes at 350°. Sprinkle with powdered sugar. While still warm, cut into squares.

Recipes for Rain or Shine (New Mexico)

Sour Cream Apple Squares

2 cups all-purpose flour
2 cups brown sugar, packed
½ cup butter or margarine
1 cup chopped nuts
1 or 2 teaspoons cinnamon
1 teaspoon baking soda

½ teaspoon salt
1 cup sour cream
1 teaspoon vanilla
1 egg
2 cups finely chopped peeled
  apples (2 medium)

Preheat oven to 350°. Combine flour, brown sugar and margarine. Blend until crumbly. Stir in nuts. Press 2¾ cups mixture into 13x9-inch pan. To remaining mixture, add cinnamon, baking soda, salt, sour cream, vanilla, and egg. Blend well. Stir in apples. Spoon evenly over base. Bake 25–35 minutes until toothpick comes out clean. Cut into squares. Serve with whipped cream.

Repast (Texas)

Raspberry Snow Bars

¾ cup shortening
¾ cup sugar, divided
¼ teaspoon salt
¼ teaspoon almond extract
2 egg yolks

1½ cups all-purpose flour
1 cup raspberry preserves
1 cup flaked coconut
2 egg whites

Cream the shortening, ¼ cup sugar, and salt in a mixer bowl until light and fluffy. Beat in the almond extract and egg yolks. Add the flour and mix well. Pat the dough over the bottom of a 9x13-inch pan. Bake at 350° for 15 minutes. Spread the preserves over the hot crust. Top with the coconut.

Beat the egg whites in mixer bowl until foamy. Add the remaining ½ cup sugar gradually, beating constantly until the egg whites form stiff peaks. Spread over the coconut. Bake for 25 minutes. Cool in the pan on wire rack. Cut into 24 bars.

Tucson Treasures (Arizona)

Desert Dream Bars

½ cup butter or margarine, softened
½ cup brown sugar
1 cup all-purpose flour
2 eggs
1 cup brown sugar

1 cup flaked coconut
1 cup chopped pecans
2 tablespoons flour
¼ teaspoon salt
½ teaspoon baking powder
1 teaspoon vanilla extract

In medium bowl, mix butter, ½ cup brown sugar, and flour. Press into greased 9x13-inch pan. Bake in a 350° oven for 15 minutes. In large bowl, combine remaining ingredients and spread over baked first mixture. Bake another 25–30 minutes. Cut into bars while still warm.

Sedona Cook Book (Arizona)

Crunchy Bars

1 stick butter	1 cup flaked coconut
1 cup graham cracker crumbs	1 cup Grapenuts
1 (6-ounce) package semisweet chocolate chips	1 (14-ounce) can sweetened condensed milk

1. In 325° oven, melt butter in 9x13-inch pan.
2. Remove from oven and sprinkle evenly over butter in this order: graham cracker crumbs, chocolate bits, coconut, and Grapenuts.
3. Drizzle can of milk over all.
4. Bake at 325° for 30 minutes.
5. Cut into bars.

Double recipe for freezing day. Freezes well. You may want to cut into squares and separate into packages of 6–8 before freezing for easy defrosting.

Easy Does It Cookbook (Texas)

Chocolate Peanut Popcorn Squares

1 bag microwave popcorn, popped or ⅓ cup popcorn, popped	1 (10½-ounce) package miniature marshmallows
2 tablespoons butter	½ cup milk chocolate chips
	½ cup peanuts

Remove and discard unpopped kernels. Place butter in a 4-quart microwavable bowl or casserole. Microwave on HIGH until melted, 1–2 minutes. Stir in marshmallows and chips until coated. Microwave on HIGH just until mixture can be stirred smooth, 2–4 minutes, stirring once each minute. Carefully fold in peanuts and popcorn until coated. Press mixture into greased 9x13-inch pan with wooden spoon. Drizzle with Chocolate Glaze. Makes about 24 (2-inch) squares.

CHOCOLATE GLAZE:

½ cup milk chocolate chips	2 teaspoons butter or shortening

Place chips and butter in 1-cup microwavable measure. Microwave, uncovered, on HIGH until melted, 1–3 minutes, stirring every 30 seconds.

Heavenly Delights (Arizona)

Chocolate Brickle Brownies

1 cup butter
½ cup cocoa
4 eggs
2 cups sugar
1½ cups unbleached all-purpose
   flour

⅛ teaspoon salt
1 teaspoon vanilla
1 cup chopped pecans
½ cup semisweet chocolate chips
½ cup Heath Bits or Brickle
   chips or chopped Heath Bars

Preheat oven to 350°. Melt butter and dissolve cocoa in the butter and set aside. Beat eggs and sugar together until fluffy. Beat in flour, salt and vanilla. Add cocoa and butter. Stirring well add pecans, chocolate and brickle chips. Bake in a greased and floured 9x13-inch metal pan for 30 minutes or until done. Makes 2 dozen.

The Wild Wild West (Texas II)

Deluxe Brownies

1 package Duncan Hines
   brownie mix
Milk
½–1 cup chopped pecans

Chocolate chips
Butter or margarine
Light brown sugar

Mix brownies according to package directions for chewy brownies, substituting milk for water. Add pecans, reserving a few to sprinkle on top. Place brownie mixture in a pan. Sprinkle chocolate chips over batter. Melt equal parts butter and sugar, 2–4 tablespoons each depending on size of mix, and drizzle over batter. Bake according to package directions.

Flavors (Texas)

Gypsy Raspberry Brownies

¾ cup butter, melted
1½ cups sugar
2 teaspoons vanilla
3 eggs, slightly beaten

¾ cup all-purpose flour
½ cup unsweetened cocoa
½ teaspoon baking powder
½ teaspoon salt

Cream butter, sugar, and vanilla. Beat in eggs. In another bowl, stir together flour, cocoa, baking powder, and salt with fork. Blend dry ingredients into egg mixture. Do not overbeat. Spread batter into ungreased 8-inch square baking pan.

FILLING:

1 (8-ounce) package cream
  cheese, softened
1 egg
½ teaspoon baking powder

1 tablespoon sugar
1 (12-ounce) jar raspberry
  preserves
Powdered sugar

Combine cream cheese, egg, baking powder, and sugar thoroughly. Swirl (use back of spoon to make trenches) cream cheese mixture and raspberry preserves through chocolate batter before baking. Bake 50–60 minutes in oven preheated to 350° until brownie pulls away from edges of pan. Cool completely. Dust with powdered sugar and cut into squares.

Raspberry Enchantment House Tour Cookbook (New Mexico)

MUSEUM OF NEW MEXICO MEDIA CENTER

Santa Fe is the capital of New Mexico. Having been established in the early 1600s while it was still under Spanish rule, Santa Fe holds the distinction of being the seat of government longer than any other capital in the United States. The Palace of the Governors in Santa Fe, built by the Spanish in 1610, is the oldest public building in the country. This ancient adobe palace, one of the most unique structures in the United States, is a National Historic Landmark and now houses the Museum of New Mexico.

Biscochitos

This is New Mexico's traditional cookie.

6 cups all-purpose flour
3 teaspoons baking powder
¼ teaspoon salt
1 pound (2 cups) lard
1½ cups sugar

2 teaspoons anise seeds
2 eggs
¼ cup brandy
¼ cup sugar
1 tablespoon cinnamon

Sift flour with baking powder and salt. Cream lard with sugar and anise seeds until fluffy. Beat in eggs one at a time. Mix in flour and brandy until well blended. Turn dough out on floured board and pat or roll to ¼ or ½-inch thickness. Cut into shapes. (The fleur-de-lis is traditional.) Dust with mixture of sugar and cinnamon. Bake 10 minutes at 350° or until browned.

The Best from New Mexico Kitchens (New Mexico)

Orange Biscotti

The addition of orange juice and tequila to this classic Italian cookie makes this a perfect pastry to serve with after-dinner coffee or at teatime.

1 cup sugar
½ cup butter, at room
   temperature
2 eggs, lightly beaten
2 tablespoons tequila
2 tablespoons orange juice

1 teaspoon grated orange peel
2½ cups all-purpose flour
2 teaspoons baking powder
¼ teaspoon salt
⅓ cup slivered almonds

Mix sugar and butter together, then add eggs, tequila, orange juice, and orange peel; beat well. Stir in flour, baking powder, and salt. Then stir in the almonds. Place the mixture on a lightly floured pastry board and knead until the dough makes a ball—approximately 5 minutes. Divide dough into 2 halves and roll the halves into a rope about the length of a cookie sheet. Place each rope on an ungreased cooking sheet and bake in a 325° oven for 20–30 minutes or until golden brown. Remove from the baking sheet and let cool for 6–7 minutes. Slice diagonally to ½-inch pieces; lay the pieces flat on the cookie sheet and bake in a 325° oven for 5 minutes. Turn over and bake for 5 more minutes. Let cool to room temperature and store in a covered container. Makes approximately 3 dozen.

The Tequila Cook Book (New Mexico)

Clouds

A light, practically fat-free, meringue cookie. Clouds make excellent use of extra egg whites and are loved for their delicate texture and just the right amount of chocolate.

**4 egg whites, room
  temperature**
¼ teaspoon cream of tartar
1 cup sugar

Dash of salt
½ teaspoon vanilla extract
**1 (12-ounce) package chocolate
  chips**

Preheat oven to 325°. With an electric mixer, beat the egg whites and cream of tartar until stiff. Gradually add the sugar, salt, and vanilla extract. Fold in the chocolate chips. Drop dough by table-spoonfuls onto brown paper bag which has been placed on a standard cookie sheet. Bake for 20 minutes. Turn oven off and keep cookies in the oven for another 20 minutes. Store in an airtight container. Makes 4 dozen "Clouds."

Inn on the Rio's Favorite Recipes (New Mexico)

Mexican Honey Dainties

⅓ cup cooking oil
**½ cup unsalted butter,
  softened**
⅓ cup sugar
1 tablespoon orange juice
1 teaspoon baking powder

½ teaspoon baking soda
1¾–2 cups all-purpose flour
¾ cup sugar
½ cup water
⅓ cup honey
⅓ cup finely chopped pecans

In mixer bowl, beat together cooking oil and butter until blended. Beat in the sugar. Add orange juice, baking powder, and baking soda. Mix well. Add enough of the flour, a little at a time, to make a medium-soft dough. Shape dough into 2-inch ovals and place on an ungreased baking sheet. Bake in preheated 350° oven for 20–25 minutes or until cookies are golden.

Meanwhile, in a saucepan, combine sugar, water, and honey. Boil gently uncovered for 5 minutes. Cool. Dip face of cookies into warm syrup and then press into chopped nuts. Let dry. Store in covered container or freeze for later use. Yields 2½–3 dozen.

Fiesta Mexicana (New Mexico)

Chocolate Pecan Toffee

1 cup (2 sticks) butter
1⅓ cups granulated sugar
3 tablespoons water
1 tablespoon corn syrup
1 cup chopped pecans
8 ounces semisweet or
    bittersweet chocolate

Butter a 9x13-inch pan and set aside. Melt the butter in a heavy saucepan. Add sugar, water, and corn syrup; place a candy thermometer in the pan. Cook at a low boil, stirring occasionally. When the mixture reaches 300°, quickly add the pecans. Swirl the pan vigorously, and pour the mixture into the buttered pan. Spread the candy out when cool; invert onto wax paper and wipe away any excess butter from the bottom side.

Melt the chocolate over hot water. Spread on the smooth bottom side of toffee and let harden. Break candy into pieces and refrigerate. Can also be made with coarsely chopped macadamia nuts. Yields 2 pounds.

The Very Special Raspberry Cookbook (New Mexico)

Best in the World Peanut Brittle

Oh! So good!

1 cup white corn syrup
2 cups white sugar
½ cup water
2 cups raw peanuts
2 teaspoons margarine
2 teaspoons vanilla
2 teaspoons baking soda
½ teaspoon salt

Place syrup, sugar, and water in iron skillet and cook to soft-ball stage (230°). Add raw peanuts. Stir and cook these ingredients on medium-high to the crack stage (301°–302°), stirring constantly. Turn off heat. Stir in margarine, vanilla, baking soda, and salt until well blended. This will want to foam over. Keep stirring fast until well blended. Pour into large platter that is well buttered. As soon as possible, start pulling over the edges of platter. Work on Formica or tile counter. You can't pull this out thin until it reaches the right temperature. (If it's too hot, it will not be clear, so just keep working with it.) You can make it as thin as you like, and break it into pieces.

Peanut Palate Pleasers from Portales (New Mexico)

PIES and OTHER DESSERTS

After many years of Spain and then Mexico's rule, some Texans demanded independence—and the Texas Revolution began, leading to the Battle of the Alamo. There on March 6, 1836, a small band of Texans held out for 13 days before falling to Mexico's forces. Among the casualties were non-Texans, Davy Crockett and Jim Bowie. That defeat inspired others to "Remember the Alamo" and win Texas independence.

Fresh Strawberry Pie

3 pints fresh strawberries
1 cup sugar
½ cup boiling water
3 tablespoons cornstarch

3–4 drops red food coloring
1 (9-inch) pie shell, baked
1 pint whipping cream, whipped

Mash enough strawberries to make 1 cup. Combine mashed strawberries with sugar and cornstarch and add ½ cup boiling water. Cook over medium heat, stirring constantly, until thick. Add food coloring. Place glaze in refrigerator to cool. Wash remaining berries, slice to desired pieces, and place in baked pie shell. When ready to serve, pour cooled glaze over sliced berries and top with whipped cream.

Feast of Goodness (Texas II)

Praline Apple Pie

2½ cups sliced peeled pie
   apples
⅓ cup sugar
¼ teaspoon nutmeg
¼ teaspoon cinnamon
Unbaked 9-inch pie shell

2 tablespoons honey
½ cup brown sugar, packed
2 tablespoons butter
1 egg, beaten
½ cup chopped pecans

Combine apples, sugar, and spices. Place apple mixture in unbaked pie shell. Bake at 400° for 15 minutes. Mix honey, brown sugar, and butter in a saucepan. Bring to a boil. Add egg and nuts. Remove the pie from the oven and pour honey mixture over the top. Return the pie to the oven for 10 minutes at 400°, then reduce the heat to 325°. Bake 25–30 minutes until set and apples soft. Serve warm.

The Blue Denim Gourmet (Texas)

Skillet Apple Pie à la Mode

This is a delicious "quicky" when you're in a hurry. The Butter Rum Sauce stores well.

PIE:

1 (9-inch) apple pie (from a bakery, frozen and baked or, if you feel ambitious, made from scratch)

Vanilla ice cream

BUTTER RUM SAUCE:

1 teaspoon water

2 tablespoons unsalted butter, divided

2 tablespoons sugar

2 tablespoons Karo dark corn syrup

2 tablespoons Karo light corn syrup

1 teaspoon Myer's rum

½ teaspoon rum extract

1 teaspoon vanilla extract

In a saucepan, combine water, 1 tablespoon butter, and sugar. Bring to a boil. Add syrups to pan, bring to a boil again, and lower to a simmer. Simmer 10 minutes. Add rum, rum extract, vanilla extract, and remaining tablespoon of butter and turn off heat. Let cool for 1 hour. Stir again.

ASSEMBLY:

Preheat oven to 350°. Place heavy 10-inch skillet in oven and heat. Carefully remove pie from baking pan and place in hot skillet. Pour ½ cup Butter Rum Sauce over and around pie and place in oven. Remove when heated through and sauce is bubbling. Cut pie into wedges; place on plates with scoop of ice cream on top.

Contributed by Manuel's, Phoenix
Arizona Chefs: Dine-In Dine-Out Cookbook (Arizona)

Dutch Peach Pie

A Stonewall, Texas, "Peach Jamboree" recipe.

1 (9-inch) unbaked pastry shell
10–12 ripe peaches
1 egg, slightly beaten
1 cup sour cream
¾ cup sugar

¼ teaspoon salt
2 tablespoons flour
½ teaspoon cinnamon
½ teaspoon nutmeg

Preheat oven to 350°. Peel peaches, slice, and arrange in pastry shell. Mix egg with sour cream, sugar, salt, flour, cinnamon, and nutmeg. Pour over peaches and bake for 20 minutes. Mix Topping and sprinkle over pie; continue to bake 12–15 minutes.

TOPPING:
¼ cup brown sugar
3 tablespoons flour

2 tablespoons soft butter
½ cup chopped nuts

A Texas Hill Country Cookbook (Texas)

Margarita Pie

1 (8-ounce) package cream
 cheese, softened
2 packages Holland House
 Margarita Mix

½–¾ cup sugar
1 (8-ounce) carton Cool Whip
1 graham cracker crust

Cream the cream cheese until fluffy. Add margarita mix and sugar and beat until smooth. Add Cool Whip and mix. Freeze in graham cracker crust until ready to serve.

More of the Four Ingredient Cookbook (Texas II)

Kay's Lime Pie

1 envelope unflavored gelatin	Few drops green food coloring
½ cup sugar	4 egg whites
¼ teaspoon salt	½ cup sugar
4 egg yolks	1 cup heavy cream, whipped
½ cup fresh lime juice	1 (9-inch) pie shell, pastry or
¼ cup water	crumb
1 teaspoon grated lime peel	

1. Thoroughly mix gelatin, sugar, and salt in saucepan.
2. Beat together egg yolks, lime juice, and water and stir into gelatin mixture. Cook over medium heat, stirring constantly until mixture comes to a boil.
3. Remove from heat and stir in grated peel. Add food coloring sparingly to give a pale green color.
4. Chill, stirring occasionally, until mixture mounds slightly when dropped from a spoon.
5. Beat egg whites until soft peaks form; gradually add ½ cup sugar, beating to stiff peaks. Fold gelatin mixture into egg whites. Fold in whipped cream and pile into crust.
6. Chill until firm. Spread with additional whipped cream and edge with grated lime peel. Garnish with wedges of lime.

Morning, Noon and Night Cookbook (Texas)

KEITH ODOM

Pie Town, New Mexico—The first merchant in town had such a demand for homemade pies, and they were of such quality that they became justly famous. Local folks as well as travelers began to refer to the community as "Pie Town." And that's how it got its name. Pie Town is located along U.S. Route 60, approximately 2.5 hours' drive from Albuquerque and 5.5 hours' drive from Phoenix.

Pecan Pie

3 eggs
1 cup sugar
½ teaspoon salt
2 tablespoons melted butter
½ cup dark corn syrup

½ cup whipping cream
1 teaspoon vanilla
¼ cup brandy
1 cup chopped pecans
1 (9-inch) pie crust

In a bowl, beat the eggs, sugar, salt, melted butter, corn syrup, and whipping cream. When well blended, stir in vanilla, brandy, and pecans. Pour into pie crust and bake in preheated 375° oven for 40–50 minutes, until set. Top with whipped cream, if desired.

Bravo, Chef! (Texas)

Buttermilk Pecan Pie

1½ cups sugar
1 tablespoon flour
4 tablespoons unmelted
  margarine
4 eggs

½ cup buttermilk
1 teaspoon vanilla
1 cup chopped pecans
1 (9-inch) unbaked pie shell

Combine sugar, flour, and margarine in a bowl. Mix with electric mixer on low speed. Add eggs, 1 at a time, mixing well. Add buttermilk and vanilla. Mix well. Stir in pecans. Pour into pie shell. Bake in preheated 325° oven about 1 hour, until light brown and middle is set.

The Authorized Texas Ranger Cookbook (Texas II)

Las Cruces Pecan Pie

1 (9-inch) pie shell, frozen	1 teaspoon vanilla extract
3 eggs, beaten	3 tablespoons melted butter
1 cup sugar	(cooled)
1 cup dark karo syrup	1½ cups pecans

Slightly thaw pie shell. Combine eggs and sugar, mixing together slightly. Add karo syrup, vanilla, and melted butter to egg mixture. Fold into pie shell. Gently top with pecans. Preheat oven to 350°. Place pie pan on cookie sheet and bake at 350° for 10 minutes. Reduce heat to 325° and bake for 40–45 minutes. Cool and serve.

Fiery Appetizers (New Mexico)

Chocolate-Piñon Pie

8 ounces piñons (pine nuts)	1 cup plus 1 tablespoon sugar
7 ounces unsweetened	4 large egg yolks
chocolate squares	Zest of 1 orange
1 cup unsalted butter,	4 large egg whites
softened	

Preheat oven to 300°. Process piñons and chocolate in a food processor until ground. Beat butter at medium speed with an electric mixer until creamed; add sugar, and beat until sugar dissolves. Add egg yolks to butter mixture; add zest and piñon mixture, and beat until blended. Beat egg whites at high speed until stiff peaks form. Fold egg whites, one-third at a time, into butter mixture. Pour batter into a buttered, floured 8-inch round cake pan lined with parchment paper. Bake for 45 minutes or until pie shrinks away from edges of pan. Cool and slice with a wet knife. Makes 10 servings.

Savoring the Southwest Again (New Mexico)

Blue Ribbon Cafe's Old-Fashioned Chocolate Cream Pie

CRUST:

1 cup all-purpose flour
½ teaspoon salt

⅓ cup shortening
2 tablespoons ice water

In bowl, combine flour and salt. Cut in shortening until mixture is consistency of coarse meal. Add ice water, 1 tablespoon at a time, until mixture stays together when formed into a ball. Roll out on floured board until about ⅛ inch thick. Place in 9-inch pie pan and crimp around edges. Prick crust several times with fork. Bake in 350° oven for 10–12 minutes. Set aside to cool.

FILLING:

2 cups evaporated milk
½ cup water
2¼ cups sugar, divided
3 tablespoons flour
½ teaspoon salt

4 tablespoons cocoa
4 egg yolks, beaten
1 tablespoon butter
1 teaspoon vanilla
4 egg whites

In medium saucepan, combine milk and water. Bring to scalding (not boiling) point. In another bowl, combine 1½ cups sugar, flour, salt, and cocoa. Add egg yolks and mix into a thick batter. Add batter to milk-water mixture, stirring constantly with whisk. Cook over medium heat until thickened. Remove from heat and add butter and vanilla, stirring well to blend. Pour into baked pie shell and allow to cool.

Prepare meringue by beating egg whites at high speed in bowl until stiff. Add remaining ¾ cup sugar and beat until peaks form. Top pie with meringue. Bake in 350° oven for 6–8 minutes, until top is golden brown. Cool and serve.

Arizona's Historic Restaurants and their Recipes (Arizona)

Cookie Pie

This scrumptious pie is a simple yet delightfully different treat. The entire family will love it.

1 cup (2 sticks) unsalted butter, softened	1 teaspoon baking soda
3 cups dark brown sugar	1 cup semisweet chocolate chips
2 extra large eggs	⅔ cup white chocolate chips
1½ teaspoons vanilla extract	½ cup pecan pieces
5 cups all-purpose flour	½ cup coarsely chopped walnuts

Preheat oven to 275°.

Using an electric mixer set at medium speed, in a large bowl, cream butter and sugar until fluffy, then add eggs and vanilla. Slowly add flour and baking soda and mix well. Fold in chocolate chips.

Butter and flour a 10-inch springform pan. Pour nuts into the bottom of the pan and press cookie dough over the nuts. Bake at 275° for approximately 1 hour or until a toothpick inserted in the center comes out clean. Serves 12.

Approximate values per serving: Cal 661; Fat 30g; Chol 77mg; Carbo 94g; Sod 124mg; Cal from Fat 41%.

By Request (Arizona)

Soda Cracker Pie

3 egg whites	½ teaspoon baking powder
1 cup sugar	14 soda crackers, crumbled
1 teaspoon vanilla	1 cup chopped nuts

Beat egg whites until foamy. Gradually add sugar, beating until stiff. Add vanilla. Fold in remaining ingredients. Pour into well-buttered 9-inch pie pan. Bake at 375° for 30 minutes. Cool and top with whipped cream. Refrigerate for 4–5 hours.

Cooking with Cops (Arizona)

Lemon Tarts

1 cup all-purpose flour
½ cup sugar
Pinch of salt
1 egg yolk

½ cup butter or margarine,
   softened
½ teaspoon vanilla

Sift flour, sugar, and salt into a mixing bowl. Add remaining ingredients and mix with hands until dough is like pie dough and sticks together. After mixing, turn out on lightly floured surface. Make walnut-size dough balls and press into mini-muffin pan. Bake at 300° for 15 minutes (no longer). Fill shells with Lemon Filling.

LEMON FILLING:

2 eggs
2 egg yolks
½ cup butter or margarine
1 cup sugar

6 tablespoons lemon juice
   (2 lemons)
Zest from 2 lemons

Put whole eggs and egg yolks in the top of a double boiler. Beat gently until eggs are mixed well. Add remaining ingredients and stir with a wooden spoon. Cook over gently boiling water until it reaches the consistency of mayonnaise. Fill shells just before serving and top with whipped cream or Cool Whip.

Note: Filling can be stored in a covered jar and refrigerated up to 2 weeks.

Hospice Hospitality (Arizona)

WIKIPEDIA.ORG

Los Alamos, New Mexico, has the distinction of being the site of the world's first atomic bomb explosion (1945). Founded in 1963, the Bradbury Science Museum there allows visitors to look into the history of nuclear energy. Upon declassification, artifacts and documents from the World War II Manhattan Project were displayed. Other exhibits include full-size models of the Little Boy and Fat Man atomic bombs.

Mexican Pecan-Toffee Tartlets in Chocolate Chip Cookie Crust

Who doesn't like chocolate chip cookies? When combined with pecan-stuffed coffee-toffee ice cream, the result is a rich blend of flavors that no dessert lover can resist.

24 small or 12 medium-size
  chocolate chip cookies
4 tablespoons sweet (unsalted)
  butter, melted
1 pint coffee ice cream
1 (4-ounce) toffee candy bar
½ cup very coarsely chopped
  pecan halves

½ pint heavy whipping cream
3 tablespoons vanilla-scented
  sugar (made by storing sugar
  with a broken piece of vanilla
  bean)
½ cup thick, rich chocolate
  fudge sauce

Using a food processor, blender, or a rolling pin, crush the cookies until finely crumbled. Meanwhile, melt the butter. Butter the insides of 6 small soufflé cups, or any other suitable small serving dishes. Combine remaining butter with the cookie crumbs in a bowl. Divide the mixture evenly among the 6 cups, and then press it firmly into them. Freeze.

Soften the ice cream by scooping it into a mixing bowl and letting it sit a few minutes, then process in a food processor or mixer. Crush the toffee bar in the processor or with a rolling pin, until it is in chunks about ½ inch across, not too fine. Add to the ice cream along with ⅓ cup of the pecans. Process or mix until just combined so as not to overly crush the candy and the nuts. Divide among the cookie crusts, leaving the surface of each somewhat uneven and interesting looking as you would frosting. Whip the cream with the vanilla sugar.

Divide the chocolate fudge sauce among each of the tarts, drizzling it in a swirl in the center of each, allowing some of the ice cream filling around the edges to show. Top each with a dollop of the whipped cream. If you have too much, place the extra in dollops on a cookie sheet covered with wax paper and freeze for later garnishing for drinks or desserts. Sprinkle reserved pecan pieces over the top of the cream. Freeze until serving time.

Fiestas for Four Seasons (New Mexico)

Pistol Packin' Mama
Pecan Cups

1 (3-ounce) package cream
  cheese, softened
½ cup butter or margarine,
  softened
1 cup flour
2 eggs

1 cup brown sugar
2 tablespoons butter or margarine,
  softened
1 teaspoon vanilla
Dash of salt
1 cup broken pecans

Mix cream cheese and butter. Blend into flour with fork. Chill 1 hour or longer. Shape into 1-inch balls. Press in tiny muffin tins (12 to a tin). Combine eggs, brown sugar, butter, vanilla, and salt. Beat until smooth. Divide pecans in half. Use ½ to sprinkle on bottom of each cup. Add filling, and top with remaining pecans. Bake at 325° for 25 minutes. Remove quickly before filling hardens. Makes 24.

Cowboy Cookin' (Arizona)

KEITH ODOM

The town of Lincoln, New Mexico, is filled with memories of Billy the Kid. Though his legend bears only remote resemblance to the Billy the Kid of history, the outlaw of sunny disposition and deadly trigger finger still rides boldly across America's mental landscape. In 1881 Sheriff Pat Garrett shot Billy the Kid (alias Henry McCarty, alias Kid Antrim, alias William H. Bonney) near Ft. Sumner. La Mesilla, the one-time Mexican border town that witnessed the signing of the Gadsden Purchase in 1853, is also the site of the trial and murder conviction of Billy the Kid in 1881. His jail cell is in the nearby Gadsden Museum.

Piñon Nut Torte

CRUST:*

1¼ cups all-purpose flour
1½ teaspoons sugar
¼ teaspoon salt
1 tablespoon grated orange
  peel

½ cup chilled butter-flavored
  solid vegetable shortening,
  cut into small pieces
2 tablespoons ice water

In a food processor, combine the flour, sugar, salt, and grated orange peel. Turning the food processor on and off, cut in the vegetable shortening until coarsely blended. Add enough ice water to form moist clumps. Mold the dough into a ball, then flatten it into a disk. Wrap it in plastic wrap and refrigerate for one hour.

Bring the dough to room temperature and roll it out on a lightly floured surface to a size that will cover the torte pan (about 12 inches). Press the dough into the pan with your fingers and trim the edges. Place the Crust in the freezer for 15 minutes. Pour in the Filling and bake.

*A frozen pie crust works well if you need to save time.

FILLING:

1 cup light corn syrup
3 whole eggs, lightly beaten
⅔ cup granulated sugar

2 tablespoons butter, melted
1 teaspoon vanilla
2 cups piñon nuts, roasted**

Preheat the oven to 350°. Combine the corn syrup, eggs, sugar, melted butter, and vanilla in a medium-size bowl. Whisk until the mixture is well blended, then fold in the piñon nuts. Pour the Filling into the torte shell and bake for about one hour.

Let it cool completely. Cut into wedges. Serve with vanilla ice cream with candied orange strips (available at most candy stores) and Spanish Coffee. Serves 6–8.

**To roast Piñon nuts, preheat the oven to 400°. Spread the nuts in a single layer on a baking sheet and roast for 7–12 minutes, or until they are a rich golden brown. The nuts burn easily, so keep an eye on them and shake the pan occasionally to avoid scorching.

Christmas Celebration: Santa Fe Traditions (New Mexico)

Bread Pudding
with Whiskey Sauce

1 (1-pound) loaf French bread	1 cup raisins
1 quart milk	1 cup peeled, chopped, fresh
3 eggs	apple
2 cups sugar	3 tablespoons melted margarine
2 tablespoons vanilla	

Preheat oven to 350°. Break bread into chunks and soak in milk for about 15 minutes. Crush with hands until well mixed. Combine and beat well eggs, sugar, vanilla, and fruit. Pour these ingredients over the soaked bread and stir them lightly with a fork until well blended. Pour the margarine into 2 (1-quart) casseroles. Pour the bread pudding into the 2 casseroles. Bake at 350° for 1 hour. Allow to cool. Serve with Whiskey Sauce.

WHISKEY SAUCE:

1 stick margarine or butter	1 egg, beaten
1 cup sugar	Whiskey to taste
2 tablespoons water	

Put margarine, sugar, and water in top of double boiler and cook until sugar is dissolved. Add egg and whip quickly so that egg does not curdle. Cook for 1 minute to ensure egg is well done, stirring constantly. Cool. Add whiskey. The pudding and sauce taste best at room temperature. Serves 10–12.

From Generation to Generation (Texas II)

WIKIPEDIA.ORG

The prime-time soap, *Dallas*, which ran from 1978 to 1991, was set in Texas but primarily filmed in California. Southfork, the Ewing family mansion, is a real Texas home near Dallas, and many exterior shots were filmed there. Some of the filming was done in Dallas skyscrapers. Opening credits unscrolled over Texas fields, cattle, and oil wells.

Cherry Pudding

1 cup sugar
1 tablespoon real butter
1 egg, beaten
1 cup all-purpose flour
½ cup chopped pecans

½ teaspoon baking soda
1 cup canned pitted sour cherries, drained
Heavy cream, whipped

Heat oven to 350°; cream sugar and butter. Add egg and mix until well blended. Blend 1 tablespoon flour into nuts; set aside. Mix remaining flour and baking soda. Add cherries alternately with flour mixture to batter. Stir in nuts. Pour pudding into a well-greased, 9- or 10-inch tube cake pan. Bake for 45 minutes. Serve with whipped cream. Serves 8–10.

The Dallas Pecan Cookbook (Texas)

Log Cabin Pudding

When sugar was limited during the war, this was our dessert.

1 cup milk
1 tablespoon Knox gelatine
¼ cup cold water
1 cup Log Cabin syrup

1 cup finely chopped pecans
1½ cups whipped cream
Vanilla wafers (about 25)

Bring the milk to a boil. Soak the gelatine in cold water and add to milk; stir until dissolved. Add Log Cabin syrup; set it aside to partly congeal. Add pecans and stiffly whipped cream. Butter a 9x13-inch pan. Line it with crushed vanilla wafers. Pour in the pudding and top with crushed wafers. Refrigerate for several hours.

Red River's Cookin' (New Mexico)

Ricotta Almond Flan

1½ cups slivered almonds
1 (15-ounce) carton ricotta
   cheese
¾ cup sugar
6 large eggs, beaten

Grated zest of 2 large oranges
¼ cup dark rum
1 teaspoon vanilla extract
½ teaspoon nutmeg

Spread almonds on a baking sheet and bake at 300° until lightly browned, about 10 minutes. Remove from oven and cool. Increase oven temperature to 325°.

Grind almonds fine in a food processor, then blend in ricotta, sugar, eggs, orange zest, rum, vanilla, and nutmeg. Butter a deep pie dish, pour in ricotta mixture, and bake for 30–35 minutes or until center of flan is set. Cool before cutting into wedges. Serves 10.

The Mozzarella Company, Dallas.
Dallas Cuisine (Texas II)

Strawberry Almond Crème

To make this great dip for fluffy pieces of angel food cake nonfat, use nonfat sour cream and yogurt.

½ cup puréed strawberries
   (process 12–15 small
   berries in a blender or food
   processor)

½ cup sour cream
½ cup plain yogurt
¼ teaspoon almond extract
2 tablespoons confectioners' sugar

In a small bowl, fold strawberries into sour cream. Fold in yogurt. Gently stir in almond extract and sugar. Chill in the freezer for 20 minutes (set a timer!) then move to the refrigerator for 1 hour. Serve with cake or mixed berries. Makes 1½ cups.

Chips, Dips, & Salsas (Arizona)

Jay's Glory

1½ cups crumbled almond
  macaroons
½ cup sugar

½ cup Cognac or Tia Maria
1 pint heavy cream, stiffly
  whipped

Mix first 3 ingredients and fold in whipped cream. Place in dessert or custard cups and put in freezer for at least 3 hours. Mixture stiffens but will not freeze. Add a drop or two of food coloring for whatever season or reason. Serves 8.

Hospitality (Texas)

Chocolate Velvet Mousse Cake

This recipe is from a special customer who loves the dessert, but prefers that someone else make it.

1 pound semisweet chocolate
2 whole eggs
4 egg yolks
2 cups heavy cream

6 tablespoons confectioners'
  sugar
1 cup egg white
¼ cup grated white chocolate

Melt semisweet chocolate in double boiler over simmering water. Cool slightly. Add whole eggs and yolks and mix thoroughly. Whip cream with sugar until stiff. Whip egg whites to medium-stiff peaks. Gently fold whipped cream and egg whites alternately into melted chocolate mixture.

CRUST:

1 (9-ounce) box chocolate
  wafers

1½ cup butter, melted

Crush chocolate wafers in food processor. Add melted butter and combine. Press mixture into bottom of a 10-inch springform pan. Top with chocolate mousse. Refrigerate for 2 hours. Top with grated white chocolate. Serves 10–12.

Variation: Egg substitute can be used in place of whole eggs, 4 cups Cool Whip instead of heavy cream, and ½ the amount of white chocolate and butter.

Cafe Matthew, Fort Worth
Fort Worth is Cooking! (Texas II)

Mexican Kahlúa Soufflé

1 tablespoon cornstarch
1 cup evaporated milk
3 eggs, separated
5 tablespoons sugar, divided

1 tablespoon unflavored gelatin
½ cup Kahlúa
¼ teaspoon vanilla
Pinch of salt

Mix cornstarch with a little water and add to milk. Cook over low heat, stirring constantly, until thickened. Beat egg yolks lightly with 4 tablespoons sugar. Soften gelatin in ¼ cup water. Add yolks and gelatin to milk and cook for 5 minutes, stirring constantly. Allow to cool slightly and add Kahlúa and vanilla. Add salt and remaining 1 tablespoon sugar to egg whites, and beat until standing in peaks. Fold into the yolk mixture, pour into soufflé dish, and chill until set. Serves 6.

San Antonio Cookbook II (Texas)

White Magic Mousse

¼ cup sugar
1 envelope unflavored gelatin
1¼ cups milk
4 ounces white chocolate, chopped
4 egg yolks, beaten

¼ cup white crème de cacao
4 egg whites
2 tablespoons sugar
½ cup whipping cream, whipped
White chocolate curls
Fresh strawberries

In saucepan, combine ¼ cup sugar and gelatin. Stir in milk; add white chocolate. Cook and stir over low heat until chocolate melts. Gradually stir half of mixture into egg yolks; return to saucepan. Cook and stir 1–2 minutes or until mixture thickens slightly; do not boil. Remove from heat; stir in white crème de cacao. Chill gelatin mixture until partially set, stirring occasionally.

Beat egg whites until soft peaks form; gradually add 2 tablespoons sugar, beating until stiff peaks form. Fold into white chocolate along with whipping cream. Attach a buttered foil collar to a buttered and sugared 1-quart soufflé dish. Turn mixture into soufflé dish; chill until firm. To serve, remove collar and garnish with white chocolate curls and strawberries. Serves 6–8.

The Dallas Symphony Cookbook (Texas)

Four-Layer Chocolate Dessert

2 cups vanilla wafers, crushed
½–1 cup chopped pecans
  (optional)
1 stick margarine, melted
1 (8-ounce) package cream
  cheese, softened
1 large carton Cool Whip,
  divided

1 cup powdered sugar
2 small packages chocolate
  instant pudding
3 cups milk
1 teaspoon vanilla
Shaved chocolate

Mix vanilla wafer crumbs, pecans, and margarine together. Line bottom of 9x13-inch glass dish and bake for 10 minutes at 350°. Mix cream cheese, one cup Cool Whip, and powdered sugar together; spread on cooled crust.

Mix chocolate instant pudding, milk, and vanilla until thick; spread over layer of cream cheese mixture. On top of chocolate pudding layer, spread balance of Cool Whip. On top of this, use chocolate shavings. Keep refrigerated. Makes approximately 15 servings.

Red River's Cookin' (New Mexico)

Death by Chocolate

A beautiful dessert, and rated off the chart by our testers.

1 (9-ounce) box Jell-O
  Chocolate Mousse Mix
1 teaspoon vanilla
¼ cup sugar
2 cups whipping cream,
  whipped

1 pan brownies (homemade or
  bakery purchased)
¼ cup Kahlúa liqueur
3 Skor candy bars, crushed

Prepare mousse only from box mix, and refrigerate. (Save the crumb mixture for another use.) Add vanilla and sugar to whipped cream. Soak brownies with Kahlúa. Assemble in a glass trifle or fruit bowl. Using ½ of each ingredient at a time, layer in the following order: brownies, mousse, whipped cream, candy bars. Repeat layers. Refrigerate. Yields 10–12 servings.

Homecoming (Texas II)

Floating Islands

A family member recalls being intrigued and charmed as a child by such an exotic name.

3 egg whites
3 cups milk
½ cup sugar
⅛ teaspoon salt

2 tablespoons cornstarch
4 ounces grated chocolate
3 egg yolks, beaten well
1 teaspoon vanilla

Beat egg whites to a froth. Drop by the teaspoonful in boiling sweet milk. When done, place on a plate. Combine sugar, salt, and cornstarch in top of double boiler. Add milk, stir in chocolate, and boil 8–10 minutes. Remove from fire and stir, adding beaten egg yolks. Place again over fire and stir, but do not let boil. Add vanilla. Put in shallow dish and slip the islands on the cream.

Perfectly Splendid (Texas II)

The Jerome Grille's
Deep-Fried Ice Cream

½ pound cornflakes
1½ quarts French vanilla
  soft-serve ice cream
4 cups vegetable oil
6 pre-formed tortilla bowls
  (optional, available in specialty
  stores)

⅔ cup honey
1 tablespoon ground cinnamon
6 tablespoons sugar
1 cup whipped cream
6 sweet, fresh cherries, for
  garnish

Crush cornflakes with rolling pin or mash flakes into small pieces in large bowl. Use ice cream scoop and hand to form ice cream into 6 round balls. Roll ice cream balls in crushed flakes, covering completely. Freeze overnight or until hard.

In 2-quart pan, heat oil to boiling. Drop frozen ice cream balls, one at a time, into oil for 5 seconds only. Remove with slotted spoon or tongs. Place each ball in a tortilla bowl or ice cream sundae dish. Pour an equal amount of honey over each ice cream ball. Mix cinnamon and sugar together and sprinkle over each serving. Top each serving with dollop of whipped cream and a cherry. Serves 6.

Arizona's Historic Restaurants and their Recipes (Arizona)

Butter Pecan Ice Cream

A food authority once claimed that Texans consume almost all the butter pecan ice cream made in the country. If you try this recipe, you'll understand why.

¼ cup unsalted butter
1 cup chopped pecans
5 egg yolks
1 pint half-and-half

1 cup whipping cream
¾ cup sugar
1 tablespoon vanilla

Melt the butter in a small skillet over medium heat. Add the pecans, and cook until the nuts are coated with the butter and lightly crisped. Strain the excess butter into the top of a double boiler. Add the egg yolks, half-and-half, whipping cream, sugar, and vanilla. Set the pan over its water bath. Warm the custard mixture over medium-low heat, whisking until the mixture is well blended. Continue heating, frequently stirring up from the bottom, until the mixture thickens. (Make sure it does not come to a boil; the egg yolks should poach, not scramble.) This process takes about 15 minutes. Remove the pan from the heat and pour the custard through a strainer into a bowl. Chill it thoroughly.

Transfer the custard to an ice cream maker, and process it according to the manufacturer's directions. After churning, stir in the pecans, and place the ice cream in the freezer until serving time.

This ice cream is best eaten within several days. Makes about 1 quart.

Texas Home Cooking (Texas II)

Ruggles' Chocolate Parfait

Ruggles Grill, Houston, chef/owner Bruce Molzan got inspiration for this lay-ered, chocolate-on-chocolate dessert on a trip to Paris, where he worked in the kitchens of some of its most celebrated restaurants. "This is my absolute favorite chocolate dessert," says the CIA honors graduate.

CHOCOLATE CAKE:

1 cup cocoa	1 cup butter
2¾ cups all-purpose flour	2½ cups granulated sugar
2 teaspoons baking soda	4 eggs
½ teaspoon salt	1½ teaspoons vanilla
½ teaspoon baking powder	2 cups water

Preheat oven to 350°. In a mixing bowl, sift together the cocoa, flour, baking soda, salt, and baking powder. In a separate bowl, using an electric mixer, cream the butter with the sugar, eggs, and vanilla. Combine the 2 mixtures alternately in a 3rd bowl, adding the water. Pour into a greased jellyroll pan and bake for 25–30 minutes. Cool and reserve.

MOUSSE MIXTURE:

1 pound semisweet chocolate, coarsely chopped	2 cups heavy cream, lightly whipped
4 ounces unsalted butter	

Melt the chopped semisweet chocolate with the butter over medi-um-low heat. Fold in the lightly whipped cream; reserve.

1½ ounces Chambord	Almond Brittle (recipe follows)
1½ ounces simple syrup (equal parts sugar and water)	Raspberry, mango, and chocolate sauce (optional) garnish
1 pint raspberries	
2 ounces shaved white chocolate	
2 ounces shaved semisweet chocolate	

Take four circular tin molds, 2 inches deep and 3 inches in diame-ter (they are kind of like deep biscuit cutters), and line with parch-ment paper. (Bruce Molzan found these molds in Paris, but says that you can also use PVC piping material.)

Place a layer of chocolate cake at bottom of each mold. Drizzle each layer of cake with Chambord and some of the simple syrup. Place raspberries on top of cake. Divide the chocolate mousse evenly on top of each mold and pack down. Chop up leftover

(continued)

(Ruggles' Chocolate Parfait continued)

chocolate cake into cubes and sprinkle on top of chocolate mixture. Sprinkle white and semisweet chocolate shavings over each dessert and refrigerator for 2 hours. Unmold and top with chopped Almond Brittle. Serve at room temperature. Serves 4.

ALMOND BRITTLE:

1 cup granulated sugar	**½ cup chopped almonds**

Over medium heat, cook sugar until brown but not burned. Add almonds and continue cooking about 5 minutes more. Pour mixture into buttered sheet pan. Let cool and chop into small pieces.

Top Chefs in Texas (Texas II)

Tortilla Apple Strudel

2 quarts cooking apples, pared and cut fine	**2 teaspoons cinnamon**
4 ounces chopped nuts	**1 package large flour tortillas**
1 cup raisins	**½ cup butter, melted**
¾ cup sugar	**½ cup crushed cornflakes**

Mix apples, nuts, and raisins. Stir in sugar mixed with cinnamon. Place tortilla on flat surface and spread with melted butter, using brush. Sprinkle some crushed cornflakes lightly over buttered tortilla and then spread with some of apple mixture.

Fold ⅓ of tortilla over mixture, brush with butter; fold both sides of tortilla to center, brush with melted butter and then roll. Brush entire outside with melted butter. Repeat for each tortilla. Place rolled tortillas on buttered baking pan and bake at 350° until brown and crisp. They can be frozen after baking.

Fruits of the Desert Cookbook (Arizona)

Raspberry Pizza

CRUST:

1 cup all-purpose flour   ½ cup powdered sugar
1 stick butter or margarine,
    softened

Blend and knead into dough. Spread on pizza pan and bake 10 minutes at 350°.

FILLING:

1 (8-ounce) package cream   1 teaspoon vanilla
    cheese, softened   ⅓ cup lemon juice
1 can sweetened condensed milk   1 pint fresh raspberries

Combine cream cheese, milk, vanilla, and lemon juice. Spread over cooled Crust. Top with raspberries and cover with Raspberry Glaze.

RASPBERRY GLAZE:

1 cup raspberries   1 cup water
1 cup sugar, divided   2½ tablespoons cornstarch

In a saucepan, combine raspberries, ¾ cup sugar, and water. Cook until berries are soft. Add ¼ cup sugar mixed with cornstarch. Cook until thick and glazed.

Contributed by The Honorable Joe Skeen, congressman from New Mexico.
The Very Special Raspberry Cookbook (New Mexico)

Gail Borden, a Texas surveyor and patriot, discovered that milk could be condensed by evaporation, and patented condensed milk in 1856. The product was initially meant to combat food poisoning and other illnesses related to lack of refrigeration and preservation techniques of milk. Eagle Brand Sweetened Condensed Milk was credited with significantly lowering the infant mortality rate in North America at that time. In 1931, a Borden Kitchens' promotion offered homemakers $25 for their original recipes. The rules called for "recipes in which Eagle Brand Sweetened Condensed Milk makes cooking quicker, easier, and surer." Over 80,000 recipes were submitted. Quick and easy foolproof recipes have been a key benefit of Eagle Brand® through the decades.

Jeannine's Fruit Pizza

Doctors, like school teachers, are recipients of cherished gifts and sayings from children. One of my favorite patients, Susie, age five, gave me a coffee mug with the picture of a cow grazing in the field. The inscription said "Someone Outstanding in the Field." As she handed it to me she said, "Here, Dr. Hill, to someone standing out in the field."

1 box yellow cake mix
¼ cup water
¼ cup margarine
¼ cup brown sugar
½ cup finely chopped pecans
1 (8-ounce) package cream
  cheese, room temperature

1 pint whipped cream
Sliced strawberries, blueberries,
  bananas
Chunked pineapple, sliced in
  half
1 small jar apricot preserves
1½ tablespoons water

Combine cake mix, water, margarine, brown sugar, and pecans. Press into 2 pizza pans which have been greased and floured. Bake at 375° until brown. Whip cream cheese and fold into whipped cream. This takes awhile. Spread over cake crust. Drain fruit several hours before using. Soak bananas in pineapple juice and drain. Arrange fruit on crust in pie wedge design or in rows. Combine apricot preserves with water. Glaze fruit. This is a beautiful dessert; looks like a stained glass window.

A Doctor's Prescription for Gourmet Cooking (Texas)

Ancho: Dried form of the green Poblano. Anchos vary in pungency from almost mild to medium, with smoky flavors reminiscent of coffee, prunes, and tobacco.

Cascabel Chile: A dried, dark reddish-brown chile with smooth, tough skin and a round shape about 1½ inches in diameter.

Chile Caribe: Crushed form of New Mexican dried red chile pods along with the seeds.

Chipotles: Dried and smoked form of a fresh jalapeño chile that is dusty brown in color. It is ridged, with wrinkly skin, measuring 2–2½ inches long and ¾–1 inch wide. The chipotle has a rich, smoky, tobacco-like flavor with a very pronounced heat.

Chipotles in Adobo: Canned chipotle chiles in a sauce of tomatoes, vinegar, garlic, onion, and spices.

De Arbol: A dried, bright red chile measuring 2-3 inches long and related to the cayenne chile. It is very hot with intense flavor.

Guajillo: Dried red chile pod similar in look to a dried New Mexican pod but smaller and smoother in texture. It has an earthy flavor.

Jalapeño: Fresh, small, thick-fleshed green chile approximately 2 inches long and 1 inch wide. It is the most popular hot green chile.

Moritals: Another type of dried, smoked jalapeño chile that is deep red to red-brown in color. It measures 1–2 inches long and about ⅜ inch wide.

New Mexico Green Chile: Fresh New Mexican variety of chile in its green form, measuring 4-6 inches long. There are a variety of types of New Mexican chiles distinguished by heat level from mild to hot. When New Mexican green chile is called for, it is assumed the chile has been roasted and peeled.

New Mexico Red Pods: The form of the green chile that has ripened to its red state and dried. The traditional method for storing these chiles is to tie them in a long bunch called a ristra.

New Mexico or Chimayó Chili Powder: Dried version of the New Mexican green chile that has been ripened (turned red) and ground into powder without additional ingredients.

Mulato: A type of poblano chile, dried, browner in color than the ancho chile and slightly smokier, but without the depth. It is one of the three chiles (ancho, mulato, pasilla) used in traditional Mole Poblano.

Pasilla: Also called Chile Negro. Pasilla, a dried chile, translated as "little raisin." It is brownish-black in color, wrinkled, long, and tapered.

Poblano: Fresh form of the ancho chile measuring 3-4 inches. This is a good chile for chile rellenos due to its size and the thickness of its flesh. A dark green color, the poblano is usually charred and peeled to enhance its full flavor.

Serrano: Fresh, small green chile, cylindrical in shape and measuring 1–2 inches long and ½–¾ inch in width. It is a crisp, hot chile used extensively in salsas.

LIST of CONTRIBUTORS

GWEN McKEE

Built approximately 1610, San Miguel Mission in Santa Fe, New Mexico, is claimed to be the oldest church in the United States. Though the church has been repaired and rebuilt numerous times over the years, its original adobe walls are still largely intact. Sunday mass is still held at this United States National Historic Landmark.

Listed below are the cookbooks that have contributed recipes to this book, along with copyright, author, publisher, city, and state.

The Aficiondado's Southwestern Cooking, by Ronald Johnson, Living Batch Press, Albuquerque, NM

Amarillo Junior League Cookbook ©1979 Amarillo Junior League, Amarillo, TX

Amazing Graces ©1993 The Texas Conference United Methodist Ministers' Spouses Assn., Houston, TX

Amistad Community Recipes, Amistad Community Members, Amistad, NM

The Arizona Celebrity Cookbook ©1997 by Eileen Bailey, Northland Publishing, Flagstaff, AZ

Arizona Chefs: Cooking at Home with 36 Arizona Chefs ©1999 by Elin Jeffords, Phoenix, AZ

Arizona Chefs: Dine-In Dine-Out Cookbook ©1997 by Elin Jeffords, Phoenix, AZ

Arizona Heart Institute Foundation Cookbook ©1993 Arizona Heart Institute Foundation, Phoenix, AZ

Arizona Highways Heritage Cookbook ©1988 Arizona Highways Magazine, Phoenix, AZ

Arizona Small Game and Fish Recipes ©1992 by Evelyn Bates, Golden West Publishers, Phoenix, AZ

Arizona's Historic Restaurants and their Recipes ©1995 by Karen Surina Mulford, John F. Blair, Publisher, Winston-Salem, NC

The Authorized Texas Ranger Cookbook ©1994 by Johnny and Cheryl Harris, Harris Farms Publishing, Hamilton, TX

Becky's Brunch & Breakfast Book ©1983 by Rebecca Walker, Austin, TX

The Best from New Mexico Kitchens, New Mexico Magazine, Santa Fe, NM

Best of Friends Two ©1987 by Dee Reiser and Teresa Dormer, Kingwood, TX

Beyond Loaves and Fishes, St. Paul's Episcopal Churchwomen, Artesia, NM

Billy the Kid Cook Book ©1998 by Lynn Nusom, Golden West Publishers, Phoenix, AZ

The Blue Denim Gourmet, Junior League of Odessa Publications, Odessa, TX

Boardin' in the Thicket ©1990 by Wanda A. Landrey, University of North Texas Press, Denton, TX

Bon Appétit de Las Sandias, by Aleen Freeman, Rico Rancho, NM

Bon Appétit: Healthy Recipes, by Diane Holloway, ph. D. Editor, Sun City West, AZ

Bravo, Chef! ©1983 The Dallas Opera Guild, Dallas, TX

By Request ©1998 by Betsy Mann, Northland Publishing, Flagstaff, AZ

Calf Fries to Caviar ©1983 by Janet Franklin and Sue Vaughn, Lamesa, TX

Canyon Echoes ©1994 Texas Panhandle Star Co., Wildorado, TX

A Casually Catered Affair ©1980 by Carole Curlee, Lubbock, TX

Celebrate San Antonio ©1986 San Antonio Junior Forum, San Antonio, TX

Central Texas Style ©1988 Junior Service League of Killeen, Inc., Killeen, TX

Changing Thymes ©1995 Austin Junior Forum Publications, Austin, TX

Chips, Dips, & Salsas ©1999 by Judy Walker and Kim MacEachern, Northland Publishing, Flagstaff, AZ

Christmas Celebration: Santa Fe Traditions ©1996 by Richard Clawson/Jann Arrington Wolcott, Clear Light Publishers, Santa Fe, NM

Christmas in Arizona Cook Book, by Lynn Nusom, Golden West Publishers, Phoenix, AZ

Chuck Wagon Cookin' ©1974 by Stella Hughes, University of Arizona Press, Tucson, AZ

Coastal Cuisine ©1993 Junior Service League of Brazosport, Lake Jackson, TX

Cocinas de New Mexico ©1994 Public Service Company of New Mexico, Albuquerque, NM

Collectibles II ©1983 by Mary Pittman, Van Alstyne, TX

Collectibles III, by Mary Pittman, Van Alstyne, TX

Comida Sabrosa ©1982 by Irene Barraza Sanchez and Gloria Sanchez Yund, University of New Mexico Press, Albuquerque, NM

Cook 'em Horns ©1981 The Ex-Students' Association of The University of Texas, Austin, TX

Cook 'em Horns: The Quickbook ©1986 The Ex-Students' Association, Austin, TX

Cookin' Wise ©1980 YWCA, Texarkana, TX

Cooking at the Natural Café in Santa Fe ©1992 by Lynn Walters, The Crossing Press, Freedom, CA

Cooking with Cops, Kingman Police Department, Kingman, AZ

Cooking with Kiwanis, Kiwanis Club of Los Alamos, Santa Fe, NM

Corazón Contento ©1999 by Madeline Gallego Thorpe and Mary Tate Engels, Texas Tech University Press, Lubbock, TX

Cowboy Cookin' ©1990 by Sharon Wilson Walton, Outlaw Books, Cave Creek, AZ

Cowtown Cuisine, St. Joseph's Hospital Guild Volunteer Office

Crème of the Crop, by Jane Neely Winchell, Waco, TX

'Cross the Border ©1993 by Janel Franklin and Sue Vaughn, Lamesa, TX

Cuckoo Too ©1982 by Nancy Allen, Kay Bruce, Fran Fauntleroy, Pat Glauser, Isla Reckling, and Mary Whilden, Houston, TX

Dallas Cuisine ©1993 Two Lane Press, Inc., Dallas, TX

The Dallas Pecan Cookbook © Zonta Club of Dallas, TX

The Dallas Symphony Cookbook ©1983 Junior Group of the Dallas Symphony Orchestra League, Dallas, TX

Decades of Mason County Cooking ©1992 Riata Service Organization, Mason, TX

Delicioso! ©1982 The Junior League of Corpus Christi, Inc., TX

A Different Taste of Paris, McCuistion Regional Medical Center Auxiliary, Paris, TX

Dishes from the Deep, Arizona Perch Base Submarine Veterans, Sun City West, AZ

Down-Home Texas Cooking ©1994 by James Stroman, National Book Network, Blue Ridge Summit, PA

Duck Creek Collection, Junior League of Garland, TX

Dutch Oven and Campfire Cookbook, Boy Scouts of America, Troop 211, Tucson, AZ

The Eagle's Kitchen, Belen Middle School M.E.S.A., Belen, NM

Easy Does It Cookbook, Woman Time Management

Eats: A Fold History of Texas Foods ©1989 TCU Press, Fort Worth, TX

Enjoy! ©1980 Women's Symphony League of Austin, TX

Entertaining at Aldredge House ©1980 Dallas County Medical Society Auxiliary, Dallas, TX

Entertaining in Texas ©1982 Junior League of Victoria, TX

Families Cooking Together ©1998 Georgia O'Keeffe Elementary Friends of the Library, Albuquerque, NM

Favorite Recipes from the Foothills of Carefree, Arizona, Our Lady of Joy Catholic Church, Carefree, AZ

Favorites for All Seasons, Desert Foothills Library, Cave Creek, AZ

Feast of Goodness, Gruver United Methodist Women, Gruver, TX

Fiery Appetizers ©1991 The Crossing Press, Freedom, CA

Fiesta Mexicana, by Toby Arias and Elaine Frassanito, Albuquerque, NM

Fiestas for Four Seasons ©1998-99 by Jane Butel, Clear Light Publishers, Santa Fe, NM

First Baptist Favorites, First Baptist Church, Bisbee, AZ

The First Texas Cook Book ©1986 Eakin Press, Austin, TX

Flavor Favorites ©1979 Baylor University Alumni Association, Waco, TX

Flavors ©1978 Junior League of San Antonio, Inc., San Antonio, TX

Flavors of the Southwest ©1998 by Robert Oser, The Book Publishing Co., Summertown, TN

A Fork in the Road, Mimbres Regional Arts Council, Silver City, NM

Fort Worth is Cooking! ©1993 by Renie Steves, Fort Worth, TX

The Four Ingredient Cookbook, Coffee and Cale, Kerrville, TX

From Generation to Generation ©1992 Sisterhood of Temple Emanu-El, Dallas, TX

From My Apron Pocket, by Suzanne L. Collins, Dallas, TX

Fruits of the Desert Cookbook ©1981 by Sandal English, The Arizona Daily Stir, Tucson, AZ

Gallery Buffet Soup Cookbook ©1983 Dallas Museum of Art League, Dallas, TX

The Galveston Island Cookbook ©1975 The Women of Trinity Episcopal Church, Galveston, TX

The Garden Patch, by Kay Hauser, St. Johns, AZ

Gatherings ©1987 Caprock Girl Scout Council, Lubbock, TX

Gingerbread . . . and all the trimmings ©1987 Waxahachie Junior Service League, Inc., Waxahachie, TX

Good Sam Celebrates 15 Years of Love, Socorro Good Samaritan Village, Socorro, NM

Gourmet Grains, Beans, and Rice ©1992 by Dotty Griffith, Taylor Publishing Co., Dallas, TX

Gourmet Gringo ©1996 by Mari Meyers, Golden West Publishers, Phoenix, AZ

Great Flavors of Texas ©1992 by Barbara C. Jones, Bonham, TX

Great Salsas by the Boss of Sauce, The Crossing Press, Freedom, CA

Great Tastes of Texas ©1994 by Barbara C. Jones, Bonham, TX

Green Chile Bible ©1996-99 by Albuquerque Tribune, Clear Light Publishers, Santa Fe, NM

The Happy Camper's Cookbook ©1999 by Marilyn Abraham and Sandy MacGregor, Clear Light Publishers, Santa Fe, NM

Heard in the Kitchen ©1994 The Heard Museum Guild, Phoenix, AZ

Heavenly Delights, United Methodist Women, Page, AZ

Homecoming ©1994 Baylor Alumni Association, Waco, TX

Hopi Cookery ©1980 by Juanita Tiger Kavena, University of Arizona Press, Tucson, AZ

Hospice Hospitality, by Sharon J. Chessum & Karen Griffin, Yuma, AZ

Hospitality ©1983 Harvey Woman's Club, Palestine, TX

Houston Junior League Cookbook ©1992 Junior League of Houston, Houston, TX

Hullabaloo in the Kitchen, Dallas A&M University Mother's Club, Dallas, TX

I Cook - You Clean ©1993 by Barbara C. Jones, Bonham, TX

I'm Glad I Ate When I Did, 'Cause I'm Not Hungry Now ©1984 Crazy Sam Enterprises, TX

Inn on the Rio's Favorite Recipes, by Julie Cahalane, Taos, NM

Jane Long's Brazoria Inn ©1992 Coldwater Productions, Inc., Dallas, TX

Janos: Recipes and Tales from a Southwest Restaurant ©1989 by Janos Wilder, Ten Speed Press, Berkeley, CA

The Joy of Sharing, First United Methodist Women, Artesia, NM

Keepers! ©1980 by Helen Randolph Moore, New Braunfels, TX

Kingman Welcome Wagon Club Cookbook, Welcome Wagon Club of Kingman, AZ

Kosher Kettle ©1996 Five Star Publications, Inc., Chandler, AZ

La Galerie Perroquet Food Fare, by Carolyn M. Abney, Marshall, TX

La Piñata ©1976 The Junior League of McAllen, TX

Lean Star Cuisine ©1993 Lake Austin Spa Resort, Austin, TX

Leaving Home ©1984 by Lulu Muse, Seven Points, TX

The Light Switch ©1992 by June McLean Jeter, Arlington, TX

License to Cook New Mexico Style, Penfield Press, Iowa City, IA

A Little Southwest Cookbook ©1993 by Chronicle Books, San Francisco, CA

The Little Taste of Texas ©1990 by Barbara C. Jones, Bonham, TX

Loin's Club of Globe Cookbook, Globe Lion's Club, Miami, AZ

Lone Star Legacy ©1981 Austin Junior Forum Publications, Austin, TX

M. D. Anderson Volunteers Cooking for Fun ©1991 M. D. Anderson Volunteer Service, Houston, TX

Ma's in the Kitchen ©1994 by Carl R. McQueary and May Nelson Paulissen, Eakin Press, Austin, TX

March of Dimes Gourmet Gala Cookbook ©1983 Women's Auxiliary of the March of Dimes, Dallas, TX

The Mexican Collection ©1992 by Carole Curlee, Lubbock, TX

More Calf Fries to Caviar ©1988 by Janel Franklin and Sue Vaughn, Lamesa, TX

More of the Four Ingredient Cookbook, Coffee and Cale, Kerrville, TX

More Tastes & Tales ©1987 by Peggy E. Hein, Austin, TX

Morning, Noon and Night Cookbook ©1963 by Gerald Ramsey, Dallas, TX

Mrs. Blackwell's Heart of Texas Cookbook ©1980 by Louise B. Dillow and Deenie B. Carver, Corona Publishing, Co, San Antonio, TX

Necessities and Temptations ©1987 Junior League of Austin, TX

New Mexico Cook Book ©1990 by Lynn Nusom, Golden West Publishers, Phoenix, AZ

New Tastes of Texas ©1994 by Peggy E. Hein, Austin, TX

Not Just Bacon & Eggs ©1991 Straw Hat Publications, Houston, TX

Of Magnolia and Mesquite ©1985 by Suzanne Corder and Gay Thompson, Plainview, TX

The Only Texas Cookbook ©1981 by Linda West Eckhardt, Gulf Publishing, Houston, TX

Our Best Home Cooking, Roosevelt County Family and Community Educators, Portales, NM

Padre Kino's Favorite Meatloaf, Community Food Bank, Inc., Tucson, AZ

Par Excellence, Pinetop Lakes Golf & Country Club, Pinetop, AZ

Pass it On... ©1994 Delta Delta Delta National Fraternity, Arlington, TX

The Peach Tree Tea Room Cookbook ©1990 by Cynthia Collins Pedregon, The Peach Tree, Fredericksburg, TX

Peanut Palate Pleasers from Portales, Portales Woman's Club, Portales, NM

Perfectly Splendid ©1992 McFaddin-Ward House, Beaumont, TX

A Pinch of This and A Handful of That ©1988 Daughters of the Republic of Texas District VIII, Eakin Press, Austin, TX

Pleasures from the Good Earth, Rock of Ages LWML, Sedona, AZ

Portal's Best Little Cookbook, Portal Rescue, Portal, AZ

Potluck on the Pedernales ©1991 Community Garden Club of Johnson City, TX

The Pride of Texas ©1984 Texas Federation of Women's Clubs Historical Foundation Trustees, Austin, TX

Purple Sage and Other Pleasures ©1986 Junior League of Tucson, AZ

Raider Recipes, by David and Dawn Fleming, Lubbock, TX

The Rancho de Chimayó Cookbook ©1991 by Cheryl Jamison and Bill Jamison, Harvard Common Press, Boston, MA

Rare Collection ©1985 Junior League of Galveston County, Inc., Galveston, TX

Raspberry Enchantment House Tour Cookbook, Carrie Tingley Hospital Foundation, Albuquerque, NM

Ready to Serve ©1984 National Guard Auxiliary of Austin, TX

Recipes for Rain or Shine, First Christian Church, Artesia, NM

Recipes from Hatch: Chile Capitol of the World, Hatch, NM

Recipes from the Cotton Patch, St. Luke's Episcopal Church, El Paso, TX

Red Chile Bible ©1998-99 by Kathleen Hansell and Audrey Jenkins, Clear Light Publishers, Santa Fe, NM

Red River's Cookin', Red River Women's Club, NM

Reflections Under the Sun ©1999 Junior League of Phoenix, AZ

Rehoboth Christian School Cookbook, ©1981 Tse Yaaniichi Promoters, Rehoboth, NM

Repast ©1979 Harris County Heritage Society, Houston, TX

Saint Joseph's Really Grande Cookbook, Saint Joseph Parish, Albuquerque, NM

San Antonio Conservation Society Cookbook ©1982 San Antonio Conservation Society, San Antonio, TX

San Antonio Cookbook II ©1976 The San Antonio Symphony League, San Antonio, TX

The Santa Fe School of Cooking Cookbook ©1995 by Susan Curtis, Gibbs Smith Publisher, Layton, UT

Sassy Southwest Cooking: Vibrant New Mexico Foods ©1997 by Clyde W. Casey, Pecos Valley Pepper Company, Roswell, NM

Savor the Southwest, by Barbara Pool Fenzl, San Francisco, CA

Savoring the Southwest ©1983 Roswell Symphony Guild Publications, Roswell, NM

Savory Southwest ©1990 by Judy Hille Walker, Northland Publishing, Flagstaff, AZ

Scrumptions ©1980 Houston Junior Forum, Houston, TX

The Second Typically Texas Cookbook ©1989 Texas Electric Cooperatives, Inc., Austin, TX

Seconds of A Pinch of This and A Handful of That ©1994 Daughters of the Republic of Texas District VIII, Eakin Press, Austin, TX

Sedona Cook Book ©1994 by Susan K. Bollin, Golden West Publishers, Phoenix, AZ

South Texas Mexican Cookbook ©1982 by Lucy Garza, Eakin Press, Austin, TX

Southwest Indian Cookbook ©1978-99 by Macia Keegan, Clear Light Publishers, Santa Fe, NM

Southwest Sizzler ©1990 by Barbara C. Jones, Bonham, TX

Spindletop International Cooks ©1984 Spindletop Oilmen's Golf Charities, Inc., Houston, TX

Square House Museum Cookbook ©1973 Carson County Square House Museum, Panhandle, TX

Sweets . . . From Marina with Love . . . ©1984 by Marina Reed Gonzalez, San Antonio, TX

Taste & Tales From Texas . . . With Love ©1984 Heinco, Austin, TX

A Taste of Victoria ©1974 Nazareth-St. Joseph Schools Project, Victoria, TX

Tasteful Traditions ©1983 Women for Abilene Christian University, Abilene, TX

The Tequila Cook Book ©1993 by Lynn Nusom, Golden West Publishers, Phoenix, AZ

Texas Barbecue ©1994 by Paris Permenter and John Bigley, Pig Out Publications, Inc., Kansas City, MO

Texas Border Cookbook ©1992 by W. Park Kerr and Norma Kerr, The El Paso Chile Company, El Paso, TX

Texas Celebrity Cookbook ©1984 Gardner-Farkas Press, Inc., Fort Worth, TX

The Texas Experience ©1992 Richardson Woman's Club, Richardson, TX

A Texas Hill Country Cookbook ©1976 San Antonio, TX

Texas Historic Inns Cookbook ©1985 by Ann Ruff and Gail Drago, Austin, TX

Texas Home Cooking ©1993 by Cheryl Alters Jamison and Bill Jamison, Harvard Common Press, Boston, MA

Texas Sampler ©1995 Junior League of Richardson, TX

Through Our Kitchen Door ©1978 Dallas County Heritage Society Guild, Dallas, TX

Top Chefs in Texas ©1990 by Sarah Jane English, Austin, TX

Trading Secrets, Beaumont Heritage Society, Beaumont, TX

Tucson Treasures ©1999 Tucson Medical Center Auxiliary, Tucson, AZ

The Very Special Raspberry Cookbook, Carrie Tingley Hospital Foundation, Albuquerque, NM

Vistoso Vittles II, Sun City Vistoso, Tucson, AZ

What's Cookin' at Casa, Casa Arena Blanca, Alamogordo, MN

What's Cooking Inn Arizona ©1996 by Tracy and Phyllis Winters, Winters Publishing, Greensburg, IN

Wild About Texas ©1989 Cypress Woodlands Junior Forum, Spring, TX

The Wild Wild West ©1991 Junior League of Odessa, TX

Wild-n-Tame Fish-n-Game ©1981 by Lynn M. Moore, Cypress, TX

INDEX

Big Bend National Park in Brewster County, Texas, covers 801,163 acres and exhibits dramatic contrasts in both topography and climate. The southern park boundary includes spectacular canyons carved by 118 miles of the Rio Grande/Rio Bravo rivers.

INDEX

INDEX

INDEX

Collect the Series!
Best of the Best State Cookbook Series

Cookbook collectors love this Series! The forty-two cookbooks, covering all fifty states (see next page for listing), contain over 15,000 of the most popular local and regional recipes collected from approximately 3,000 of the leading cookbooks from these states. The Series not only captures the flavor of America, but saves a lot of shelf space!

To assist individuals who wish to collect the Series, we are offering a **Collect the Series Discount Coupon Booklet.** With the Booklet you get:

Collect the Series!
BEST OF THE BEST STATE COOKBOOK SERIES
With this Special *Collect the Series* Discount Coupon Booklet

OVER 3 MILLION STATE COOKBOOKS SOLD!   *continued inside...*

Call **1-800-343-1583** to order a free, no-obligation Discount Coupon Booklet. A free catalog of all QRP cookbooks is also available on request.

- **25% discount off the list price ($16.95 minus 25% = $12.70 per copy)**
- **With a single order of five copies, you receive a sixth copy free. A single order of ten cookbooks, gets two free copies, etc.**
- **Only $4.00 shipping cost for any number of books ordered (within contiguous United States).**

Recipe Hall of Fame Cookbook Collection
is also included in the **Collect the Series Discount Coupon Booklet.**

| 304 pages • $19.95 | 304 pages • $19.95 | 304 pages • $19.95 | 240 pages • $16.95 |

The four cookbooks in this collection consist of over 1,200 of the most exceptional recipes collected from the entire
BEST OF THE BEST STATE COOKBOOK SERIES.
The Hall of Fame Collection can be bought
as a four-cookbook set for $40.00.
This is a 48% discount off the total individual cost of $76.80.

QUAIL RIDGE PRESS
P. O. Box 123 • Brandon, MS 39043 • 1-800-343-1583
E-mail: info@quailridge.com • www.quailridge.com

BEST OF THE BEST STATE COOKBOOK SERIES

ALABAMA
ALASKA
ARIZONA
ARKANSAS
BIG SKY
Includes Montana, Wyoming
CALIFORNIA
COLORADO
FLORIDA
GEORGIA
GREAT PLAINS
Includes North Dakota, South Dakota, Nebraska, and Kansas

HAWAII
IDAHO
ILLINOIS
INDIANA
IOWA
KENTUCKY
LOUISIANA
LOUISIANA II
MICHIGAN
MID-ATLANTIC
Includes Maryland, Delaware, New Jersey, and Washington, D.C.

MINNESOTA
MISSISSIPPI
MISSOURI
NEVADA
NEW ENGLAND
Includes Rhode Island, Connecticut, Massachusetts, Vermont, New Hampshire, and Maine
NEW MEXICO
NEW YORK
NO. CAROLINA
OHIO
OKLAHOMA

OREGON
PENNSYLVANIA
SO. CAROLINA
TENNESSEE
TEXAS
TEXAS II
UTAH
VIRGINIA
VIRGINIA II
WASHINGTON
WEST VIRGINIA
WISCONSIN

All BEST OF THE BEST COOKBOOKS are 6x9 inches, are comb-bound, contain approximately 400 recipes, and total 264–352 pages. Each contains illustrations, photographs, an index, and a list of contributing cookbooks, a special feature that cookbook collectors enjoy. Scattered throughout the cookbooks are short quips that provide interesting information about each state, including historical facts and major attractions along with amusing trivia. Retail price per copy $16.95.

To order by credit card, call toll-free **1-800-343-1583**, visit **www.quailridge.com**, or use the Order Form below.